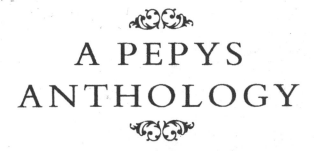

A PEPYS
ANTHOLOGY

A PEPYS
ANTHOLOGY

Passages from the Diary of
SAMUEL PEPYS

Selected and edited by
ROBERT AND LINNET
LATHAM

University of California Press
Berkeley   Los Angeles   London

University of California Press
Berkeley and Los Angeles, California

University of California Press, Ltd.
London, England

First Paperback Printing 1999

The selection in this volume is taken
from THE DIARY OF SAMUEL PEPYS, A NEW AND
COMPLETE TRANSCRIPTION, edited by Robert
Latham and William Matthews, Volumes I–XI,
1970–83, published by
the University of California Press

Library of Congress Cataloging-in-Publication Data
Pepys, Samuel, 1633–1703.
 1. Pepys, Samuel, 1633–1703—Diaries. 2. Statesmen—
Great Britain—Diaries. 3. Authors, English—Early
modern, 1500–1700—Diaries. 4. Great Britain—Social
life and customs—17th century. I. Latham, Robert,
1912–   . II. Latham, Linnet. III. Title.
DA447.P4A3 1988 941.06'6'0924 87-30022
ISBN-13: 978-0-520-22167-3

Printed in the United States of America
08 07
    10 9 8 7 6 5 4

Dedicated to

Mary Coleman and Aude Fitzsimons

Contents

Acknowledgement   vii

Preface   ix

I
THE DIARY BEGINS   I
Pepys and the Restoration   3

II
PEPYS THE MAN   II
The Booklover   13
The Churchman   19
Country Outings and River Excursions   27
Dinners and Parties   35
Encounters with Children   47
The Householder   51
The Husband   58
The King's Servant   68
The Man of Fashion   83
The Musician   87
The Neighbour   96
Pictures and Portraits   101
The Rising Man   106
The Theatre-goer   112
The Virtuoso   118

III
PEPYS'S WORLD   127
Ceremonies and Processions   129
Christmas   136
Church Uniformity Restored   138
The Court   143

CONTENTS

The Fire of London	154
Houses and Gardens	162
Marvels and Mysteries	167
Matters of State	173
The Navy: Officers and Seamen	183
The Navy at War	191
The Plague	200
Popular Entertainments	205
St Valentine's Day	209
Sports and Contests	211
Street Life	215
Travellers' Tales	220

IV

PEPYS THE STORY-TELLER	229
The Bashful Lovers	231
Buried Gold	240
The Dancing Master	247
Deb Willet	255

V

ANECDOTES, OBSERVATIONS AND REFLECTIONS	271

VI

THE DIARY ENDS	283
Select Glossary	285

Acknowledgement

We are grateful to Mary Coleman and Aude Fitzsimons of the Pepys Library for their help in the preparation of this volume.

Preface

❧❧

PEPYS WAS BORN in London in 1633 and died in 1703, highly esteemed for his achievements as a public servant in the Admiralty, and in his private life known in intellectual circles as an accomplished amateur of music and learning. His greatest fame, however, was yet to come. Between 1660 and 1669, as a young man living in London, he had secretly kept a shorthand diary. It was preserved in his library, which he left to his old college, Magdalene, Cambridge, and in 1825 was published (in selection – for it was almost 1½ million words long) by the 3rd Lord Braybrooke, from a transcription by John Smith. It was immediately recognised as a work of unusual interest. Never before had any part of the English past been evoked in such lively detail. Walter Scott praised it in terms that were later echoed by Lord Macaulay and by Robert Louis Stevenson. It became a classic: one of the best known and best loved books in the language. Since 1825 it has been published in many forms, large and small, on both sides of the Atlantic, and translated into several languages. In 1970–83 the first complete edition appeared in eleven volumes.[1]

In this *Anthology* we attempt a fresh presentation. We have broken the chronological mould of the diary and gathered together extracts, arranged under subjects, which we take to be representative of the whole work. Our organisation of the extracts (principally into those that illustrate the man himself and those that illustrate the

[1] *The Diary of Samuel Pepys*, ed. Robert Latham and William Matthews.

world he lived in) reflects the fact that the diary is both autobiography and history. Between the two and within each we have tried to strike a balance. In the auto-biographical material the balance lies between his private and his public life, and between his intellectual interests and his emotional experience. In the historical material it lies between the great events (like the Plague and the Fire and the high politics of the Court) and the everyday life of Restoration London. Some subjects – Pepys's relations with his family and with the Earl of Sandwich, his patron, for instance – have been omitted because they are difficult to illustrate briefly. For the rest, we have tried to select passages which give the flavour of the diary, and which reflect in particular its candour and vivacity.

In making the selection we found that the significant themes suggested themselves. The difficulty lay in choosing the most telling extracts to illustrate them from among so many of apparently equal merit. Another consideration was to choose passages as far as possible that explained themselves, so that any further information needed by the reader could be accommodated in a brief headnote to each section. In part IV, 'Pepys as Story-teller', once we had decided on the stories themselves, which was not difficult, it was much easier to select passages; we had simply to peel away what was irrele-vant. The result is, we believe, to make the episodes even more vivid and to reveal more clearly than before Pepys's powers as a narrator.

Our method has necessarily involved taking liberties with the text of the diary. The passages are in some cases compressed to save space or to ensure that they are clear and coherent. Marks of omission would have spoilt the appearance of the page: they have therefore not been insetted. All interpolations made by the editors are signalled by the use of square brackets. These interpolations are of two kinds: where they employ Pepys's own words (e.g. where to make Pepys's meaning clear a pronoun is replaced by a name – 'he' by 'Mr Coventry') the words supplied are printed in roman type, but where the editors have needed to use words of their own, these are printed in italic.

The text we have used is based on the transcription made, principally by Professor Matthews, for the eleven-volume edition. Pepys wrote mainly in shorthand, using the Shelton system which he learnt from an instructional manual[2] and which was current, though (like other systems) not widely used, until the early eighteenth century. But he also wrote longhand occasionally, and this mixture of shorthand and longhand accounts for the mixture of seventeenth- and twentieth-century spellings in our text. The longhand words are reproduced in Pepys's spelling; so are those shorthand words for which there is a known Pepysian spelling – known, that is, from longhand examples (themselves often variable – he was not consistent) or deducible from the phonetic evidence of the shorthand. Elsewhere words are spelt in modern style. Pepys used very few marks of punctuation because

[2] Thomas Shelton, *A Tutor to Tachygraphy, or Short-Writing* (1642). Pepys's copy survives in his library. A modern reprint, with an introduction by Professor Matthews, has been published by the Augustan Reprint Society (William Andrews Clark Memorial Library, University of California, Los Angeles, 1970). It is clear from the concluding words of the diary (below, p. 284) that Pepys's main purpose in using shorthand was to preserve the secrecy of its contents. In some of the amorous passages he went further by garbling the shorthand and by writing in a comic mixture of languages (see, for example, below, p. 54).

of the danger of confusion with the shorthand. They have therefore been supplied where necessary. Another peculiarity of the original text arises from Pepys's wayward treatment of capital letters when he is writing in longhand: he can insert them in the middle of a word, and, equally, he can fail to use them at the beginning of a sentence. Here we have adopted modern usage.

A Select Glossary is provided at the end of the volume.

Cambridge, 1987

Pepys: a biographical note

Born 23 February 1633 in Salisbury Court off Fleet Street, son of a tailor. Educated at St Paul's School and Magdalene College, Cambridge; employed from *c.*1654 as man of business to his cousin Edward Mountagu (Councillor of State under Oliver Cromwell; later Earl of Sandwich); junior clerk in the Exchequer 1655–60; Clerk to the Navy Board 1660–73; member of the Tangier Committee 1662–79 (and its Treasurer 1665–79); Secretary to the Admiralty 1673–9 and Secretary to the King for Naval Affairs 1684–9. Member of Parliament 1673–9, 1679 and 1685–8. Fellow of the Royal Society from 1665; President 1684–6. He resigned from the Admiralty at the Revolution, in February 1689, and died on 26 May 1703. In 1655 he had married Elizabeth St Michel, daughter of a refugee Huguenot; she died childless in 1669. Pepys never married again, but in his will left a legacy to Mary Skynner, daughter of a London merchant, who had been his companion for thirty-three years.

I

THE DIARY BEGINS

Pepys and the Restoration

¶ IT WAS ONE OF THE GREATEST MIRACLES in our history that in 1660 the Puritan Revolution was overthrown and the monarchy restored without foreign intervention or civil war. It was also a remarkable piece of good luck for our understanding of the miracle that many of the crucial events in the process were observed and recorded in detail by Pepys, whose life at this time seems almost to have run parallel to the nation's history.

He began his diary during the Christmas season of 1659–60 – the very time when the revolutionary cause began finally to collapse – and wrote from his home in Westminster, at the heart of the political world. On 26 December the rule of the army officers under Lambert had been successfully challenged by the return of the Rump (the remnant of the last legitimately elected House of Commons), and on 1 January Monck, who commanded the army in Scotland and had dissociated himself from Lambert, began to move his forces south across the Tweed. On 3 February he arrived in London and with the support of the City demanded (11 February) that the Rump should admit the 'secluded' members – the moderate M.P.s deprived of their seats shortly before Charles I's execution – so that the Parliament could vote its own dissolution and authorise fresh elections. A new Council of State which included Monck and Mountagu, Pepys's patron, was formed, and the Parliament met on 27 April. On 1 May, having received with approval a conciliatory Declaration from the King, issued in Holland (see 3 May), Parliament voted for Charles II's return and the restoration of government by King, Lords and Commons.

Meantime, a squadron of ships had been stationed off the coast ready to sail to Holland to bring back the King. Mountagu was in command, with Pepys as his Secretary (6 March). They sailed for Scheveningen on 13 May, and ten days later began the voyage home, with the King and his entourage on board the Admiral's ship. There on the quarter-deck Pepys listened to the King's stories of his adventures in flight from Cromwell's army after the Battle of Worcester (3 September 1651; see 23 May below). By the

25th the fleet was off Dover and the King, with his brothers the Dukes of York and Gloucester, went ashore. Pepys landed alongside them in a little boat that carried the servants and the King's pet dog.

By temperament and conviction Pepys was a monarchist rather than a revolutionary, and through his association with Mountagu was attached to the group of moderate politicians who had joined with the royalists to bring back the King. His account of events bears witness to the strength of popular feeling against military rule and in favour of a return to traditional government by King and Parliament.

Blessed be God, at the end of the last year I was in very good health. I lived in Axe Yard, having my wife and servant Jane, and no more in family then us three. The condition of the State was thus. *Viz.* the Rump was lately returned to sit again, and Monke is with his army in Scotland. The new Common Council of the City doth speak very high; and hath sent to Monke their sword-bearer, to acquaint him with their desires for a free and full Parliament, which is at present the desires and the hopes and expectation of all. (*January 1660*)

I went up to the Lobby, where I saw the Speaker reading of the letter [*Monck's letter demanding the admission of the 'secluded' members*]; and after it was read, Sir A. Haslerig came out very angry. Hence I went alone to Guildhall to see whether Monke was come yet or no, and met him coming out of the chamber where he had been with the Mayor and Aldermen; but such a shout I never heard in all my life, crying out "God bless your Excellence!" And endeed I saw many people give the soldiers drink and money, and all along in the streets cried, "God bless them!" and extraordinary good words. In Cheapside there was a great many bonefires, and Bow bells and all the bells in all the churches as we went home were a-ringing. Hence we went homewards, it being about 10 a-clock. But the common joy that was everywhere to be seen! The number of bonefires – there being fourteen between St Dunstan's and Temple Bar. And at Strand Bridge I could at one view tell 31 fires. In King Streete, seven or eight; and all along burning and roasting and drinking for rumps – there being rumps tied upon sticks and carried up and down. The buchers at the Maypole in the Strand rang a peal with their knifes when they were going to sacrifice their rump. On Ludgate Hill there was one turning of the spit, that had a rump tied upon it, and another basting of it. Indeed, it was past imagination, both the greatness and the suddenness of it. At one end of the street, you would think there was a whole lane of fire, and so hot that we were fain to keep still on the further side merely for heat. (*11 February 1660*)

To Westminster by water, only seeing Mr Pinkny at his own house, where he showed me how he hath alway kept the Lion and Unicorne in the back of his chimney bright, in expectation of the King's coming again. Great hopes of the King's coming again. (*5 March 1660*)

[My Lord] asked me whether I could without too much inconvenience go to sea as his Secretary, and bade me think of it. He also begin to talk of things of state, and told me that he should now want one in that capacity at sea that he might trust in. And therefore he would have me to go. He told me also that he did believe the King would come in, and did discourse with me about it and about the affection of the people and City – at which I was full glad. Everybody now drink the King's health without any fear, whereas before it was very private that a man dare do it. (*Shrove Tuesday, 6 March 1660*)

[*The remaining entries are written on board ship.*]

This day dined Sir John Boys and some other gentlemen, formerly great Cavaliers; and among the rest, one Mr Norwood, for whom my Lord gave a convoy to carry him to the Brill; but he is certainly going to the King – for my Lord commanded me that I should not enter his name in my book. My Lord doth show them and that sort of people great civility. All their discourse and others' are of the King's coming, and we begin to speak of it very freely. And heard how in many churches in London and upon many signs there and upon merchants' ships in the river they have set up the King's arms. (*21 April 1660*)

This morning my Lord showed me the King's Declaration and his letter to the two Generalls to be communicated to the fleet. The contents of the letter are his offer of grace to all that will come in within 40 days, only excepting them that the Parliament shall hereafter except. That the sales of lands during these troubles, and all other things, shall be left to the Parliament, by which he will stand. The letter dated at Breda, April$\frac{4}{14}$ 1660, in the 12th year of his raigne. Upon the receipt of it this morning by an express, my Lord summoned a Council of War, and in the meantime did dictate to me how he would have the vote ordered which he would have pass this Council. Which done, the commanders all came on board, and the Council set in the coach, where I read the letter and declaration; and while they were discoursing upon it, I seemed to draw up a vote; which being offered, they passed. Not one man seemed to say no to it, though I am confident many in their hearts were against it. After this was done, I went up to the quarter-deck with my Lord and the commanders, and there read both the papers and the vote; which done, and demanding their opinion, the seamen did all of them cry out "God bless King Charles!" with the greatest joy imaginable. (*3 May 1660*)

I wrote this morning many letters, and to all the copies of the vote of the Council of Warr I put my name; that if it should come in print, my name may be at it. I sent a copy of the vote to Doling, inclosed in this letter:

"Sir,

He that can fancy a fleet (like ours) in her pride, with pendants loose, guns roaring, caps flying, and the loud *Vive le Roy's* echoed from one ship's company to another, he and he only can apprehend the joy this enclosed vote was received with, or the blessing he thought himself possessed of that bore it, and is

Your humble servant." (*4 May 1660*)

This afternoon Mr Ed. Pickering told me in what a sad, poor condition for clothes and money the King was, and all his attendants, when he came to him first from my Lord – their clothes not being worth 40s, the best of them. And how overjoyed the King was when Sir J. Greenville brought him some money; so joyful, that he called the Princesse Royall and Duke of Yorke to look upon it as it lay in the portmanteau before it was taken out. (*16 May 1660*)

We weighed ancre, and with a fresh gale and most happy weather we set sail for England – all the afternoon the King walking here and there, up and down, very active and stirring. Upon the quarter-deck he fell in discourse of his escape from Worcester. Where it made me ready to weep to hear the stories that he told of his difficulties that he had passed through. As his travelling four days and three nights on foot, every step up to the knees in dirt, with nothing but a green coat and a pair of country breeches on and a pair of country shoes, that made him so sore all over his feet that he could scarce stir. Yet he was forced to run away from a miller and other company that took them for rogues. His sitting at table at one place, where the master of the house, that had not seen him in eight years, did know him but kept it private; when at the same table there was one that had been of his own regiment at Worcester, could not know him but made him drink the Kings health and said that the King was at least four fingers higher than he. Another place, he was by some servants of the house made to drink, that they might know him not to be a Roundhead, which they swore he was. In another place, at his inn, the master of the house, as the King was standing with his hands upon the back of a chair by the fireside, he kneeled down and kissed his hand privately, saying that he would not ask him who he was, but bid God bless him whither that he was going. Then the difficulty of getting a boat to get into France, where he was fain to plot with the master thereof to keep his design from the four men and a boy (which was all his ship's company), and so got to Feckam

[8]

in France. At Roane he looked so poorly that the people went into the rooms before he went away, to see whether he had not stole something or other. (*23 May 1660*)

By the morning we were come close to the land and everybody made ready to get on shore. The King and the two Dukes did eat their breakfast before they went, and there being set some shipps diet before them, only to show them the manner of the shipps diet, they eat of nothing else but pease and pork and boiled beef. I went, and Mr Mansell and one of the King's footmen, with a dog that the King loved (which shit in the boat, which made us laugh and me think that a King and all that belong to him are but just as others are) went in a boat by ourselfs; and so got on shore when the King did, who was received by Gen. Monke with all imaginable love and respect at his entrance upon the land at Dover. Infinite the croud of people and the gallantry of the horsmen, citizens, and noblemen of all sorts. The Mayor of the town came and gave him his white staffe, the badge of his place, which the King did give him again. The Mayor also presented him from the town a very rich Bible, which he took and said it was the thing that he loved above all things in the world. A canopy was provided for him to stand under, which he did; and talked awhile with Gen. Monke and others; and so into a stately coach there set for him; and so away straight through the towne toward Canterbury without making any stay at Dover. The shouting and joy expressed by all is past imagination. (*25 May 1660*)

II

PEPYS THE MAN

The Booklover

¶ PEPYS DID SOMETHING MORE than collect books – he collected a library. Being a man of system, he soon came to have regard to the total design of his collection. Bindings mattered a great deal since books were normally sold unbound and were later given leather covers of the purchaser's choice. (Cloth covers did not come in until the 1820s.) Pepys aimed to collect examples of foreign binding (15 May 1660; Dutch publishers issued their products in vellum for the international market); he once considered having virtually all his books bound in a uniform style (18 January 1665 – fortunately he soon abandoned this idea); he devised a policy for discards as well as accessions (2 February 1668); he contrived bookcases that were aesthetically pleasing as well as efficient (23 July 1666; they are glazed presses made for him free of charge in the dockyards); he drew up lists and catalogues (19, 25 December 1666). All these features of the library which he built up in the 1660s survive in the much larger collection which he had gathered by the time of his death. By his bequest it passed in 1724 into the possession of his old college, Magdalene, Cambridge, where it remains to this day virtually unaltered and in its original furniture. The diary is the best known of its many treasures.

As these passages show, Pepys read a wide variety of books, reading early and late, indoors and outdoors. He loved writing too – or the diary itself would not exist. He once wrote – or at any rate started – a novel (30 January 1664): but all we can say with confidence about it, since he destroyed it, is that it was almost certainly easier to read than the only book he ever published (*Memoires relating to the State of the Royal Navy*, 1690) which reads like an office memorandum. He meant to write something on the history of the navy, but never did so, perhaps because he knew too much about it.

[*At The Hague.*] To a bookseller's and bought, for the love of the binding, three books – the French Psalms in four parts – Bacon's *organon*, and Farnaby's *Rhetoric*. (*15 May 1660*)

[13]

Mr Greatorex did show me the manner of the lamp glasses which carry the light a great way. Good to read in bed by and I intend to have one of them. (*24 October 1660*)

To Pauls Churchyard, and there I met with Dr Fullers *Englands Worthys* – the first time that I ever saw it; and so I sat down reading in it, till it was 2 a-clock before I thought of the time's going. And so I rose and went home to dinner, being much troubled that (though he had some discourse with me about my family and armes) he says nothing at all, nor mentions us either in Cambrige or Norfolke. But I believe endeed, our family were never considerable. (*10 February 1662*)

Up by 4 a-clock in the morning and read Cicero's *Second Oracion against Cataline*, which pleased me exceedingly; and more I discern therein then ever I thought was to be found in him. But I perceive it was my ignorance, and that he is as good a writer as ever I read in my life. (*13 June 1662*)

Hither came Mr Battersby; and we falling into a discourse of a new book of drollery in verse called *Hudebras*, I would needs go find it out; and met with it at the Temple, cost me 2s.-6d. But when I came to read it, it is so silly an abuse of the Presbyter-Knight going to the warrs, that I am ashamed of it; and by and by meeting at Mr Townsends at dinner, I sold it to him for 18d. (*26 December 1662*)

By water to Whitehall, all our way by water, both coming and going, reading a little book said to be writ by a Person of Quality concerning English gentry to be preferred before titular honours; but the most silly nonsense, no sense nor grammar, yet in as good words that ever I saw in all my life, that from beginning to end you meet not with one entire and regular sentence. (*22 May 1663*)

To St Paul's Churchyard to my booksellers; and having gained this day in the office, by my stationer's bill to the King, about 40s. or 3*l*, I did here sit two or three hours, calling for twenty books to lay this money out upon; and found myself at a great loss where to choose, and do see how my nature would gladly returne to the laying out of money in this trade. I could not tell whether to lay out my money for books of pleasure, as plays, which my nature was most earnest in; but at last, after seeing Chaucer, Dugdales *History of Pauls*, Stow's *London*, Gesners *History of Trent*, besides Shakespeare, Johnson, and Beaumonts plays, I at last chose Dr Fuller's *Worthys*, *The Cabbala or Collections of Letters of State* – and a little book, *Delices de Hollande*, with another little book or two, all of good use or serious pleasure; and *Hudibras*, both parts, the book now in greatest fashion for drollery, though I cannot, I confess, see enough where the wit lies. (*10 December 1663*)

This evening, being in an humour of making all things even and clear in the world, I tore some old papers; among others, a romance which (under the title of *Love a Cheate*) I begun ten year ago at Cambrige; and at this time, reading it over tonight, I liked it very well and wondered a little at myself at my vein at that time when I wrote it, doubting that I cannot do so well now if I would try. (*30 January 1664*)

Walked with Mr Coventry to St James's. After dinner, we did talk of a History of the Navy of England, how fit it were to be writ; and he did say that it hath been in his mind to propose to me the writing of the history of the late Dutch warr [*of 1654–8*] – which I am glad to hear, it being a thing I much desire and sorts mightily with my genius – and if done well, may recommend me much. So he says he will get me an order for making of searches to all records &c. in order thereto, and I shall take great delight in doing of it. (*13 June 1664*)

To Paul's Churchyard about books – and to the binders and directed the doing of my Chaucer, though they were not full neat enough for me, but pretty well it is – and thence to the clasp-makers to have it clasped and bossed. (*8 July 1664*)

Up, and by and by to my bookseller's and there did give thorough direction for the new binding of a great many of my old books, to make my whole study of the same binding, within very few. (*18 January 1665*)

I walked quite over the fields home, by light of link, one of my watermen carrying it and I reading by the light of it, it being a very fine clear dry night. (*27 December 1665*)

Up and to my chamber, doing several things there of moment. And then comes Simpson [*master-joiner of Deptford dockyard*], and he and I with great pains contriving presses to put my books up in; they now growing numerous, and lying one upon another on my chairs, I lose the use, to avoid the trouble of removing them when I would open a book. (*23 July 1666*)

Up, and despatched several businesses at home in the morning; and then comes Sympson to set up my other new presse for my books; and so he and I fell in to the furnishing of my new closet, and taking out the things out of my old. I kept him with me all day, and he dined with me; and so all the afternoon, till it was quite dark, hanging things; that is, my maps and picture[s] and draughts, and setting up my books, and as much as we could do – to my most extraordinary satisfaction; so that I think it will be as noble a closet as any man hath. (*24 August 1666*)

I to my chamber and there to ticket a good part of my books, in order to the numbring of them for my easy finding them to read, as I have occasion. (*19 December 1666*)

And so back home, and there with my brother, reducing the names of all my books to an alphabet, which kept us till 7 or 8 at night; and then to supper. (*Christmas Day, 1666*)

I by coach to the Temple and there did buy a little book or two; and it is strange how Rycaut's discourse of Turky, which before the Fire I was asked but 8*s* for, there being all but 22 or thereabouts burnt, I did now offer 20*s*, and he demands 50*s*; and I think I shall give it him, though it be only as a monument of the Fire. (*20 March 1667*)

[17]

I all day at home, and all the morning setting my books in order in my presses for the fallowing year, their number being much encreased since the last, so as I am fain to lay by several books to make room for better, being resolved to keep no more than just my presses will contain. (*Lord's Day, 2 February 1668*)

Up, and at my chamber all the morning and the office, doing business and also reading a little of *L'Escolle des Filles*, which is a mighty lewd book, but yet not amiss for a sober man once to read over to inform himself in the villainy of the world. (*Lord's Day, 9 February 1668*)

The Churchman

¶ PEPYS'S MOTHER and probably his brother Tom were sectarian Puritans (4 March 1660; 30 May 1663), but Pepys himself was a middle-of-the-road, rather tepid, Anglican. (He rarely, for example, took Communion: 30 March 1662.) In the first of these extracts he was attending one of the Anglican services which, although illegal, were commonly enough held in London in the later years of the Commonwealth. Within the Anglican church, he disapproved of extremes, whether of doctrine or ceremonial, and outside it he favoured toleration for peaceable Protestant Dissenters. He attended Roman Catholic services at the Queen's Chapel, mainly out of curiosity, and his comments (15 April 1666; 24 December 1667) show that he was critical of the behaviour of the congregation rather than of the services themselves. Most of the services described here were held in his parish church, St Olave's Hart St, where he and his colleagues of the Navy Board had a gallery erected for their use by workmen from Deptford dockyard (11 November 1660). The Rector, Daniel Milles, was no favourite of Pepys (who seems to have been a lifelong anticlerical); still less was the unnamed Scotsman who served as curate (21 June 1663).

Pepys for all his worldliness was a man of sincere piety. The diary bears frequent marks of his religious feelings, and his interest in theology and church history is evident in the books he chose for his library. On his deathbed he asked for a High Church clergyman to attend him, who administered extreme unction. But this may only imply political sympathy with the High Church clergy who had, like him, suffered dismissal from office after the Revolution of 1689 rather than swear obedience during the lifetime of James II to the new sovereigns.

To church in the afternoon, and in Mrs Turners pew my wife took up a good black hood and kept it. A stranger preached a poor sermon, and so I read over the whole book of the story of Tobit. (*Lord's Day, 5 February 1660*)

Then to my mother again; and after supper, she and I talked very high about religion, I in defence of the religion I was born in. (*Lord's Day, 4 March 1660*)

[*On board the* Naseby.] I and Will Howe, the surgeon, parson, and Balty supped in the Lieutenant's cabin and afterward sat disputing, the parson for and I against extemporary prayer very hot. (*8 April 1660*)

Today at noon (God forgive me), I strung my lute, which I have not touched a great while before. (*Lord's Day, 21 October 1660*)

[Sir W. Batten] and I went to church into our new gallery (the first time that ever it was used and it not being yet quite finished); there came after us Sir W. Pen, Mr Davis, and his eldest son. There being no women this day, we sat in the foremost pew and behind us our servants; but I hope it will not be always so, it not being handsome for our servants to sit so equal with us. (*Lord's Day, 11 November 1660*)

By coach [*from Chatham*] to Greenwich church, where a good sermon, a fine church, and a great company of handsome women. (*13 January 1661*)

A most tedious, unseasonable, and impertinent sermon by an Irish Doctor. His text was "Scatter them, O Lord, that delight in warr." Sir Wm Batten and I very much angry with the parson. (*Lord's Day, 17 February 1661*)

Very merry at dinner. Among other things, because Mrs Turner and her company eate no flesh at all this Lent and

I had a great deal of good flesh, which made their mouths water. (*26 March 1661*)

We went to Mrs Brown's, where Sir W. Pen and I were godfathers and Mrs Jordan and Shipman godmothers to her boy. And there, before and after the christening, we were with the women above in her chamber. One passage, of a lady that eate wafers with her dog, did a little displease me. I did give the midwife 10s. and the nurse 5s. and the maid of the house 2: but forasmuch as I expected to give the name to the childe, but did not, it being called John, I forbore then to give my plate – till another time, after a little more advice. (*29 May 1661*)

To church; and before sermon there was a long psalm and half another sung out while the sexton gathered what the church would give him for this last year (I gave him 3s., and have the last week given the clerke 2s., which I set down that I may know what to do the next year, if it please the Lord that I live so long); but the jest was, the clerke begins the 25 psalm, which hath a proper tune to it, and then the 116, which cannot be sung with that tune, which seemed very ridiculous. (*Lord's Day, 5 January 1662*)

Early to Whitehall to the Chappell; where by Mr Blagrave's means, I got into his pew and heard Dr Creeton, the great Scochman, preach before the King and Duke and Duchesse upon the words of Michah: "Roule yourselves in dust." He made a most learned sermon upon the words; but in his applicacion, the most comicall man that ever I heard in my life. He discoursed much against a man's lying with his wife in Lent, saying that he might be as incontinent during that time with his own wife as at another time in another man's bed. (*7 March 1662*)

This morning, till churches were done, I spent going from one church to another and hearing a bit here and a bit there. (*Lord's Day, 16 March 1662*)

To church in the morning. And so home, leaving the two Sir Wms to take the sacrament – which I blame myself that I have hitherto neglected all my life, but once or twice at Cambrige. (*Easter Day, 30 March 1662*)

[*At Southampton.*] On board the *Swallow* in the dock, hear our navy chaplin preach a sad sermon, full of nonsense and false Latin – but prayed for the Right Honourable the Principal Officers. (*Sunday, 27 April 1662*)

Then came Mr Mills the Minister to see me – which he hath but rarely done to me, though every day almost to others of us; but he is a cunning fellow and knows where the good victualls is and the good drink, at Sir W. Batten. (*9 July 1662*)

So to my brother's and there was a fellow that said grace so long, like a prayer; I believe the fellow is a cunning fellow, and yet I by my brother's desire did give him a crowne, he being in great want and it seems a parson among the fanatiques and a cousin of my poor aunts – whose prayers, she told me, did do me good among the many good souls that did by my father's desires pray for me when I was cut of the stone, and which God did hear;

which I also in complaisance did owne, but God forgive me, my mind was otherwise. (*30 May 1663*)

So to church and slept all the sermon, the Scott, to whose voice I am not to be reconciled, preaching. (*Lord's Day, 21 June 1663*)

To [Whitehall] Chapel and heard the famous young Stillingfleete, who I knew at Cambridge and is now newly admitted one of the King's chaplains – and was presented, they say, to my Lord Treasurer for St Andrews Holborne, where he is now minister, with these words: that they (the Bishops of Canterbury, London, and another) believed he is the ablest young man to preach the gospel of any since the Apostles. He did make the most plain, honest, good, grave sermon, in the most unconcerned and easy yet substantial manner, that ever I heard in my life – upon the words of Samuell to the people – "Fear the Lord in truth with all your heart, and remember the great things that he hath done for you" – it being proper to this day, the day of the King's coronation. (*Lord's Day, 23 April 1665*)

My wife and I the first time together at church since the Plague, and now only because of Mr Mills his coming home to preach his first sermon, expecting a great excuse for his leaving the parish before anybody went, and now staying till all are come home; but he made but a very poor and short excuse, and a bad sermon. (*Lord's Day, 4 February 1666*)

Walked into [St James's] Park to the Queen's chapel and there heard a good deal of their mass and some of their musique, which is not so contemptible, I think, as our people would make it, it pleasing me very well – and indeed, better then the anthemne I heard afterward at Whitehall at my coming back. I stayed till the King went down to receive the Sacrament; and stood in his closett with a great many others and there saw him receive it – which I did never see the manner of before. But do see very little difference between the degree of the ceremonies used by our people in the administration thereof and that in the Roman church, saving that methought our chapel was not so fine, nor the manner of doing it so glorious, as it was in the Queenes chapel. (*15 April 1666*)

Up and with my wife to church, where Mr Mills made an unnecessary sermon upon originall sin, neither understood by himself nor the people. (*Lord's Day, 10 February 1667*)

To Hackny church, where very full; and found much difficulty to get pews, I offering the sexton money and he could not help me – so my wife and Mercer ventured into a pew, and I into another. A knight and his lady very civil to me when they came, and the like to my wife in hers, being Sir George Viner's; and his lady rich in jewells, but most in beauty; almost the finest woman that ever I saw. That which we went chiefly to see was the young ladies of the schools, whereof there is great store, very pretty; and also the organ, which is handsome and tunes the psalm and plays with the people; which is mighty pretty and makes me mighty earnest to have a pair at our church, I having almost a mind to give them a pair if they would settle a maintenance on them for it – I am mightily taken with them. (*Lord's Day, 21 April 1667*)

I walked toward Whitehall; but being weary, turned into
St Dunstan's church, where I hear an able sermon of the
minister of the place. And stood by a pretty, modest
maid, whom I did labour to take by the hand and body;
but she would not, but got further and further from me,
and at last I could perceive her to take pins out of her
pocket to prick me if I should touch her again; which
seeing, I did forbear, and was glad I did espy her design.
And then I fell to gaze upon another pretty maid in a pew
close to me, and she on me; and I did go about to take her
by the hand, which she suffered a little and then withdrew. So the sermon ended and the church broke up, and
my amours ended also. (*Lord's Day, 18 August 1667*)

Through the park to [*the Queen's*] chapel, where I got in
up almost to the rail and with a great deal of patience,
stayed from 9 at night to 2 in the morning in a very great
crowd; and there expected, but found nothing extraordinary, there being nothing but a High Masse. The Queen
was there and some ladies. But Lord, what an odde thing
it was for me to be in a crowd of people, here a footman,
there a beggar, here a fine lady, there a zealous poor
Papist, and here a Protestant, two or three together, come
to see the show. I was afeared of my pocket being picked
very much. Their music very good endeed, but their
service I confess too frivolous, that there can be no zeal go
along with it; and I do find by them themselfs, that they
do run over their beads with one hand, and point and
play and talk and make signs with the other, in the midst
of their Messe. But all things very rich and beautiful. And
I see the Papists had the wit, most of them, to bring
cushions to kneel on; which I wanted, and was mightily
troubled to kneel. All being done, and I sorry for my

coming, missing of what I expected; which was to have had a child borne and dressed there and a great deal of do, but we broke up and nothing like it done; and there I left people receiving the Sacrament, and the Queen gone, and ladies; only my [Lady] Castlemayne, who looks prettily in her night-clothes. And so took my coach, which waited, and away through Covent Garden to set down two gentlemen and a lady, who came thither to see also and did make mighty mirth in their talk of the folly of this religion. (*24 December 1667*)

Back to church and heard a good sermon of Mr Gifford's at our church, upon "Seek ye first the Kingdom of Heaven and its righteousness, and all these things shall be added to you." A very excellent and persuasive, good and moral sermon; showed like a wise man that righteousness is a surer moral way of being rich then sin and villainy. (*Lord's Day, 23 August 1668*)

Country Outings and River Excursions

¶ LONDONERS IN SEARCH OF A CHANGE from the town had not far to go. There were within easy distance country villages such as Hackney and Islington, and riverside resorts such as Barn Elms, a house and park near to the modern Barnes. Further afield to the south lay the Downs at Epsom and Banstead. Altogether, Pepys considered (14 July 1667) that it was not necessary to go to the expense and trouble of having a country house for week-ends. Later, he changed his mind and rented a villa in Parson's Green in 1677–9 and 1681.

[*At Brampton.*] We took horse and got early to Baldwick [*Baldock*]; where there was a fair, and we put in and eat a mouthful of porke, which they made us pay 14*d* for, which vexed us much. And so away to Stevenage and stayed till a showre was over; and so rode easily to Welling [*Welwyn*] – where we supped well and had two beds in the room and so lay single; and must remember it that, of all the nights that ever I slept in my life, I never did pass a night with more epicurisme of sleep – there being now and then a noise of people stirring that waked me; and then it was a very rainy night; and then I was a little weary, that what between waking and then sleeping again, one after another, I never had so much content in all my life. And so my wife says it was with her. (*23 September 1661*)

[*At Brampton.*] With my father took a walk to Portholme, seeing the country-maids milking their cowes there (they being there now at grasse) and to see with what mirth they come all home together in pomp with their milk, and sometimes they have musique go before them. (*13 October 1662*)

Having directed it last night, I was called up this morning before 4 a-clock. It was full light, enough to dress myself; and so by water against tide, it being a little coole, to Greenewich and thence (only that it was somewhat foggy till the sun got to some heighth) walked with great pleasure to Woolwich, in my way staying several times to listen to the nightingales. (*22 April 1664*)

I took my wife by coach out through the City, discoursing how to spend the afternoon -- and conquered, with much ado, a desire of going to a play. But took her out at Whitechapel and to Bednell Green; so to Hackny, where I have not been many a year, since a little child I boarded there. Thence to Kingsland by my nurse's house, Goody Lawrence, where my brother Tom and I was kept when young. Then to Newington Green and saw the outside of Mrs Herberts house where she lived, and my aunt Ellen with her. But Lord, how in every point I find myself to over-value things when a child. Thence to Islington, and so to St John's to the Red Bull and there saw the latter part of a rude prize fight -- but with good pleasure enough. And thence back to Islington and at the Kings Head, where Pitts lived, we light and eat and drunk for remembrance of the old house sake. And so through Kingsland again and so to Bishopsgate, and so home with great pleasure -- the country mighty pleasant; and we with great content home, and after supper to bed. (*25 April 1664*)

Up very betimes, and my wife also, and got us ready; and about 8 a-clock, having got some bottles of wine and beer and neat's tongues, we went to our barge at the Towre, where Mr Pierce and his wife and a kinswoman and his sister, and Mrs Clerke and her sister and cousin were to expect us. And so set out for the Hope, all the way down playing at cards and other sports, spending our time pretty merry. Came to the Hope about one, and there showed them all the ship[s] and had a collacion of anchoves, gammon &c.; and after an hour's stay or more imbarked again for home, and so to cards and other sports till we came to Greenwich; and there Mrs Clerke and my wife and I on shore to an alehouse for them to do their business, and so to the barge again, having shown them the King's pleasure-boat. And so home to the Bridge, bringing night home with us and it raining hard, but we got them on foot to the Beare and there put them into a boat; and I back to my wife in the barge and so to the Tower Wharf and home – being very well pleased today with the company, especially Mrs Pierce, who continues her complexion as well as ever, and hath at this day, I think, the best complexion that ever I saw on any woman, young or old, or child either, all days of my life. Also, Mrs Clerkes kinswoman sings very prettily, but is very confident in it. Mrs Clerke herself witty, but spoils all in being so conceited and making so great a flutter with a few fine clothes and some bad tawdry things worn with them. But the charge of the barge lies heavy upon me, which troubles me; but it is but once, and I may make Pierce do me some courtesy as great. (*6 July 1664*)

To Windsor to the Guarter, and thither sent for Dr Childe – who came to us, and carried us to St Georges Chapel and there placed us among the Knights' stalls (and pretty the observation, that no man, but a woman, may sit in a Knight's place where any brasse-plates are set). And hither comes cushions to us, and a young singing-boy to bring us a copy of the anthemne to be sung. And here, for our sakes, had this anthem and the great service sung extraordinary, only to entertain us. It is a noble place endeed, and good quire of voices. After prayers, we to see the plate of the Chapel and the robes of Knights, and a man to show us the banners of the several Knights in being, which hang up over the stalls. And so to other discourse, very pretty, about that Order. Was shown where the late [King] is buried, and King Henry the 8, and my Lady Seymour. This being done, to the King's house and to observe the neatness and contrivance of the house and gates; it is the most romantique castle that is in the world. But Lord, the prospect that is in the balcone in the Queen's lodgings, and the tarrace and walk, are strange things to consider, being the best in the world, sure. Infinitely satisfied, I and my wife with all this; she being in all points mightily pleased too, which added to my pleasure. And so giving a great deal of money to this and that man and woman, we to our tavern and there dined, the Doctor with us; and so took coach and away to Eaton, the Doctor with me. At Eaton I left my wife in the coach, and he and I to the college and there find all mighty fine. The school good, and the custom pretty of boys cutting their names in the shuts of the window when they go to Cambrige; by which many a one hath lived to see himself Provost and Fellow, that had his name in the window standing. To the hall, and there find the boys' verses, *De peste*; it being their custom to make verses at Shrovetide. I read several, and very good they were, and better I think then ever I made when I was a boy – and in rolls as long and longer then the whole hall by much. Here is a picture of Venice hung up, given, and a monument made of Sir H. Wottons giving it, to the college. Thence to the Porters, in the absence of the butler, and did drink of the college beer, which is very good, and went into the back fields to see the scholars play. Thence took leave of the Doctor; and so took coach, and finely, but sleepy, away home, and got thither about 8 at night; and after a little at my office, I to bed. (*26 February 1666*)

After dinner, with my wife and Mercer and Jane by water all the afternoon up as high as Moreclacke, with great pleasure, and a fine day – reading over the second part of *The Siege of Rhodes* with great delight. We landed and walked at Barne Elmes; and then at the Neat Houses I landed and bought a millon (and we did also land and eat and drink at Wandsworth); and so to the Old Swan, and there walked home – it being a mighty fine evening. (*5 August 1666*)

I away to my boat, and up with it as far as Barne Elmes, reading of Mr Eveling's late new book against solitude, in which I do not find much excess of good matter, though it be pretty for a by-discourse. I walked the length of the Elmes, and with great pleasure saw some gallant ladies and people, come with their bottles and basket[s] and chairs and form[s] to sup under the trees by the waterside, which was mighty pleasant. (*26 May 1667*)

Up, and my wife, a little before 4, and to make us ready; and by and by Mrs Turner came to us by agreement, and she and I stayed talking below while my wife dressed herself; which vexed me that she was so long about it, keeping us till past 5 a-clock before she was ready. She ready, and taking some bottles of wine and beer and some cold fowle with us into the coach, we took coach and four horses which I had provided last night, and so away – a very fine day; and so towards Epsum, talking all the way pleasantly, and perticularly of the pride and ignorance of Mrs Lowther in having of her train carried up. The country very fine; only, the way very dusty. We got to Epsum by 8 a-clock to the Well, where much company; and there we light and I drank the water. [*After dinner*] the women and W. Hewer and I walked upon the Downes, where a flock of sheep was, and the most pleasant and innocent sight that ever I saw in my life; we find a shepheard and his little boy reading, far from any houses or sight of people, the Bible to him. So I made the boy read to me, which he did with the forced tone that children do usually read, that was mighty pretty; and then I did give him something and went to the father and talked with him; and I find he had been a servant in my Cosen Pepys's house, and told me what was become of their old servants. He did content himself mightily in my liking his boy's reading and did bless God for him, the most like one of the old Patriarchs that ever I saw in my life, and it brought those thoughts of the old age of the world in my mind for two or three days after. We took notice of his woolen knit stockings of two colours mixed, and of his shoes shod with iron shoes, both at the toe and heels, and with great nails in the soles of his feet, which was mighty pretty; and taking notice of them, "Why," says the poor man, "the Downes, you see, are full of stones, and we are fain to shoe ourselfs thus; and these," says he, "will make the stones fly till they sing before me." I did give the poor man something, for which he was mighty thankful, and I tried to cast stones with his horne crooke. He values his dog mightily, that would turn a sheep any way which he would have him when he goes to fold them. Told me there was about 18 scoare sheep in his flock, and that he hath 4s. a week the year round for keeping of them. So we parted thence, with mighty pleasure in the discourse we had with this poor man; and Mrs Turner, in the common fields here, did gather one of the prettiest nosegays that ever I saw in my life. So to our coach, and through Mr Minnes's wood and looked upon Mr Eveling's house; and so over the common and through Epsum towne to our inne, in the way stopping a poor woman with her milk-pail and in one of my gilt tumblers did drink our bellyfuls of milk, better than any creame; and so to our inne and there had a dish of creame, but it was sour and so had no pleasure in it; and so paid our reckoning and took coach, it being about 7 at night, and passed and saw the people walking with their wifes and children to take the ayre; and we set out for home, the sun by and by going down, and we in the cool of the evening all the way with much pleasure home, talking and pleasing ourselfs with the pleasure of this day's work; and Mrs Turner mightily pleased with my resolution, which I tell her is never to keep a country-house, but to keep a coach and with my wife on the Saturday to go sometimes for a day to this place and then quite to another place; and there is more variety, and as little charge and no trouble, as there is in a country-house. Anon it grew dark, and as it grew dark we had pleasure to see several glow wormes, which was mighty pretty. (*Lord's Day, 14 July 1667*)

[*Pepys travels from Chatham to Maidstone.*] So away, it being a mighty cold and windy, but clear day, and had the pleasure of seeing the Medway running, winding up

and down mightily, and a very fine country. Thence to
Maydstone, which I had a mighty mind to see, having
never been there; and walked all up and down the town,
and up to the top of the steeple and had a noble view, and
then down again and in the town did see an old man
beating of flax, and did step into the barn and give him
money and saw that piece of husbandry, which I never
saw, and it is very pretty. In the street also, I did buy and
send to our inne, the Bell, a dish of fresh fish; and so
having walked all round the town, and find it very pretty
as most towns I ever saw, though not very big, and
people of good fashion in it, we to our inne to dinner, and
had a good dinner; and after dinner a barber came to me
and there trimmed me, that I might be clean against night
to go to Mrs Allen; and so staying till about 4 a-clock, we
set out, I alone in the coach going and coming; and in our
way back, I light out of the way to see a Saxon
monument [*Kit's Coty House*], as they say, of a king;
which is three stones staying upright and a great round
one lying on them, of great bigness, although not so big
as those on Salsbury-plain, but certainly it is a thing of
great antiquity, and I mightily glad to see it. (*24 March
1669*)

Dinners and Parties

¶ GRAND DINNERS CONSISTED of several courses each of which included a variety of dishes. It was usual for all of these to be put on the table together, but Pepys also records the more modern practice of serving a succession of courses (13 January 1663), and of bringing in one dish at a time (23 January 1669). The French habit of beginning with soup and proceeding to entrée and then roast makes its appearance at 12 May 1667. The absence of vegetables and fruit is illusory: although part of the meal they were rarely mentioned in Pepys's account, being treated as garnishes or accompaniments. Pepys was fond of oysters which, as in Dickens's London, were a popular food rather than a luxury. For Pepys, venison pasty was a favourite party dish.

A special feast day in Pepys's calendar was his 'stone feast', when, on or about 26 March, he celebrated his recovery from his operation for the stone in 1658. The company often included his surgeon, Thomas Hollier; on 26 March 1662 it included his cousin Jane Turner, in whose house in Salisbury Court the operation had been performed.

The 'earthen pitchers and wooden dishes' at the Lord Mayor's Dinner of 1663 are reminders of the losses suffered by the City during the Interregnum.

I went home and took my wife and went to my Cosen Tho. Pepys's and found them just sat down to dinner, which was very good; only the venison pasty was palpable beef, which was not handsome. (*6 January 1660*)

I met with Osborne and with Shaw and Spicer, and then we went to the Sun tavern in expectation of a dinner, where we had sent us only two trencherfuls of meat, at which we were very merry, while in came Mr Wade and his friend Capt. Moyse, and here we stayed till 7 at night, I winning a quart of sack of Shaw that one trencherful that was sent us was all lamb, and he that it was veale. I, by having but 3*d.* in my pocket, made shift to spend no more; whereas if I had had more I had spent more, as the rest did. So that I see it is an advantage to a man to carry little in his pocket. (*16 February 1660*)

Mr Moore and I and several others being invited today by Mr Goodman, a friend of his, we dined at the Bull Head upon the best venison pasty that ever I eat of in my life; and with one dish more, it was the best dinner I ever was at. Here ris in discourse at table a dispute between Mr Moore and Dr Clerke, the former affirming that it was essentiall to a tragedy to have the argument of it true, which the Doctor denyed and left to me to be judge – and the cause to be determind next Tuesday morning at the same place upon the eating of the remains of the pasty, and the loser to spend 10*s*. (*1 September 1660*)

After dinner [Sir J. Mennes] begun some sports; among others, the nameing of people round, and afterward demanding questions of them that they are forced to answer their names to; which doth make very good sport. And here I took pleasure to take the forfeits of the ladies who could not do their duty, by kissing of them – among others, a pretty lady who I found afterward to be wife to Sir W. Battens son. (*4 February 1661*)

To the Dolphin to a dinner of Mr Harris's, where Sir Wms both and my Lady Batten and her two daughters and other company – where a great deal of mirth. And there stayed till 11 a-clock at night. And in our mirth I sang and sometimes fiddled (there being a noise of fiddlers there) and at last we fell to dancing – the first time that ever I did in my life – which I did wonder to see myself to do. At last we made Mingo, Sir W. Battens blaqk, and Jack, Sir W. Pens, dance; and it was strange how the first did dance with a great deal of seeming skill. (*27 March 1661*)

I stayed at the Miter, whither I had invited all my old acquaintance of the Exchequer to a good chine of beefe – which with three barrels of oysters and three pullets and plenty of wine and mirth, was our dinner. There was about twelve of us. And here I made them a foolish promise to give them one this day twelvemonth, and so for ever while I live. But I do not entend it. (*30 December 1661*)

At noon I dined with Sir W. Batten with many friends more, it being his wedding day. And among other froliques, it being their third year, they had three pyes, whereof the middlemost was made of an ovall form in an ovall hole within the other two which made much mirth and was called the middle peace; and above all the rest, wc had great striving to steal a spoonefull out of it; and I remember Mrs Mills the minister's wife did steal one for me and did give it me; and to end all, Mrs Shippman did fill the pie full of white wine (it holding at least a pint and a half) and did drink it off for a health to Sir Wm and my Lady, it being the greatest draught that ever I did see a woman drink in my life. Before we had dined came Sir G. Carteret, and we went all three to the office and did business there till night. And then to Sir Wm Batten again, and I went along with my Lady and the rest of the gentlewomen to Maj. Holmes's, and there we had a fine supper; among others, excellent lobsters, which I never eat at this time of the year before. Here we stayed late, and at last home. And being in my chamber, we do hear great noise of mirth at Sir Wm Battens, tearing the ribbands from my Lady and him. So I to bed. (*3 February 1662*)

Up earely – this being, by God's great blessing, the fourth solemne day of my cutting for the stone this day four year. And am by God's mercy in very good health, and like to do well, the Lord's name be praised for it. To the office and Sir G. Carterets all the morning, about business. At noon came my good guest[s], Madame Turner, The[oph]., and Cosen Norton, and a gentleman, one Mr Lewin of the King's Life-guard. I had a pretty dinner for them – *viz*: a brace of stewed carps, six roasted chicken, and a jowle of salmon hot, for the first course – a tanzy and two neats' tongues and cheese the second. And were very merry all the afternoon, talking and singing and piping on the flagelette. In the evening they went with great pleasure away; and I with great content, and my wife, walked half an houre in the garden; and so home to supper and to bed. (*26 March 1662*)

So my poor wife rose by 5 a-clock in the morning, before day, and went to market and bought fowle and many other things for dinner – with which I was highly pleased. And the chine of beef was done also before 6 a-clock, and my own jacke, of which I was doubtful, doth carry it very well. Things being put in order and the cooke come, I went to the office, where we sat till noon; and then broke up and I home, whither by and by comes Dr Clerke and his lady, his sister and a she-cosen, and Mr Pierce and his wife, which was all my guest[s]. I had for them, after oysters – at first course, a hash of rabbits and lamb, and a rare chine of beef; next, a great dish of

roasted fowl, cost me about 30s., and a tart; and then fruit
and cheese. My dinner was noble and enough. I had my
house mighty clean and neat, my room below with a
good fire in it – my dining-room above, and my chamber
being made a withdrawing-chamber, and my wife's a
good fire also. I find my new table very proper, and will
hold nine or ten people well, but eight with great room.
After dinner, the women to cards in my wife's chamber
and the Doctor [and] Mr Pierce in mine, because the
dining-room smokes unless I keep a good charcole fire,
which I was not then provided with. At night to supper;
had a good sack-posset and cold meat and sent my guests
away about 10 a-clock at night – both them and myself
highly pleased with our management of this day. And
indeed, their company was very fine and Mrs Clerke a
very witty, fine lady, though a little conceited and proud.
So weary to bed. I believe this day's feast will cost me
near 5l. (*13 January 1663*)

Home to dinner whither by and by comes Roger Pepys,
Mrs Turner, her daughter, Joyce Norton and a young
lady, a daughter of Coll. Cockes, my uncle Wight, his
wife and Mrs Anne Wight – this being my feast, in lieu of
what I should have had a few days ago, for my cutting of
the stone, for which the Lord make me truly thankful.
Very merry before, at, and after dinner, and the more for
that my dinner was great and most neatly dressed by our
own only mayde. We had a fricasse of rabbets and
chicken – a leg of mutton boiled – three carps in a dish – a
great dish of a side of lamb – a dish [of] roasted pigeons –
a dish of four lobsters – three tarts – a lampry pie, a most
rare pie – a dish of anchoves – good wine of several sorts;
and all things mighty noble and to my great content.

After dinner to Hide Parke. Here about an hour; and so leaving all by the way, we home and find the house as clean as if nothing had been done there today from top to bottom – which made us give the cooke 12*d*. a piece, each of us. (*4 April 1663*)

Our dinner, it being Good Friday, was only sugar sopps and fish; the only time that we have had a Lenten dinner all this Lent. (*17 April 1663*)

Up and to the office, where we sat; and at noon Sir G. Carteret, Sir J. Mennes and I to dinner to my Lord Mayors, being invited; where was the Farmers of the Customes, my Lord Chancellors three sons, and other great and much company, and a very great noble dinner, as this Mayor is good for nothing else. No extraordinary discourse of anything, every man being intent upon his dinner. (*20 October 1663*)

At noon I went forth, by coach to Guild Hall, where under every salt there was a bill of fare, and at the end of the table the persons proper for that table. Many were the tables, but none in the Hall but the Mayors and the Lords of the Privy Councell that had napkins or knives – which was very strange. We went into the Buttry and there stayed and talked, and then into the Hall again. By and by met with Creed; and we with the others went within the several Courts and there saw the tables prepared for the ladies and Judges and Bishops – all great sign of a great dinner to come. By and by, about one a-clock, before the Lord Mayor came, came into the Hall, from the room where they were first led into, the Lord Chancellor (Archbishopp before him), with the Lords of the Council and 'other Bishopps, and they to dinner. Anon comes the Lord Mayor, who went up to the Lords and then to the other tables to bid wellcome; and so all to dinner. I set near Proby, Baron, and Creed at the Merchant Strangers table – where ten good dishes to a messe, with plenty of wine of all sorts, of which I drunk none; but it was very unpleasing that we had no napkins nor change of trenchers, and drunk out of earthen pitchers and wooden dishes. It happened that, after the Lords had half dined, came the French Ambassador up to the Lords' table, where he was to have sat; but finding the table set, he would not sit down nor dine with the Lord Mayor, who was not yet come, nor have a table to himself, which was offered; but in a discontent went away again. After I had dined, I and Creed rose and went up and down the house, and up to the ladies room and there stayed gazing upon them. But though there were many and fine, both young and old, yet I could not discern one handsome face there, which was very strange. I expected musique, but there was none; but only trumpets and drums, which displeased me. The dinner, it seems, is made by the Mayor and two Sheriffs for the time being, the Lord Mayor paying one half and they the other – and the whole, Proby says, is reckoned to come to about 7 or 800*l* at most. Being wearied with looking upon a company of ugly women, Creed and I went away; and took coach and through Cheapside and there saw the pageants, which were very silly. (*Lord Mayor's Day, 29 October 1663*)

I to Capt. Cocke's where I find my Lord Brouncker and his mistress and Sir J. Mennes – where we supped (there was also Sir W. Doyly and Mr Eveling); but the receipt of this news [*of Sandwich's capture of several Dutch merchantmen*] did put us all into such an extasy of joy, that it inspired into Sir J. Mennes and Mr Eveling such a spirit of mirth, that in all my life I never met with so merry a two hours as our company this night was. Among other humours, Mr Eveling's repeating of some verses made up of nothing but the various acceptations of 'may' and 'can', and doing it so aptly, upon occasion of something of that nature, and so fast, did make us all die almost with laughing, and did so stop the mouth of Sir J. Mennes in the middle of all his mirth (and in a thing agreeing with his own manner of genius) that I never saw any man so out-done in all my life; and Sir J. Mennes's mirth too, to see himself out-done, was the crown of all our mirth. In this humour we sat till about 10 at night; and so my Lord and his mistress home, and we to bed – it being one of the times of my life wherein I was the fullest of true sense of joy. (*Lord's Day, 10 September 1665*)

I to my chamber, till in the evening our company came to supper we had invited to a venison pasty – Mr Batelier and his sister Mary, Mrs Mercer, her daughter Anne, Mr Le Brun, and W. Hewers. And so we supped, and very merry. And then about 9 a-clock, to Mrs Mercers gate, where the fire and boys expected us and her son had provided abundance of serpents and rockets; and there mighty merry (my Lady Pen and Pegg going thither with us and Nan Wright) till about 12 at night, flinging our fireworks and burning one another and the people over the way. And at last, our businesses being most spent – we into Mrs Mercers, and there mighty merry, smutting one another with candlegresse and soot, till most of us were like devils; and that being done, then we broke up and to my house, and there I made them drink; and upstairs we went, and then fell into dancing (W. Batelier dancing well) and dressing, him and I and one Mr Banister (who with his wife came over also with us) like women; and Mercer put on a suit of Toms, like a boy, and mighty mirth we had, and Mercer danced a jigg, and Nan Wright and my wife and Pegg Pen put on periwigs. Thus we spent till 3 or 4 in the morning, mighty merry; and then parted and to bed. (*Thanksgiving Day, 14 August 1666, appointed to celebrate the victory of the Battle of St James's Day, 25 July*)

[My wife] and I homeward; and in our way bethought ourselfs of going alone, she and I, to a French house to dinner, and so enquired out Monsieur Robins my periwig-maker, who keeps an ordinary, and in an ugly street in Covent Garden did find him at the door, and so we in; and in a moment almost have the table covered, and clean glasses, and all in the French manner, and a mess of potage first and then a couple of pigeons *a l'esteuvé*, and then a piece of *bœuf-a-la-mode*, all exceeding well seasoned and to our great liking; at least, it would have been anywhere else but in this bad street and in a periwig-maker's house; but to see the pleasant and ready attendance that we had, and all things so desirous to please and ingenious in the people, did take me mightily – our dinner cost us 6s. (*12 May 1667*)

Up, and again to look after the setting things right against dinner, which I did to very good content; and so to the office, where all the morning till noon, when word brought me to the Board that my Lord Sandwich was come; so I presently rose, leaving the Board ready to rise, and there I found my Lord Sandwich, Peterburgh, and Sir Ch. Herberd; and presently after them come my Lord Hinchingbrooke, Mr Sidny, and Sir Wm Godolphin; and after greeting them, and some time spent in talk, dinner was brought up, onc dish after another, but a dish at a time; but all so good, but above all things, the variety of wines, and excellent of their kind, I had for them, and all in so good order, that they were mightily pleased, and myself full of content at it; and endeed it was, of a dinner of about six or eight dishes, as noble as any man need to have I think – at least, all was done in the noblest manner that ever I had any, and I have rarely seen in my life better anywhere else – even at the Court. After dinner, my Lords to cards, and the rest of us sitting about them and talking, and looking on my books and pictures and my wife's drawings, which they commend mightily; and mighty merry all day long, with exceeding great content, and so till 7 at night; and so took their leaves, it being dark and foul weather. Thus was this entertainment over, the best of its kind, and the fullest of honour and content to me that ever I had in my life, and shall not easily have so good again. So to my wife's chamber, and there supped and got her cut my hair and look my shirt, for I have itched mightily these six or seven days; and when all came to all, she finds that I am louzy, having found in my head and body above 20 lice, little and great; which I wonder at, being more then I have had I believe almost these 20 years. I did think I might have got them from the little boy, but they did presently look him, and found none – so how they came, I know not; but presently did shift myself, and so shall be rid of them, and cut my hayre close to my head. And so, with much content to bed. (*23 January 1669*)

Up and at the office till noon, when home; and there I find my company come – *viz.* Madam Turner, Dike, The[oph]. and Betty Turner, and Mr Bellwood, formerly their father's clerk but now set up for himself, a conceited silly fellow but one they make mightily of, my Cosen Roger Pepys and his wife and two daughters. And I had a noble dinner for them as I almost ever had, and mighty merry; and perticularly, myself pleased with looking on Betty Turner who is mighty pretty. After dinner we fell one to one talk, and another to another, and looking over my house and closet and things, and The[oph]. Turner to write a letter to a lady in the country, in which I did now and then put in half a dozen words, and sometimes five or six lines, and then she as much, and made up a long and good letter, she being mighty witty really, though troublesome-humoured with it. And thus till night, that our music came and the office ready, and candles; and also W. Batelier and his sister Susan came, and also Will How and two gentlemen more, strangers, which at my request yesterday he did bring to dance, called Mr Ireton and Mr Starkey; we fell to dancing and continued, only with intermission for a good supper, till 2 in the morning, the music being Greeting and another most excellent violin and theorbo, the best in town; and so, with mighty mirth and pleased with their dancing of jiggs afterward, several of them, and among others Betty Turner, who did it mighty prettily; and lastly, W. Batelier's blackmore and blackmore-maid, and then to a country-dance again; and so broke up with extraordinary pleasure, as being one of the days and nights of my life spent with the greatest content, and that which I can but hope to repeat again a few times in my whole life. This done, we parted, the strangers home, and I did lodge my cousin Pepys and his wife in our blue chamber – my cousin Turner, her sister, and The[oph]. in our best chamber – Babb, Betty, and Betty Turner in our own chamber; and myself and my wife in the maid's bed, which is very good – our maids in the coachman's bed – the coachman with the boy in his settle-bed; and Tom where he uses to lie; and so I did to my great content lodge at once in my house, with great ease, fifteen, and eight of them strangers of quality. My wife this day put on first her French gown, called a *Sac*, which becomes her very well, brought her over by W. Batelier. (*2 March 1669*)

Encounters with Children

¶ PEPYS HAD THE SENSIBILITIES of his time. He had not the least compunction in thrashing a disobedient young servant boy till his arm ached (below, p. 53, 21 June 1662), and he was not at all shocked by the sight of young children at work in a reformatory (4 October 1664). Nevertheless, his love of children was deep and real, and declares itself at many points in the diary.

The little James Pearse (Pierce), whose pert wit Pepys found irresistible, became a clerk in the Navy Office and later a purser. The children of the Duke and Duchess of York (14 May 1667) were the young Dukes of Cambridge and Kendal who died shortly afterwards. Their mother was Anne Hyde, Clarendon's daughter. As for the promising 12-year-old twin sons of his patron Sandwich, so fluent with their Horatian odes, John became Master of Trinity and Dean of Durham, and Oliver became Solicitor-General to Queen Mary.

At about 9 a-clock, after we had breakfasted, we sett forth [*on horseback from Chatham*] for London. But of all the journeys that ever I made, this was the merriest, and I was in a strange moode for mirth. I met two little schooleboys, going with pichers of ale to their schoolmaster to break up against Easter; and I did drink of some of one of them and give him two pence. By and by we came to two little girls keeping cowes; and I saw one of them very pretty, so I had a minde to make her aske my blessing. And telling that I was her godfather, she asked me innocently whether I was not Ned Wooding, and I said that I was; so she kneeled down and very simply cried, "Pray, godfather, pray to God to bless me" – which made us very merry and I gave her twopence. In several places I asked women whether they would sell me their children; that they denied me all, but said they would give me one to keep for them if I would. (*11 April 1661*)

To dinner to my Lady Sandwich; and Sir Tho. Crewes children coming thither, I took them and all my Lady's to the Tower and showed them the lions and all that was to be shown, and so took them to my house and there made much of them; and so saw them back to my Lady's – Sir Th. Crewes children being as pretty and the best behaved that ever I saw of their age. (*3 May 1662*)

[*At the New Bridewell Workhouse*] I did with great pleasure see the many pretty works and the little children imployed, everyone to do something; which was a very fine sight and worthy incouragement. I cast away a crowne among them, and so to the Change. (*4 October 1664*)

At last we got a fisherboy by chance and took him into the boat; and being an odd kind of boy, did vex us too, for he would not answer us aloud when we spoke to him; but did carry us safe though with a mistake or two, but I wonder they were not more. We went to the Crowne Inne at Rochester, and there to supper and made ourselfs merry with our poor fisherboy, who told us he had not been in a bed in the whole seven year since he came to prentice, and hath two or three year more to serve. (*25 September 1665*)

I walked into the park, with [Mrs Pierce's] little boy James with me, who is the wittiest boy, and the best company in the world. And so back again through Whitehall both coming and going. And people did generally take him to be my boy – and some would ask me. (*15 April 1666*)

To Putny church, where I saw the girls of the schools, few of which pretty. And there I came into a pew and met with little James Pierce; which I was much pleased at, the little rogue being very glad to see me. Here was a good sermon and much company, but I sleepy and a little out of order for my hat falling down through a hole underneath the pulpit; which however, after sermon, by a stick and the help of the clerk, I got up again. And then walked out of the church with the boy, and then left him, promising him to get him a play another time. (*Lord's Day, 28 April 1667*)

It was pretty to observe how when my Lord [Chancellor] sent down to St James's to see why the Duke of York came not, and Mr Povy, who went, returned, my Lord did ask (not how the Princes or the Dukes do, as other people do) but "How do the children?" which me-thought was mighty great, and like a great man and grandfather. (*14 May 1667*)

Here [*at Hinchingbrooke, the Sandwichs' country house*] I spent alone with my Lady, after dinner, the most of the afternoon; and anon the two twins were sent for from schoole at Mr Taylors to come to see me; and I took them into the garden and there in one of the summer-houses did examine them; and do find them so well advanced in their learning, that I was amazed at it, they repeating a whole Ode without book out of Horace, and did give me a very good account of anything almost, and did make me very readily very good Latin and did give me good account of their Greek grammer, beyond all possible expectation; and so grave and manly as I never saw, I confess, nor could have believed – so that they will be fit to go on to Cambridge in two years at most. They are but little, but very like one another; and well-looked children. (*10 October 1667*)

The Householder

¶ FROM JULY 1660 Pepys and his wife lived in official lodgings in the Navy Office building in Seething Lane not far from the Tower. The house, as far as we can judge, had about ten rooms and was three or four storeys high. There was a garden to the south, enjoyed in common by all the resident officers of the Navy Board, and a forecourt protected by entrance gates and a porter's lodge. At the time of their moving to Seething Lane the Pepyses had two servants – a maid and a footboy; the number grew to six by December 1668 – a lady's companion, a cook, two maids, a boy and a coachman who doubled as waiter. The Pepyses' difficulty seems to have been not in finding servants but in managing and retaining them. Perhaps Elizabeth was at fault – Pepys certainly thought so. For his part he applied a strict discipline – as did most householders. But he also delighted in the company of his 'family' of servants. Two of them became his lifelong friends and allies – Jane Birch, his first servant ('our old little Jane'), and Tom Edwards, who came into Pepys's service in 1664 from the Chapel Royal, after his voice had broken. Tom and Jane married, much to the Pepyses' delight, and called their first son Samuel. He ultimately became a lieutenant in the navy and Tom, the father, became navy agent at Dover.

The number of occasions on which Pepys had workmen in the house reflects not only his pride in improving it, but also the fact that the King paid for the work.

By coach home – where the playsterers being at work in all the rooms in my house, my wife was fain to make a bed upon the ground for her and I; and so there we lay all night. (*25 September 1660*)

At home with the workmen all the afternoon, our house being in a most sad pickle. (*26 September 1660*)

All the afternoon at home among my workmen; work till 10 or 11 at night; and did give them drink and were very merry with them – it being my luck to meet with a sort of drolling workmen upon all occasions. (*28 September 1660*)

This morning, observing some things to be laid up not as they should be by the girl, I took a broom and basted her till she cried extremely, which made me vexed. (*1 December 1660*)

At dinner and supper, I drank, I know not how, of my owne accord, so much wine, that I was even almost foxed and my head aked all night. So home, and to bed without prayers, which I never did yet since I came to the house of a Sonday night: I being now so out of order that I durst not read prayers, for fear of being perceived by my servants in what case I was. So to bed. (*Lord's Day, 29 September 1661*)

This day I did give my man Will a sound lesson about his forbearing to give us the respect due to a master and mistress. (*25 October 1661*)

At my coming home, I am sorry to find my wife displeased with her maid Doll:, whose fault is that she cannot keep her peace, but will alway be talking in an angry manner, though it be without any reason and to no purpose. Which I am sorry for – and do see the inconvenience that doth attend the increase of a man's fortune, by being forced to keep more servants, which brings trouble. (*30 October 1661*)

All morning in the sellar with the colliers, removing the coles out of the old coal-hole into the new one, which cost me 8s. the doing; but now the cellar is done and made clean, it doth please me exceedingly, as much as anything that was ever yet done to my house. I pray God keep me from setting my mind too much upon it. About 3 a-clock, the colliers having done, I went up to dinner (my wife having often urged me to come, but my mind is so set upon these things that I cannot but be with the workmen to see things done to my mind; which if I am not there is seldom done); and so to the office. (*8 February 1662*)

Home and to bed, my mind troubled about the charge of money that is in my house, which I had forgot. But I made the maids to rise and light a candle and set it in the dining room to scare away thiefs. And so to sleep. (*3 June 1662*)

Having from my wife and the maids complaints made of the boy, I called him up and with my whip did whip him till I was not able to stir, and yet I could not make him confess any of the lies that they tax him with. At last, not willing to let him go away a conqueror, I took him in task again and pulled off his frock to his shirt, and whipped him till he did confess that he did drink the whay, which he hath denied. And pulled a pinke, and above all, did lay the candlesticke upon the ground in his chamber, which he hath denied this quarter of this year. I confess it is one of the greatest wonders that ever I met with, that such a little boy as he could possibly be able to suffer half so much as he did to maintain a lie. But I think I must be forced to put him away. So to bed, with my arme very weary. (*21 June 1662*)

I do live at my lodgings in the Navy Office – my family being, besides my wife and I, Jane Gentleman, Besse our excellent good-natured cook-maid, and Susan, a little girl – having neither man nor boy, nor like to have again a good while – living now in most perfect content and quiet and very frugally also. (*31 December 1663*)

Home and there find my boy Tom Edwards come – sent me by Captain Cooke, having [been] bred in the King's Chapel these four years. I purpose to make a clerk of him; and if he deserves well, to do well by him. [I] find [him] a very schoole-boy that talks inocently and impertinently; but at present it is a sport to us, and in a little time he will leave it. So sent him to bed, he saying that he used to go to bed at 8 a-clock. And then all of us to bed, myself pretty well pleased with my choice of a boy. (*27 August 1664*)

At supper, hearing by accident of my mayds their letting in a rogueing Scotch woman that haunts the office, to help them to wash and scour in our house, and that very lately, I fell mightily out, and made my wife, to the disturbance of the house and neighbours, to beat our little girle; and then we shut her down into the cellar and there she lay all night. So we to bed. (*19 February 1665*)

Dressed and had my head combed by my little girle, to whom I confess que je sum demasiado kind, nuper ponendo sæpe mes mains in su dos choses de son breast. Mais il faut que je leave it, lest it bring me to alguno major inconvenience. (*Lord's Day, 6 August 1665*)

[54]

It being fast-day [*for the Plague*], I stayed at home all day long to set things to rights in my chamber, by taking out all my books and putting my chamber in the same condition it was before the Plague. But in the morning, doing of it and knocking up a nail, I did bruise my left thumb, so as broke a great deal of my flesh off, that it hung by a little. It was a sight frighted my wife – but I put some balsam of Mrs Turners to it, and though in great pain, yet went on with my business; and did it to my full content, setting everything in order. (*7 February 1666*)

This day poor Jane, my old little Jane, came to us again, to my wife's and my great content; and we hope to take mighty pleasure in her, she having all the marks and qualities of a good and loving and honest servant – she coming by force away from the other place where she hath lived ever since she went from us, and at our desire – her late mistress having used all the stratagems she could to keep her. (*29 March 1666*)

By and by home and there find our Luce drunk, and when her mistress told her of it, would be gone; and so put up some of her things and did go away of her accord, nobody pressing her to it; and the truth is, though she be the dirtiest and homeliest servant that ever I kept, yet I was sorry to have her go, partly through my love to my servants and partly because she was a very drudging, working wench; only, she would be drunk. (*18 May 1667*)

Waked about 7 a-clock this morning with a noise I supposed I heard near our chamber, of knocking, which by and by increased, and I more awake, could distinguish it better; I then waked my wife and both of us wondered at it, and lay so a great while, while that encreased; and at last heard it plainer, knocking as if it were breaking down a window for people to get out – and then removing of stools and chairs, and plainly by and by going up and down our stairs. We lay both of us afeared; yet I would have rose, but my wife would not let me; besides, I could not do it without making noise; and we did both conclude that thiefs were in the house, but wondered what our people did, whom we thought either killed or afeared as we were. Thus we lay till the clock struck 8, and high day. At last I removed my gown and slippers safely to the other side of the bed over my wife, and there safely rose and put on my gown and breeches, and then with a firebrand in my hand safely opened the door, and saw nor heard anything. Then (with fear, I confess) went to the maid's chamber-door, and all quiet and safe. Called Jane up, and went down safely and opened my chamber, where all well. Then more freely about, and to the kitchen, where the cook-maid up and all safe. So up again, and when Jane came and we demanded whether she heard no noise, she said, "Yes, and was afeared," but rose with the other maid and found nothing, but heard a noise in the great stack of chimneys that goes from Sir J. Mennes's through our house; and so we sent, and their chimneys have been swept this morning, and the noise was that and nothing else. It is one of the most extraordinary accidents in my life, and gives ground to think of Don Quixot's adventures how people may be surprized – and the more from an accident last night, that our young gibb-cat did leap down our stairs from top to bottom at two leaps and frighted us, that we could not tell well whether it was the cat or a spirit, and do sometimes think this morning that the house might be haunted. Glad to have this so well over, and endeed really glad in my mind, for I was much afeared. (*29 November 1667*)

This night our poor little dogg Fancy was in a strange fit of madness through age, of which she hath had five or six. (*2 December 1667*)

This day, my father's letters tell me of the death of poor Fancy in the country, big with puppies, which troubles me, as being one of my oldest acquaintances and servants. (*16 September 1668*)

My wife abroad with Jane, who was married yesterday; and I to the office busy, till by and by my wife comes home; so home and there hear how merry they were yesterday; and I glad at it, they being married it seems very handsomely, at Islington, and dined at the [King's Head] and lay in our blue chamber, with much company and wonderful merry. The[ophila] Turner and Mary Battalier bridemaids, and Talb[ot] Pepys and W. Hewers bridemen. (*27 March 1669*)

Lay long, talking with pleasure with my wife, and so up and to the office with Tom, who looks mighty smug upon his marriage, as Jane also doth, [to] both of whom I did give joy. (*Lord's Day, 29 March 1669*)

The Husband

¶ THE DIARY CAN BE READ as the history of a marriage, and
the extracts chosen here are meant to illustrate its varied
fortunes. As is well known, Pepys was frequently unfaithful,
but there is no doubt of the depth and sincerity of his
affection for his wife. Their tiffs and quarrels make vivid
reading, but taken alone they give an incomplete picture:
the diary also provides a wealth of evidence of their
enjoying life together.

Perhaps the greatest source of their marital difficulties was
what may be called the theoretical basis on which the
marriage was founded – the Divine Right of Husbands.
There are many signs of Pepys's authoritarianism in these
passages – he was self-centred, as perhaps all diarists are, and
it may well be significant that in the diary he never mentions
Elizabeth's birthday, though with one exception he always
records his own. Another source of difficulty arose from the
different circumstances of their daily lives. Elizabeth
resented the fact that while Pepys's duties left him free to
roam over London, her duties kept her at home and too
dependent on the company of servants (9 January, 27
August 1663). The company of children might have helped.

Emotions ran deep between them: Pepys had fallen
violently in love with her (below, p. 95, 27 February 1668),
and had married her when she was only 15. In the early days
of their marriage they had had 'differences' which are never
explained but which had led to Elizabeth's leaving him for a
while (below, 4 July 1664). In the diary years each was
capable of provoking the other to fits of jealousy. In
Elizabeth's case these were only too well founded, although
she uncovered only one of Pepys's outright infidelities – the
most serious affair of all, that with her young companion,
Deb Willet (see below, pp. 255–69).

Pepys's mistresses mentioned here were two sisters, Doll
Lane and Betty Martin, who had stalls in Westminster Hall.
Betty Mitchell was the wife of an innkeeper.

I went up to put my papers in order; and finding my
wife's clothes lie carelessly laid up, I was angry with her,
which I was troubled for. (*19 August 1660*)

I went by water home, where I was angry with my wife for her things lying about, and in my passion kicked the little fine baskett which I bought her in Holland and broke it, which troubled me after I had done it. (*13 October 1660*)

My wife seemed very pretty today, it being the first time that I have given her leave to weare a black patch. (*Lord's Day, 4 November 1660*)

At night to bed; and my wife and I did fall out about the dog's being put down into the sellar, which I have a mind to have done because of his fouling the house; and I would have my will. And so we went to bed and lay all night in a quarrell. This night I was troubled all night with a dream that my wife was dead, which made me that I slept ill all night. (*6 November 1660*)

Among other things, my Lady [Sandwich] did mightily urge me to lay out money upon my wife, which I perceived was a little more earnest than ordinary; and so I seemed to be pleased with it and do resolve to bestow a lace upon her – and what with this and other talk, we were exceeding merry. (*9 November 1660*)

So to the Wardrobe, where I find my Lady hath agreed upon a lace for my wife, of 6*l.*, which I seemed much glad of that it was no more, though in my mind I think it too much, and I pray God keep me so to order myself and my wife's expenses that no inconvenience in purse or honour fallow this my prodigality. (*11 November 1660*)

At the office all the morning; and coming home, find Mr Hunt with my wife in the chamber alone; which God forgive me, did trouble my head; but remembering that it was washing-day and that there was no place else with a fire for him to be in, it being also cold weather, I was at ease again. (*19 November 1661*)

Lay long with pleasure, talking with my wife – in whom I never had greater content, blessed be God, then now; she continuing with the same care and thrift and innocence (so long as I keep her from occasions of being otherwise) as ever she was in her life, and keeps the house as well. (*2 November 1662*)

Sat late talking with my wife about our entertaining Dr Clarkes lady and Mrs Pierce shortly, being in great pain that my wife hath never a winter gowne; being almost ashamed of it that she should be seen in a taffata one when all the world wears moyre. So to prayers and to bed. But we could not come to any resolution what to do therein, other then to appear as she is. (*29 December 1662*)

My wife and I home and find all well. Only, myself somewhat vexed at my wife's neglect in leaving of her scarfe, waistcoat, and night-dressings in the coach today that brought us from Westminster, though I confess she did give them to me to look after – yet it was her fault not to see that I did take them out of the coach. (*6 January 1663*)

My wife begun to speak again of the necessity of her keeping somebody to bear her company; for her familiarity with her other servants is it that spoils them all, and other company she hath none (which is too true); and called for Jane to reach her out of her trunk, giving her the keys to that purpose, a bundle of papers; and pulls out a paper, a copy of what, a pretty while since, she had writ in a discontent to me, which I would not read but burned. She now read it, and was so picquant, and wrote in English and most of it true, of the retirednesse of her life and how unpleasant it was, that being writ in English and so in danger of being met with and read by others, I was vexed at it and desired her and then commanded her to teare it – which she desired to be excused it. I forced it from her and tore it, and withal took her other bundle of papers from her and leapt out of the bed and in my shirt clapped them into the pockets of my breeches, that she might not get them from me; and having got on my stockings and breeches and gown, I pulled them out one by one and tore them all before her face, though it went against my heart to do it, she crying and desiring me not to do it. But such was my passion and trouble to see the letters of my love to her, and my will, wherein I had given her all I have in the world when I went to sea with my Lord Sandwich, to be joyned with a paper of so much disgrace to me and dishonour if it should have been found by anybody. Having tore them all, saving a bond of my Uncle Robts which she hath long had in her hands, and our marriage licence and the first letter that ever I sent her when I was her servant, I took up the pieces and carried them into my chamber, and there, after many disputes with myself whether I should burn them or no, and having picked up the pieces of paper she read today and of my will which I tore, I burnt all the rest. (*9 January 1663*)

In Westminster Hall fell in talk with Mrs Lane and after great talk that she never went abroad with any man as she used heretofore to do, I with one word got her to go with me and to meet me at the further Rhenish wine-house – where I did give her a lobster and do so towse her and feel her all over, making her believe how fair and good a skin she had; and endeed, she hath a very white thigh and leg, but monstrous fat. When weary, I did give over, and somebody having seen some of our dalliance, called aloud in the street, "Sir, why do you kiss the gentlewoman so?" and flung a stone at the window – which vexed me – but I believe they could not see my towsing her; and so we broke up and went out the back way, without being observed, I think. (*29 June 1663*)

Up, after much pleasant talk with my wife and a little that vexes me, for I see that she is confirmed in it that all that I do is by design, and that my very keeping of the house in dirt, and the doing of this and anything else in the house, is but to find her imployment to keep her within and from minding of her pleasure. In which, though I am sorry to see she minds it, is true enough in a great degree. (*27 August 1663*)

By and by I home to my office till 9 or 10 at night, and so home to supper and to bed – after some talk and arithmetique with my poor wife, with whom nowadays I live with great content, out of all trouble of mind by jealousy (for which God forgive me), or any other distraction. (*5 December 1663*)

So my wife rise anon, and she and I all the afternoon at arithmetique; and she is come to do addicion, substraction and multiplicacion very well – and so I purpose not to trouble her yet with division, but to begin with the globes to her now. (*Lord's Day, 6 December 1663*)

At home find my wife this day of her own accord to have lain out 25s. upon a pair of pendances for her eares; which did vex me and brought both me and her to very high, and very foul words from her to me, such as trouble me to think she should have in her mouth, and reflecting upon our old differences [*their separation*] which I hate to have remembered. I vowed to break them, or that she should go and get what she could for them again. I went with that resolution out of doors. The poor wretch afterward, in a little while, did send out to change them for her money again. I fallowed Besse her messenger at the Change and there did consult and sent her back; I would not have them changed, being satisfied that she yielded. (*4 July 1664*)

At noon to Anth. Joyces to our gossips dinner; I had sent a dozen and a half bottles of wine thither and paid my double share besides, which is 18s. Very merry we were, and when the women were merry and ris from table, I above with them, ne'er a man but I, I begin discourse of my not getting of children and prayed them to give me their opinions and advice; and they freely and merrily did give me these ten among them. 1. Do not hug my wife too hard nor too much. 2. Eat no late suppers. 3. Drink juyce of sage. 4. Tent and toast. 5. Wear cool Holland-drawers. 6. Keep stomach warm and back cool. 7. Upon my query whether it was best to do at night or morn, they answered me neither one nor other, but when we have most mind to it. 8. Wife not to go too strait-laced.

9! Myself to drink mum and sugar. 10. Mrs Ward did give me to change my plat. The 3rd, 4th, 6th, 7th, and 10th they all did seriously declare and lay much stress upon them, as rules fit to be observed indeed, and especially the last: to lie with our heads where our heels do, or at least to make the bed high at feet and low at head. Very merry all. (*26 July 1664*)

Coming home tonight, I did go to examine my wife's house-accounts; and finding things that seemed somewhat doubtful, I was angry, though she did make it pretty plain; but confessed that when she doth misse a sum, she doth add something to other things to make it. And upon my being very angry, she doth protest she will here lay up something for herself to buy her a neckelace with – which madded me and doth still trouble me, for I fear she will forget by degrees the way of living cheap and under a sense of want. (*29 September 1664*)

This day by the blessing of God, my wife and I have been married nine years – but my head being full of business, I did not think of it, to keep it in any extraordinary manner. But bless God for our long lives and loves and health together, which the same God long continue, I wish from my very heart. (*10 October 1664*)

Going to bed betimes last night, we waked betimes. And from our people's being forced to take the key to go out to light a candle, I was very angry and begun to find fault with my wife for not commanding her servants as she ought. Thereupon, she giving me some cross answer, I did strike her over her left eye such a blow, as the poor wretch did cry out and was in great pain; but yet her spirit was such as to endeavour to bite and scratch me. But I cogging with her, made her leave crying, and sent for butter and parsley, and friends presently one with another; and I up, vexed at my heart to think what I had done, for she was forced to lay a poultice or something to her eye all day, and is black – and the people of the house observed it. (*19 December 1664*)

To church in the morning, and there saw a wedding in the church, which I have not seen many a day, and the young people so merry one with another; and strange, to see what delight we married people have to see these poor fools decoyed into our condition, every man and wife gazing and smiling at them. (*Christmas Day, 1665*)

Up, and down to the old Swan; and there called Betty Michell and her husband and had two or three long salutes from her out of sight of su marido, which pleased me mightily. (*Lord's Day, 5 August 1666*)

Old Michell and his wife came to see me, and there we drank and laughed a little; and then the young [Mitchells] and I took boat, it being fine moonshine. I did to my trouble see all the way that ella did get as close a su marido as ella could, and turn her manos away quando yo did endeavour to take one de los – so that I had no pleasure at all con ella ce night. When we landed, I did take occasion to send him back a the bateau while I did get un baiser or two, and would have taken la by la hand; but ella did turn away, and quando I said, "Shall I not tocar te?", answered, "Yo no love touching", in a slight modo. I seemed not to take notice of it, but parted kindly et su marido did andar with me almost a mi casa, and there parted; and so I home, troubled at this; but I think I shall make good use of it and mind my business more. (*17 February 1667*)

Lay long in bed, talking with pleasure with my poor wife how she used to make coal fires and wash my foul clothes with her own hand for me, poor wretch, in our little room at my Lord Sandwiches; for which I ought for ever to love and admire her, and do, and persuade myself she would do the same thing again if God should reduce us to it. (*25 February 1667*)

Before dinner making my wife to sing; poor wretch, her ear is so bad that it made me angry, till the poor wretch cried to see me so vexed at her, that I think I shall not discourage her so much again but will endeavour to make her understand sounds and do her good that way, for she hath a great mind to learn, only to please me; and therefore I am mighty unjust to her in discouraging her so much. But we were good friends, and to dinner. (*1 March 1667*)

I home to dinner, where I find my wife's flagilette-master; and I am so pleased with her proceeding, though she hath lost time by not practising, that I am resolved for the encouragement of the man to learn myself a little, for a month or so – for I do foresee, if God send my wife and I to live, she will become very good company for me. (*8 May 1667*)

Home in the evening, and there to sing and pipe with my wife; and that being done, she fell all of a sudden to discourse about her clothes and my humours in not suffering her to wear them as she pleases, and grew to high words between us. But I fell to read a book (Boyle's *Hydrostatickes*) aloud in my chamber and let her talk till she was tired, and vexed that I would not hear her; and so become friends and to bed together, the first night after four or five that she hath lain from me by reason of a great cold she had got. (*4 June 1667*)

I away and to Allgate, and walked forward toward Whitechapel till my wife overtook me with the coach, it being a mighty fine afternoon; and there we went the first time out of town with our coach and horses, and went as far as Bow, the spring beginning a little now to appear, though the way be dirty; and so with great pleasure, with the fore-part of our coach up, we spent the afternoon; and so in the evening home and there busy at the office a while; and so to bed, mightily pleased with being at peace with my poor wife and with the pleasure we may hope to have with our coach this summer, when the weather comes to be good. (*5 March 1669*)

The King's Servant

¶ IN THE DIARY Pepys not only chronicles his professional
success, but also, unconsciously, explains it. The following
passages are a few among the many which demonstrate the
qualities which led him to success – self-confidence, am-
bition, appetite for work and love of achievement. After his
appointment in June 1660 as Clerk of the Navy Board he
quickly became its most effective member. Some of the
earlier extracts show him making inventories (7 July 1660),
inspecting dockyards (15 January 1661), and mastering the
intricacies of laying a cable and measuring timber (15
January 1661; 18 August 1662). It became natural for him to
act as spokesman for the Board before the Cabinet (7
October 1666) and Parliament (5 March 1668). In Sir
George Carteret (Treasurer of the Navy) and Sir William
Coventry (Secretary to the Lord High Admiral) Pepys had
colleagues he could respect for their ability as well as for
their political influence. He thought much less highly of his
immediate colleagues on the Board – Sir William Penn
(Commissioner), Sir William Batten (the Surveyor) and Sir
John Mennes (the Comptroller). In the end he and his
confidential secretary Will Hewer agreed that if the Board
were to be reformed it might well be reorganised so as to
give Pepys ultimate responsibility for all its departments (5
April 1668).

From 1662 Pepys also served the Crown as a member of
the committee of the Council appointed to govern Tangier
(recently acquired as part of the Queen's dowry) of which
his friend Creed was secretary. In 1663 Pepys was made
responsible for its finances. Tangier was designed to become
a naval base – hence the work on the mole (27 January 1663)
– but was abandoned in 1684.

In each of these posts Pepys, like other public servants,
was paid a small salary in the expectation that he would
supplement it by charging members of the public with
whom he did business. Many officials, especially in the legal
and financial services, could charge fees – in theory on a
fixed scale. Pepys and his colleagues in the Navy Board and
Tangier committee could expect to receive benefits of
another sort – gifts in cash or kind and (best of all) retainers

or rake-offs from government contractors. There were dangers of bribery here, as Pepys recognised. He himself accepted a large number of gifts, and the annual payments made to him by government contractors such as Sir William Warren, the timber merchant and Sir Denis Gauden, the victualler for the navy and for Tangier, far exceeded his official pay. To have refused a gift would only have meant that a less scrupulous colleague would have drawn up a less favourable contract. At the same time, he recognised that if the gifts made to him were discovered by colleagues or parliamentary critics the results might involve embarrassment or dismissal. If any close enquiry had been made into his conduct, perhaps the most interesting witness, if she could have been persuaded to give evidence, would have been Mrs Bagwell of Deptford dockyard (cf. 7 August 1663).

In 1673, Pepys was promoted to the Admiralty where he no longer did business with contractors. He then became a very monster of probity.

With my Lord to my Lord Frezendorfes, where he dined today – where he told me that he had obtained a promise of the Clerk of the Acts place for me, at which I was glad (*23 June 1660*)

To the Navy Office, where I begin to take an inventory of the papers and goods and books of the office. (*7 July 1660*)

[*At Chatham.*] Up and down the yard all the morning, and seeing the seamen exercize, which they do already very handsomely. Taking our leaves of the officers of the yard, we walked to the waterside and in our way walked into the Ropeyard, where I do look into the tarr-houses and other places, and took great notice of all the several works belonging to the making of a cable. So after a cup of burnt wine at the taverne there, we took barge, and went to Blackwall and viewed the dock and the new wett dock [there]. (*15 January 1661*)

The ladies and I and Capt. Pett and Mr Castle took barge; and down we went to see the *Sovereigne*; which we did, taking great pleasure therein – singing all the way; and among other pleasures, I put my Lady, Mrs Turner, Mrs Hempson, and two Mrs Allen's into the lantern and I went in to them and kissed them, demanding it as a fee due to a Principall Officer. With all which we were exceeding merry, and drank some bottles of wine and neat's tongue, &c. Then back again home and so supped; and after much mirth, to bed. (*8 April 1661*)

Sir G. Carteret, Sir W. Pen, and myself, with our clerks, set out this morning from Portsmouth very early and got by noon to Petersfield, several of the officers of the yard accompanying us so far. Here we dined and were merry. To horse again after dinner, and got to Gilford – where after supper I to bed, having this day been offended by Sir Wm Pens foolish talk, and I offending him with my answers; among others, he in discourse complaining of want of confidence, did ask me to lend him a grain or two, which I told him I thought he was better stored with then myself, before Sir George. So that I see I must keep a greater distance then I have done. And I hope I may do it, because of the interest which I am making with Sir George. (*1 May 1662*)

Up betimes and to my office, where I find Griffens girl making it clean; but God forgive me, what a mind I have to her, but did not meddle with her. She being gone, I fell upon boring holes for me to see from my closet into the great office without going forth, wherein I please myself much. (*30 June 1662*)

About 7 a-clock took horse and rode to Bowe, and there stayed at the Kings Head and eat a breakfast of eggs till Mr Deane of Woolwich came to me; and he and I rid into Waltham [*Epping*] Forrest and there we saw many trees of the King's a-hewing. After we had been a good while in the wood, we rode to Ilford; and there, while dinner was getting ready, he and I practised measuring of the tables and other things till I did understand measure of timber and board very well. So to dinner; and by and by, being sent for, comes Mr Cooper, our officer in the Forrest, and did give me an account of things there and how the country is backward to come in with their carts. By and by comes one Mr Marshall, of whom the King hath many carriages for his timber, and they stayed and drank with me. By and by I got a-horse-back again and rode to Barking, and there saw the place where they ship this timber for Woolwich; and so Deane and I home again. Whiled away the evening at my office, trying to repeat my rules of measuring learnt this day; and so to bed – with my mind very well pleased with this day's work. (*18 August 1662*)

Up and to the office, where sat till 2 a-clock; and then home to dinner, whither by and by comes in Creede and he and I talked of our Tanger business and do find that there is nothing in the world done with true integrity but there is design along with it; as in my Lord Rutherford [*the Governor*], who designs to have the profit of victualling of the garrison himself, and others to have the benefit of making the molle. So that I am almost discouraged from coming any more to the Committee, were it not that it will possibly hereafter bring me to some acquaintance of the great men. Then to the office again, where very busy till past 10 at night; and so home to supper and bed. (*27 January 1663*)

To my Lord Sandwich and there stayed, there being a committee to sit upon the contract for the molle, which I dare say none of us that were there understood; but yet they agreed of things as Mr Cholmly and Sir J. Lawson demanded, who are the undertakers; and so I left them to go on to agree, for I understood it not. (*6 February 1663*)

Going out of Whitehall, I met Capt. Grove, who did give me a letter directed to myself from himself; I discerned money to be in it and took it, knowing, as I found it to be, the proceed of the place I have got him, to have the taking up of vessells for Tanger. But I did not open it till I came home to my office; and there I broke it open, not looking into it till all the money was out, that I might say I saw no money in the paper if ever I should be questioned about it. There was a piece in gold and 4l in silver. (*3 April 1663*)

I stayed walking up and down, discoursing with the officers of the Yard of several things; and so walked back again, and on my way young Bagwell [*a ship's carpenter*] and his wife waylayd me to desire my favour about getting him a better ship; which I shall pretend to be willing to do for them, but my mind is to know his wife a little better. (*7 August 1663*)

[72]

Up ánd to the office, where we sat all the morning and I laboured hard at Deerings business of his deals, more then I would if I did not think to get something, though I do verily believe that I did but what is to the King's advantage in it. And yet, God knows, the expectation of profit will have its force and make a man the more earnest. (*19 December 1663*)

Off to the Sun taverne with Sir W. Warren and with him discoursed long and had good advice and hints from him; and among [other] things, he did give me a pair of gloves for my wife, wrapped up in paper; which I would not open, feeling it hard, but did tell him my wife should thank him, and so went on in discourse. When I came home, Lord, in what pain I was to get my wife out of the room without bidding her go, that I might see what these gloves were; and by and by, she being gone, it proves a pair of white gloves for her and 40 pieces in good gold: which did so cheer my heart that I could eat no victuals almost for dinner for joy to think how God doth bless us every day more and more – and more yet I hope he will upon the encrease of my duty and endeavours. I was at great loss what to do, whether tell my wife of it or no; which I could hardly forbear, but yet I did and will think of it first before I do, for fear of making her think me to be in a better condition or in a better way of getting money then yet I am. After dinner to the office, where doing infinite of business till past 10 at night to the comfort of my mind; and so home with joy to supper and to bed. (*1 February 1664*)

Sir W. Rider come and stayed with me till about 12 at night, having found ourselfs work till that time about understanding the measuring of Mr Woods masts; which though I did so well before as to be thought to deal very hardly against Wood, yet I am ashamed I understood it no better and do hope yet, whatever be thought of me, to save the King some more money. And out of an impatience to break up with my head full of confused confounded notions but nothing brought to a clear comprehension, I was resolved to set up, and did, till now it is ready to strike 4 a-clock, all alone, cold, and my candle not enough left to light me to my own house; and so, with my business however brought to some good understanding and set it down pretty clear, I went home to bed, with my mind at good quiet and the girle setting up for me (the rest all a-bed); I eat and drank a little and to bed, weary, sleepy, cold, and my head akeing. (*17 February 1664*)

[Mr Hampson] told me many rogueries of Sir W. Batten. How Tom Newborne did make poor men give him 3*l* to get Sir W. Batten to cause them to be entered in the yard; and that Sir W. Batten hath oftentimes said – "By God, Tom, you shall get something and I will have some on't." (*3 May 1664*)

At noon dined, and then to the Change and there walked two hours or more with Sir W. Warren – who after much discourse in general of Sir W. Batten's dealings, he fell to talk how everybody must live by their places; and that he was willing, if I desired it, that I should go shares with him in anything that he deals in. (*2 August 1664*)

This night I received by Will 105*l* – the first fruits of my endeavours in the late contract for victualling of Tanger –

for which God be praised. For I can with a safe conscience say that I have therein saved the King 5000*l* per annum, and yet got myself a hope of 300*l* per annum without the least wrong to the King. So to supper and to bed. (*10 September 1664*)

Up, and at my office all the morning to prepare an account of the charge we have been put to extraordinary by the Dutch already; and I have brought it to appear 852,700*l*; but God knows, this is only a scare to the Parliament, to make them give the more money. (*25 November 1664*)

Finding Mrs Bagwell waiting at the office after dinner, away elle and I to a cabaret where elle and I have été before; and there I had her company toute l'après-dîner and had mon plein plaisir of elle – but strange, to see how a woman, notwithstanding her greatest pretences of love à son mari and religion, may be vaincue. (*23 January 1665*)

To the office and there found Bagwells wife, whom I directed to go home and I would do her business; which was to write a letter to my Lord Sandwich for her husband's advance into a better ship as there should be occasion – which I did; and by and by did go down by water to Deptford Yard, and then down further and so landed at the lower end of the town; and it being dark, did privately entrer en la maison de la femme de Bagwell, and there I had sa compagnie, though with a great deal of difficulty; néanmoins, enfin je avais ma volonté d'elle. (*20 February 1665*)

We to a committee of the Council to discourse concerning pressing of men; but Lord, how they meet; never sit down – one comes, now another goes, then comes another – one complaining that nothing is done, another swearing that he hath been there these two hours and nobody came. At last it came to this: my Lord Annesly, says he, "I think we must be forced to get the King to come to every committee, for I do not see that we do anything at any time but when he is here." And I believe he said the truth. And very constant he is at the council table on council days; which his predecessors, it seems, very rarely did. But thus, I perceive, the greatest affair in the world at this day is likely to be managed by us. (*27 February 1665*)

Up; and after doing a little business, down to Deptford with Sir W. Batten – and there left him, and I to Greenwich to the park, where I hear the King and Duke are come by water this morn from Hampton Court. They asked me several questions. The King mightily pleased with his new buildings there. Great variety of talk – and was often led to speak to the King and Duke. By and by they to dinner; and all to dinner and sat down to the King saving myself, which though I could not in modesty expect, yet God forgive my pride, I was sorry I was there, that Sir W. Batten should say that he could sit down where I could not – though he had twenty times more reason than I. But this was my pride and folly. The King having dined, he came down, and I went in the barge with him, I sitting at the door hearing him and the Duke talk and seeing and observing their manner of discourse; and God forgive me, though I adore them with all the duty possible, yet the more a man considers and observes them, the less he finds of difference between them and other men, though (blessed be God) they are both princes of great nobleness and spirits. (*26 July 1665*)

Up, and in my nightgown, cap, and neck-cloth, undressed all day long; lost not a minute, but in my chamber setting my Tanger accounts to rights, which I did by night, to my very heart's content; not only that it is done, but I find everything right and even beyond what, after so long neglecting them, I did hope for. The Lord of Heaven be praised for it. (*Lord's Day, 30 July 1665*)

We got by morning to Gillingham; and thence all walked to Chatham, and there with Commissioner Pett viewed the Yard; and among other things, a teame of four horses came close by us, he being with me, drawing a piece of timber that I am confident one man would easily have carried upon his back; I made the horses be taken away and a man or two take the timber away with their hands. This the Commissioner did see, but said nothing; but I think had cause to be ashamed of. (*2 October 1665*)

After dinner to the office again; and thither comes Mr Downing the anchor-smith, who had given me 50 pieces in gold the last month to speak for him to Sir W. Coventry for his being smith at Deptford. But after I had got it granted him, he finds himself not fit to go on with it, so lets it fall – so hath no benefit of my motion; I therefore in honour and conscience took him home, and though much to my grief, did yet willingly and forcibly force him to take it again, the poor man having no mind to have it. However, I made him take it, and away he went; and I glad I had given him so much cause to speak well of me. (*8 May 1666*)

I to the office, where all the afternoon very busy and doing much business. But here I had a most eminent experience of the evil of being behindhand in business; I was the most backward to begin anything, and would fain have framed to myself an occasion of going abroad, and should I doubt have done it – but some business coming in, one after another, kept me there, and I fell to the ridding away of a great deal of business; and when my hand was in it, was so pleasing a sight to [see] my papers disposed of, and letters answered which troubled my book and table, that I could have continued there with delight all night long; and did, till called away by my Lady Pen and Pegg and my wife to their house to eat with them; and there I went, and exceeding merry. (*16 August 1666*)

Presently after dinner, I with Sir J. Mennes to Whitehall, where met by W. Batten and Lord Brouncker, to attend the King and Duke of York at the Cabinet; but nobody had determined what to speak of, but only in general to ask for money – so I was forced immediately to prepare in my mind a method of discoursing. And anon we were called in to the Green Room. Nobody beginning, I did, and made a current and, I thought, a good speech, laying open the ill state of the Navy – by the greatness of the debt – greatness of work to do against next year – the time and materials it would take – and our incapacity, through a total want of money. I had no sooner done, but Prince Rupert rose up and told the King in a heat that whatever the gentleman had said, he had brought home

his fleet in as good a condition as ever any fleet was
brought home. I therefore did only answer that I was
sorry for his Highness's offence, but that what I said was
but the report we received from those entrusted in the
fleet to inform us. He muttered, and repeated what he
had said; and so after a long silence on all hands, nobody,
not so much as the Duke of Albemarle, seconding the
Prince, nor taking notice of what he said, we withdrew.
(*Lord's Day, 7 October 1666*)

Up, and to the office, where all the morning. At noon
home to dinner, and in the afternoon shut myself in my
chamber, and there till 12 at night finishing my great
letter to the Duke of York; which doth lay the ill
condition of the Navy so open to him, that it is impossible, if the King and he minds anything of their business,
but it will operate upon them to set all matters right, and
get money to carry on the war before it be too late, or
else lay out for a peace upon any tearmes. It was a great
convenience tonight, that what I had writ fowle in
shorthand, I could read to W. Hewer and he take it fair in
shorthand so as I can read it tomorrow to Sir W.
Coventry, and then come home and he read to me, while
I take it in longhand to present – which saves me much
time. (*17 November 1666*)

This morning, before I went to the office there came to
me Mr Young and Whistler, flaggmakers, and with
mighty earnestness did present me with and press me to
take a box, wherein I could not guess there was less than
100*l* in gold. But I do wholly refuse it, and did not at last
take it – the truth is, not thinking them safe men to
receive such a gratuity from nor knowing any consider-

able courtesy that ever I did do them — but desirous to keep myself free from their reports and to have it in my power to say I had refused their offer. (*5 February 1667*)

This morning came to me the collectors for my [poll-tax], for which I paid for my title as Esquire and place of Clerk of Acts, and my head and wife's, and servants' and their wages, 40*l* 17*s*. 00*d*. And though this be a great deal, yet it is a shame I should pay no more; that is, that I should not be assessed for my pay, as in the victualling business and Tanger, and for my money, which of my own accord I had determined to charge myself with 1000*l* money, till coming to the Vestry and seeing nobody of our ablest merchants, as Sir Andrew Rickard, to do it, I thought it not decent for me to do it; nor would it be thought wisdom to do it unnecessarily, but vainglory. (*5 April 1667*)

Up betimes, and down to [my] chamber, without trimming myself or putting on clean linen, thinking only to keep to my chamber to do business today; but when I came there, I find that without being shaved I am not fully awake nor ready to settle to business, and so was fain to go up again and dress myself; which I did, and so down to my chamber and fell roundly to business, and did to my satisfaction by dinner go far in the drawing up a state of my accounts of Tanger for the new Lords Comissioners. (*Lord's Day, 2 June 1667*)

At noon home to dinner with my clerks — who have of late dined frequently with me, and I do purpose to have them so still, by that means I having opportunity to talk with them about business, and I love their company very well. (*20 November 1667*)

Up and to my office, whither came my clerks; and so I did huddle up the best I could some more notes for my discourse today; and by 9 a-clock was ready and did go down to the Old Swan, and there by boat, with T. Hater and W. Hewer with me, to Westminster, where I found myself come time enough and my brethren all ready. But I full of thoughts and trouble touching the issue of this day; and to comfort myself did go to the Dogg and drink half a pint of mulled sack, and in the Hall did drink a dram of brandy at Mrs Howletts, and with the warmth of this did find myself in better order as to courage, truly. So we all up to the Lobby; and between 11 and 12 a-clock were called in, with the Mace before us, into the House; where a mighty full House, and we stood at the Barr – *viz.*, Brouncker, Sir J. Mennes, Sir T. Harvey and myself – W. Penn being in the House as a Member. I perceive the whole House was full, and full of expectation of our defence what it would be, and with great præjudice. After the Speaker had told us the dissatisfaction of the House, I begin our defence most acceptably and smoothly, and continued at it without any hesitation or losse but with full scope and all my reason free about me, as if it had been at my own table, from that time till past 3 in the afternoon; and so ended without any interruption from the Speaker, but we withdrew. And there all my fellow-officers, and all the world that was within hearing, did congratulate me and cry up my speech as the best thing they ever heard, and my fellow-officers overjoyed in it. We were called in again by and by to answer only one question, touching our paying tickets to ticket-mongers – and so out; and we were in hopes to have had a vote this day in our favour, and so the generality of the House was; but my speech being so long, many had gone out to dinner and come in again half drunk. However, it is plain we have got great ground; and everybody says I have got the most honour that any could have had opportunity of getting. And so, with our hearts mightily overjoyed at this success, we all to dinner to Lord Brouncker. (*5 March 1668*)

Up betimes, and with Sir D. Gawden to Sir W. Coventry's chamber, where the first word he said to me was, "Goodmorrow Mr Pepys, that must be Speaker of the Parliament-house" – and did protest I had got honour for ever in Parliament. He said that his brother, that sat by him, admires me; and another gentleman said that I could not get less than 1000*l* a year if I would put on a gown and plead at the Chancery bar. But what pleases me most, he tells me that the Sollicitor-Generall did protest that he thought I spoke the best of any man in England. (*6 March 1668*)

Dined at home with W. Hewers with me; and after dinner, he and I a great deal of good talk touching this office: how it is spoilt by having so many persons in it, and so much work that is not made the work of any one man but of all, and so is never done; and that the best way to have it well done were to have the whole trust in one (as myself) to set whom I pleased to work in the several businesses of the Office, and me to be accountable for the whole; and that would do it, as I would find instruments. (*Lord's Day, 5 April 1668*)

The Man of Fashion

¶ THE SELF-AWARENESS that is natural to a diarist shows itself in Pepys's approach to dress. He chose his clothes with care, and describes them, when they deserve it, in detail. At 19 October 1661 he recalls the advice of his 'father' Osborne – Francis Osborne, whose book of conduct for young men, *Advice to a Son*, published in 1658, he greatly admired. 'Weare your *Cloaths* neat', Osborne had written, 'exceeding rather than comming short of others of like fortune. *Spare all other ways rather than prove defective in this.*' As he became more prosperous and successful, Pepys spent more on clothes, keeping up with the fashion to such effect that he was soon spending much more on his own wardrobe than on Elizabeth's (31 October 1663). His outdoor wear usually included a sword (17 May 1668), for no gentleman was complete without one. His suits were sober in colour – anything ostentatious would betoken the courtier rather than the civil servant – but relieved here and there by gold buttons and silk linings, and offset by the crisp white linen of his bands and cuffs to which he attached great importance (29 October 1663).

The most striking new item of fashion was the periwig, now worn for show, not simply to cover baldness. Pepys first wore one in November 1663 shortly after the King and the Duke of York had introduced the fashion to England.

This morning came home my fine camlott cloak with gold buttons – and a silk suit; which cost me much money and I pray God to make me be able to pay for it. (*1 July 1660*)

We had a very good and handsome dinner, and excellent wine. I not being neat in clothes, which I find a great fault in me, could not be so merry as otherwise and at all times I am and can be, when I am in good habit; which makes me remember my father Osborne's rule for a gentleman, to spare in all things rather then in that. (*19 October 1661*)

This day I first did wear a muffe, being my wife's last year's muff; and now I have bought her a new one, this serves me very well. (*Lord's Day, 30 November 1662*)

Up betimes and put on a black cloth suit with white lynings under all, as the fashion is to wear, to appear under the breeches. (*10 May 1663*)

Up, it being my Lord Mayors Day, Sir Anthony Bateman. This morning was brought home my new velvet cloak; that is, lined with velvet, a good cloth the outside – the first that ever I had in my life, and I pray God it may not be too soon now that I begin to wear it. I had it this day brought home, thinking to have worn it to dinner; but I thought it would be better to go without it because of the crowde, and so I did not wear it. This morning, in dressing myself and wanting a band, I found all my bands that were newly made clean, so ill-smoothed that I crumpled them and flung them all on the ground and was angry with Jane, which made the poor girl mighty sad, so that I were troubled for it afterwards. (*29 October 1663*)

To the office, where busy till night; and then to prepare my monthly account, about which I stayed till 10 or 11 a-clock at night; and to my great sorrow, find myself 43*l* worse than I was the last month; which was then 760*l* and now is but 717*l*. But it hath chiefly arisen from my layings-out in clothes for myself and wife – *viz.*, for her, about 12*l*; and for myself, 55*l* or thereabouts – having made myself a velvet cloak, two new cloth-suits, black, plain both, a new shag-gown, trimmed with gold buttons and twist; with a new hat, and silk top[s] for my legs, and many other things, being resolved henceforward to go like myself. And also two periwigs, one whereof costs me 3*l* and the other 40*s*. I have wore neither yet, but will begin next week, God willing. So that I hope I shall not now need to lay out more money a great while. But I hope I shall with more comfort labour to get more, and with better successe then when, for want of clothes, I was forced to sneak like a beggar. (*31 October 1663*)

By and by comes Chapman the periwig-maker, and [upon] my liking it, without more ado I went up and there he cut off my haire; which went a little to my heart at present to part with it, but it being over and my periwig on, I paid him 3*l* for it; and away went he with my own hair to make up another of; and I by and by, after I had caused all my maids to look upon it and they conclude it to become me, though Jane was mightily troubled for my parting with my own hair. (*3 November 1663*)

Up; and it being late, to church. I found that my coming in a perriwigg did not prove so strange to the world as I was afeared it would, for I thought that all the church would presently have cast their eye all upon me – but I found no such thing. (*Lord's Day, 8 November 1663*)

Up; and this morning put on my new fine coloured cloth suit, with my cloak lined with plush – which is a dear and noble suit, costing me about 17*l*. (*Lord's Day, 30 October 1664*)

Up; and going down, found Jervas the barber with a periwig which I had the other day cheapened at Westminster; but it being full of nits, as heretofore his work used to be, I did now refuse it, having bought elsewhere. (*4 April 1667*)

Up, and put on my new stuff-suit with a shoulder-belt, according to the new fashion, and the bands of my vest and tunic laced with silk lace of the colour of my suit. And so, very handsome, to church, where a dull sermon of a stranger. (*Lord's Day, 17 May 1668*)

The Musician

¶ MUSIC PLAYED A LARGE PART in the cultural and social life of educated English people in the sixteenth and seventeenth centuries. It is even likely for instance that, because of the popularity of singing in parts, there were then more tenor voices than now in proportion to the total population, simply because so many men trained themselves by practice to sing high. The diary is full of music – it is remarkable how often Pepys and his circle sang and played instruments when they met. Pepys himself was something more than a lover of music – he was a serious student of it, interested in the 'doctrine' of music and the problems of notation. He composed – though only songs, and then only the voice-line (19 December 1666). Nevertheless, he had a good ear for melody and his song 'Beauty Retire' (6 December 1665) has distinct charm. The interest in echoes and echo songs, which he more than once evinces, was a common one. He had a bass voice, as is clear from the manuscripts in his library, and his favourite instruments were the lute and the flageolet, though he played others. He never developed any facility with keyboard instruments, except to use a spinet for his studies of harmony.

There were no public concerts by professionals in the modern sense in the diary period, though they appear to have begun in London in the 1670s, and the music-making at 5 October 1664, when a large room at the General Sorting Office of the Post Office was used, is a close approach to the modern model. But music-making remained predominantly amateur, except for court, church, and theatre music and at civic functions. There is a good example of theatre music at 27 February 1668. Angels and Gods were usually represented by wind (i.e. woodwind) music. The perils of amateurishness are illustrated by two of these extracts.

The only well-known composer mentioned here is Pelham Humfrey, perhaps the best English composer of anthems in the generation before Purcell.

After dinner went to the Greene Dragon, both the Mr Pinknys, Smith, Harrison, Morrice that sang the bass,

Sheply and I, and there we sang of all sorts of things and I ventured with good success upon things at first sight and after that played on my flagelette; and stayed there till 9 a-clock, very merry and drawn on with one song after another. (*16 January 1660*)

To the Exchange and thence to an ordinary over against it – where to our dinner we had a fellow play well upon the bagpipes and whistle like a bird exceeding well. And I had a fancy to learn to whistle as he doth, and did promise to come some other day and give him an angell to teach me. To the office and sat there all the afternoon till 9 at night. So home to my musique; and my wife and I sat singing in my chamber a good while together. And then to bed. (*17 May 1661*)

To Westminster; where at Mr Mountagu's chamber I heard a Frenchman play upon the gittar most extreme well; though, at the best, methinks it is but a bawble. (*27 July 1661*)

[I] went to hear Mrs Turner's daughter play on the harpsicon, but Lord, it was enough to make any man sick to hear her; yet was I forced to commend her highly. So home to supper and to bed, Ashwell playing upon the tryangle very well before I went to bed. (*1 May 1663*)

To Mr Blands, where Mr Povey, Gauden and I were invited to dinner – which we had very finely. They have a kinswoman they call daughter in the house, a short, ugly, red-haired slut that plays upon the virginalls and sings, but after such a country manner, I was weary of it but yet could not but commend it. So by and by after dinner comes Monsieur Gotier, who is beginning to teach her; but Lord, what a drolle fellow it is, to make her hold open her mouth and telling this and that so drolly, would make a man burst; but himself I perceive sings very well. (*24 July 1663*)

[*At Tunbridge Wells.*] There was, under one of the trees on the common, a company got together that sung; I, at that distance, and so all the rest, being a quarter of a mile off, took them for the waytes; so I rid up to them and find them only voices – some citizens, met by chance, that sing four or five parts excellently. I have not been more pleased with a snapp of musique, considering the circumstances of the time and place, in all my life anything so pleasant. (*27 July 1663*)

To the musique-meeting at the Post Office, where I was once before. And thither anon come all the Gresham College and a great deal of noble company. And the new instrument was brought, called the arched viall – where, being tuned with lutestrings and played on with kees like an organ – a piece of parchment is always kept moving; and the strings, which by the keys are pressed down upon it, are grated, in imitation of a bow, by the parchment; and so it is intended to resemble several vyalls played on with one bow – but so basely and harshly, that it will never do. But after three hours' stay, it could not be fixt in tune; and so they were fain to go to some other musique of instruments, which I am grown quite out of love with. (*5 October 1664*)

Mr Povy carried me to Somersett House and there down the great stone stairs to the garden and tried the brave

[89]

eccho upon the stairs – which continues a voice so long as the singing three notes, concords, one after another, they all three shall sound in consort together a good while most pleasantly. (*21 January 1665*)

Up, and before I went out of my chamber, did draw a musique scale, in order to my having it at any time ready in my hand to turn to for exercise, for I have a great mind to perfect myself in my scale, in order to my practising of composition. (*Lord's Day, 17 September 1665*)

Back to Mr Povys and there supped. And after supper to talk and to sing, his man Dutton's wife singing very prettily (a mighty fat woman), and I wrote out one song from her and pricked the tune, being very pretty. But I did never hear one sing with so much pleasure to herself as this lady doth, relishing it to her very heart – which was mighty pleasant. (*15 October 1665*)

I spent the afternoon upon a song of Solyman's words to Roxolana [*from Davenant's* Siege of Rhodes] that I have set; and so with my wife walked, and Mercer, to Mrs Pierces, where Capt. Rolt and Mrs Knipp, Mr Coleman and his wife, and Laneare, Mrs Worship, and her singing daughter met; and by and by unexpectedly comes Mr Pierce from Oxford. Here the best company for musique I ever was in in my life, and wish I could live and die in it, both for music and the face of Mrs Pierce and my wife and Knipp, who is pretty enough, but the most excellent mad-hum[ou]rd thing; and sings the noblest that ever I heard in my life, and Rolt with her, some things together most excellently – I spent the night in an ecstasy almost;

and having invited them to my house a day or two hence, we broke up. (*6 December 1665*)

Till 10 at night busy about letters and other necessary matters of the office. About 11, I home, it being a fine moonshine; and so my wife and Mercer came into the garden, and my business being done, we sang till about 12 at night with mighty pleasure to ourselfs and neighbours, by their casements opening. And so home to supper and to bed. (*5 May 1666*)

We find [Lord Lauderdale] and his lady and some Scotch people at supper – pretty odd company; though my Lord Brouncker tells me my Lord Lauderdale is a man of mighty good reason and judgment. But at supper there played one of their servants upon the viallin, some Scotch tunes only – several – and the best of their country, as they seemed to esteem them by their praising and admiring them; but Lord, the strangest ayre that ever I heard in my life, and all of one cast. But strange to hear my Lord Lauderdale say himself, that he had rather hear a catt mew then the best musique in the world – and the better the music, the more sick it makes him. And that of all instruments, he hates the lute most; and next to that, the baggpipe. (*28 July 1666*)

The porter brought my vest back from the taylors, and then to dress myself very fine, about 4 or 5 a-clock; and by that time comes Mr Batelier and Mercer, and away by coach to Mrs Pierces by appointment, where we find good company – a fair lady, my Lady Prettyman, Mrs Corbet, Knipp. And for men, Capt. Downing, Mr

Lloyd, Sir W. Coventry's clerk – and one Mr Tripp, who dances well. After our first bout of dancing, Knipp and I to sing, and Mercer and Capt. Downing (who loves and understands music) would by all means have my song of *Beauty Retire* – which Knipp hath spread abroad, and he extols it above anything he ever heard. And without flattery, I think it is good in its kind. (*9 November 1666*)

Met Mr Hingston the organist (my old acquaintance) in the court, and I took him to the Dogg tavern and got him to set me a bass to my *It is decreed*, which I think will go well; but he commends the song, not knowing the words [*from Ben Jonson's* Catiline's Conspiracy], but says the ayre is good, and believes the words are plainly expressed. He is of my mind, against having of eighths unnecessarily in composition. This did all please me mightily. (*19 December 1666*)

To my Lord Bruncker's, and there was Sir Rob. Murray, whom I never understood so well as now by this opportunity of discourse; he is a most excellent man of reason and learning, and understands the doctrine of musique and everything else I could discourse of very finely. Here came Mr Hooke, Sir George Ent, Dr Wren, and many others; and by and by the music, that is to say, Seignor Vincentio, who is the maister composer, and six more, whereof two eunuches (so tall, that Sir T. Harvy said well that he believes they did grow large by being gelt, as our oxen do) and one woman, very well dressed and handsome enough but would not be kissed, as Mr Killigrew, who brought the company in, did acquaint us. They sent two harpsicons before; and by and by, after tuning them, they begun; and I confess, very good music

they made; that is, the composition exceeding good, but
yet not at all more pleasing to me then what I have heard
in English by Mrs Knipp, Capt. Cooke and others. Nor
do I dote on the eunuchs; they sing endeed pretty high
and have a mellow kind of sound, but yet I have been as
well satisfied with several women's voices, and men also,
as Crispe of the Wardrobe. The woman sung well, but
that which distinguishes all is this: that in singing, the
words are to be considered and how they are fitted with
notes, and then the common accent of the country is to be
known and understood by the hearer, or he will never be
a good judge of the vocall music of another country. So
that I was not taken with this at all, neither understanding
the first nor by practice reconciled to the latter, so that
their motions and risings and fallings, though it may be
pleasing to an Italian or one that understands that tongue,
yet to me it did not; but do from my heart believe that I
could set words in English, and make music of them,
more agreeable to any Englishman's eare (the most
judicious) then any Italian music set for the voice and
performed before the same man, unless he be acquainted
with the Italian accent of speech. The composition as to
the musique part was exceeding good, and their justness
in keeping time by practice much before any that we
have, unless it be a good band of practised fiddlers. (*16
February 1667*)

We to church, and then home, and there comes Mr
Pelling with two men by promise, one Wallington and
Piggott; the former whereof, being a very little fellow,
did sing a most excellent bass, and yet a poor fellow, a
working goldsmith, that goes without gloves to his
hands. Here we sung several good things, but I am more

and more confirmed that singing with many voices is not singing, but a sort of instrumentall music, the sense of the words being lost by not being heard, and especially as they set them with fuges of words, one after another; whereas singing properly, I think, should be but with one or two voices at most, and that counterpoint. (*15 September 1667*)

I away home (calling at my mercer and tailor's) and there find, as I expected, Mr Cæsar and little Pellam Humphrys, lately returned from France and is an absolute Monsieur, as full of form and confidence and vanity, and disparages everything and everybody's skill but his own. The truth is, everybody says he is very able; but to hear how he laughs at all the King's Music here, as Blagrave and others, that they cannot keep time nor tune nor understand anything, and that Grebus the Frenchman, the King's Master of the Musique, how he understands nothing nor can play on any instrument and so cannot compose, and that he will give him a lift out of his place, and that he and the King are mighty great, and that he hath already spoke to the King of Grebus, would make a man piss. (*15 November 1667*)

All the morning at the office, and at noon home to dinner; and thence with my wife and Deb to the King's House to see *Virgin Martyr* [*by Dekker and Massinger*], the first time it hath been acted a great while, and is mighty pleasant; not that the play is worth much, but it is finely acted by Becke Marshall; but that which did please me beyond anything in the whole world was the wind-musique when the Angell comes down, which is so sweet that it ravished me; and endeed, in a word, did wrap up my soul so that it made me really sick, just as I have formerly been when in love with my wife; that neither then, nor all the evening going home and at home, I was able to think of anything, but remained all night transported, so as I could not believe that ever any music hath that real command over the soul of a man as this did upon me; and makes me resolve to practise wind-music and to make my wife do the like. (*27 February 1668*)

At my chamber all the evening, pricking down some things and trying some conclusions upon my viall, in order to the inventing of a better theory of musique then hath yet been abroad; and I think verily I shall do it. (*20 March 1668*)

With Lord Brouncker and several [*other Fellows of the Royal Society*] to the King's Head tavern by Chancery Lane, and there did drink and eat and talk; and above the rest, I did desire of Mr Hooke and my Lord an account of the reason of concords and discords in music – which they say is from the æquality of the vibrations; but I am not satisfied in it, but will at my leisure think of it more and see how far that doth go to explain it. (*2 April 1668*)

The Neighbour

¶ THE NAVY OFFICE BUILDING in Seething Lane housed three of Pepys's colleagues and a senior clerk, Thomas Turner, as well as Pepys himself. These were official lodgings and the arrangement was meant to facilitate business, as no doubt it did. Abutting the building on the south was the house of Sir Richard Ford, a rich and influential merchant (Lord Mayor 1670–1). It was Ford who introduced Pepys to tea drinking – a habit he had probably acquired through his connections with the Dutch East Indian trade. (See 25 September 1660 – possibly the first mention of a cup of tea in English literature.) But Pepys's principal contacts among his neighbours were with his professional colleagues, Sir William Batten, Surveyor of the Navy, and Sir William Penn, a Commissioner of the Navy Board and father of William Penn, the Quaker leader who founded Pennsylvania. Both had had considerable and distinguished experience as naval commanders, Batten during the Civil War and Penn during the Commonwealth. Both had houses in the country (at Walthamstow; Penn had an Irish estate too); both were knights and M.P.s. Neither, however, was as competent a man of business as Pepys, and Pepys did not allow himself to be overawed, though he clearly envied Batten his wealth.

Relations between the Pepyses and their neighbours had their ups and downs, but Pepys's comments on the Penns become more disparaging as the diary proceeds. In particular his references to Peg Penn, their daughter, are malicious: at 23 May 1667 he gleefully records his successful attempt at dalliance with her shortly after her marriage. The Mrs Markham mentioned at 15 September 1667 was Lady Penn's companion.

Dined at Sir W. Battens; and by this time I see that we are like to have a very good correspondency and neighbourhood, but chargeable. (*11 September 1660*)

To the office, where Sir W. Batten, Coll. Slingsby, and I sat a while; and Sir R. Ford coming to us about some business, we talked together. Sir R. Ford talked like a man of great reason and experience. And afterwards did send for a cupp of tee (a China drink of which I never had drank before) and went away. (*25 September 1660*)

To Sir W. Batten's to dinner, he having a couple of servants married today; and so there was a great number of merchants and others of good quality, on purpose after dinner to make an offering, which when dinner was done, we did; and I did give 10s. and no more, though I believe most of the rest did give more and did believe that I did so too. (*15 November 1660*)

In the afternoon to our own church and my wife with me (the first time that she and my Lady Battin came to sit in our new pew); and after sermon my Lady took us home and there we supped with her and Sir W. Batten and Pen and were much made of – the first time that ever my wife was there. (*Lord's Day, 18 November 1660*)

So home, Sir William [Penn] and I; and it being very hot weather, I took my flagilette and played upon the leads in the garden, where Sir William came out in his shirt into his leads and there we stayed talking and singing and drinking of great draughts of clarret and eating botargo and bread and butter till 12 at night, it being moonshine. And so to bed – very near fuddled. (*5 June 1661*)

Home, and I find my Lady Batten and her daughter to look something askew upon my wife, because my wife doth not buckle to them and is not sollicitous for their acquaintance, which I am not troubled at at all. (*Lord's Day, 25 August 1661*)

My wife and I to church in the afternoon and seated ourselfs, she below me; and by that means the precedence of the pew, which my Lady Batten and her daughter takes, is confounded. And after sermon she and I did stay behind them in the pew and went out by ourselfs a good while after them – which we judge a very fine project hereafter, to avoyd contention. (*Easter Day, 30 March 1662*)

In the morning my Lady Batten did send to speak with me and told me very civilly that she did not desire, nor hoped I did, that anything should pass between us but what was civill, though there was not the neighbourliness between her and my wife that was fit to be; and so complained of my maid's mocking of her when she called "Nan" to her maid within her own house; my maid Jane in my yard overheard her and mocked her. And some other such-like things she told me, and of my wife's speaking unhandsomely of her; to all which I did give her a very respectful answer, such as did please her, and am sorry endeed that this should be, though I do not desire there should be any acquaintance between my wife and her. But I promised to avoid such words and passages for the future; so home. At night I called up my maids and schooled Jane; who did answer me so humbly and drolly about it, that though I seemed angry I was much pleased with her, and wife also. (*5 November 1662*)

My wife tells me stories how she hears that by Sarahs going to live at Sir W. Penn's, all our affairs of my family are made known and discoursed of there, and theirs by my people – which doth trouble me much, and I shall take a time to let Sir W. Penn know how he hath dealt in taking her without our full consent. (*7 January 1663*)

My wife and I to see Sir W. Penn and there supped with him, much against my stomach, for the dishes were so deadly foul that I could not endure to look upon them. (*17 January 1664*)

After dinner my wife and I to Sir W. Penn's to see his lady the first time – who is a well-looked, fat, short, old Dutchwoman, but one that hath been heretofore pretty handsome; and is now very discreet and I believe hath more wit then her husband. Here we stayed talking a good while. And very well pleased I was with the old woman at first visit. (*19 August 1664*)

This day Sir W. Batten, who hath been sick four or five days, is now very bad, so as that people begin to fear his death – and I at a loss whether it will be better for me to have him die, because he is a bad man, or live, for fear a worse should come. (*7 February 1665*)

At dinner all of us, that is to say, Lord Brouncker, J. Mennes, W. Batten, T. Harvy and myself, to Sir W. Penn's house to dinner, where some other company; it is instead of a wedding dinner for his daughter, whom I saw in palterly clothes, nothing new but a bracelet that her servant hath given her, and ugly she is as heart can wish. A sorry dinner, not anything handsome nor clean but some silver plates they borrowed of me. After dinner, to talk a little; and then I away to my office, and then home to supper and to bed – talking with my wife of the poorness and meanness of all that Sir W. Penn and the people about us do, compared with what we do. (*22 February 1667*)

Up; and when ready, I to my office to do a little business; and coming homeward again, saw my door and hatch open, left so by Luce our cookmaid; which so vexed me, that I did give her a kick in our entry and offered a blow at her, and was seen doing so by Sir W. Penn's footboy, which did vex me to the heart because I know he will be telling their family of it, though I did put on presently a very pleasant face to the boy and spoke kindly to him as one without passion, so as it may be he might not think I was angry; but yet I was troubled at it. (*12 April 1667*)

This afternoon I had opportunity para jouer with Mrs Pen, tocando her mamelles and besando ella – being sola in the casa of her pater – and she fort willing. (*23 May 1667*)

Home, and dined with my wife at Sir W. Penn's, where a very good pasty of venison, better than we expected, the last stinking basely. (*5 August 1667*)

To church, where I stood in continual fear of Mrs Markham's coming to church and offering to come into our pew; to prevent which, as soon as ever I heard the great door open, I did step back and clapped my breech to our pew door, that she might be forced to shove me to come in; but as God would have it, she did not come. (*Lord's Day, 15 September 1667*)

Pictures and Portraits

¶ PEPYS'S GREAT COLLECTION of prints has survived in his Library, but after his death his pictures for the most part were scattered among his descendants and have to a large extent been lost. His portrait by John Hales (Hayls) is now in the National Portrait Gallery and has often been reproduced. The music he holds there (11 April 1666) is the song 'Beauty Retire' which he had recently composed. His wife's portrait (15 February 1666) survives only as an engraving. She was painted 'like a St Katharine', i.e. in the vogue established in compliment to Queen Catherine of Braganza. The plaster casts (10, 15 February 1669) have disappeared.

Sir Peter Lely was the most fashionable court painter of the day and his portraits of the naval commanders in the Battle of Lowestoft (see 18 July 1666) are now mostly in the National Maritime Museum, Greenwich. Samuel Cooper (30 March 1668) was the great miniaturist: the portrait mentioned here was of Frances Teresa Stewart, the court beauty. Other painters mentioned are (1 February 1669) Robert Streater and Hendrick Danckerts ('Dancres'), and (11 April 1669) Simon Verelst ('Everelst'). The 'Dr Wren' at 1 February 1669 is the architect.

With Comissioner Pett to Mr Lillys the great painter, who came forth to us; but believing that I came to bespeak a picture, he prevented us by telling us that he should not be at leisure these three weeks, which methinks is a rare thing; and then to see in what pomp his table was laid for himself to go to dinner. And here among other pictures, I saw the so much by me desired picture of my Lady Castlemayne, which is a most blessed picture and that that I must have a copy of. (*20 October 1662*)

After dinner to Whitehall and there met with Mr Pierce and he showed me the Queen's bedchamber and her closet. Thence he carried me to the King's closet; where such variety of pictures and other things of value and rarity, that I was properly confounded and enjoyed no pleasure in the sight of them – which is the only time in my life that ever I was so at a loss for pleasure in the greatest plenty of objects to give it me. (*24 June 1664*)

To Mr Hales the painter's. Here [he] begun my wife in the posture we saw one of my Lady Peters, like a St Katharine. While he painted, Knipp and Mercer and I sang. But strange, how like his very first dead colouring is, that it did me good to see it, and pleases me mightily – and I believe will be a noble picture. (*15 February 1666*)

By coach to Hales's; and there saw my wife sit, and I do like her picture mightily, and very like it will be, and a brave piece of work. But he doth complain that her nose hath cost him as much work as another's face, and he hath done it finely indeed. (*3 March 1666*)

To Hales's to see my wife's picture, which I like mighty well; and there had the pleasure to see how suddenly he draws the heavens, laying a dark ground and then lightening it when and where he will. (*10 March 1666*)

This day I begun to sit [*to Hales*], and he will make me, I think, a very fine picture. He promises it shall be as good as my wife's, and I sit to have it full of shadows, and do almost break my neck looking over my shoulder to make the posture for him to work by. (*17 March 1666*)

To Hales's, where there was nothing found to be done more to my picture but the musique; which now pleases me mightily, it being painted true. (*11 April 1666*)

To Hales's to see how my father's picture goes on, which pleases me mighty well, though I find again, as I did in Mrs Pierces, that a picture may have more of likeness in the first or second working then it shall have when finished; but so it is. And contrarily, mine was not so like at the first, second, or third sitting as it was afterward. (*18 June 1666*)

With Sir W. Pen home, calling at Lillys to have a time appointed when to be drawn among the other Commanders of Flags the last year's fight. And so full of work Lilly is, that he was fain to take his table-book out to see how his time is appointed; and appointed six days hence for him to come, between 7 and 8 in the morning. (*18 July 1666*)

To Mr Cooper's house to see some of his work; which is all in little, but so excellent, as though I must confess I do think the colouring of the flesh to be a little forced, yet the painting is so extraordinary, as I do never expect to see the like again. Here I did see Mrs Stewards picture as when a young maid, and now again done just before her having the smallpox; and it would make a man weep to see what she was then, and what she is like to be, by people's discourse, now. (*30 March 1668*)

To Mr Streeters the famous history-painter over the way, whom I have often heard of but did never see him before; and there I found him and Dr Wren and several virtuosos looking upon the paintings which he is making for the new Theatre at Oxford [*the Sheldonian*]; and endeed, they look as they would be very fine, and the rest thinks better then those of Rubens in the Banqueting House at White-

[103]

hall, but I do not so fully think so – but they will certainly be very noble, and I am mightily pleased to have the fortune to see this man and his work, which is very famous – and he a very civil little man and lame, but lives very handsomely. So thence to my Lord Bellasses to see a chimney-piece of Dancre's doing in distemper with egg [*in tempera*] to keep off the glaring of the light, which I must have done for my room; and endeed it is pretty, but I must confess I do not think it is not altogether so beautiful as the oyle pictures; but I will have some of one and some of another. (*1 February 1669*)

With [my wife] to the plasterer's at Charing Cross that casts heads and bodies in plaster, and there I had my whole face done; but I was vexed first to be forced to daub all my face over with pomatum, but it was pretty to feel how saft and easily it is done on the face, and by and by, by degrees, how hard it becomes, that you cannot break it, and sits so close that you cannot pull it off, and yet so easy that it is as soft as a pillow, so safe is everything where many parts of the body do bear alike. Thus was the mold made; but when it came off, there was little pleasure in it as it looks in the mold, nor any resemblance whatever there will be in the figure when I come to see it cast off – which I am to call for a day or two hence; which I shall long to see. (*10 February 1669*)

To the plasterers and there saw the figure of my face taken from the mold; and it is most admirably like, and I will have another made before I take it away. (*15 February 1669*)

After dinner my wife and I to Loton the landskip-drawer, a Dutchman living in St James's Market, but there saw no good pictures; but by accident he did direct us to a painter that was then in the house with him, a Dutchman newly come over, one Everelst, who took us to his lodging close by and did show us a little flower pott of his doing, the finest thing that ever I saw in my life – the drops of dew hanging on the leaves, so as I was forced again and again to put my finger to it to feel whether my eyes were deceived or no. He doth ask 70*l* for it; I had the vanity to bid him 20*l* – but a better picture I never saw in my whole life, and it is worth going twenty miles to see. (*Easter Day, 11 April 1669*)

The Rising Man

¶ PEPYS WAS BORN TO SUCCESS. Not only was he gifted with a powerful intelligence and untiring energy, but he enjoyed, at the right moment, the favour of an influential patron, his cousin Edward Mountagu. 'We will rise together,' Mountagu told him (2 June 1660). And they did – Mountagu to the earldom of Sandwich, a place at court, the command of fleets and an embassy; Pepys (though then nothing more than a temporary clerk in the Exchequer) to a series of posts in the government service which earned him the esteem of two monarchs and brought him into contact with the highest in the land. In our day he would have been a Permanent Secretary, a life peer and the Chairman of the Royal Opera House, Covent Garden.

On 2 March 1662, he told Elizabeth that his aim was to save up £2000, to have his own coach, and to become a knight. The knighthood, for reasons which remain mysterious, never came his way, but he realised the other two ambitions. His savings exceeded £2000 by July 1665, and three years later he acquired his coach a smart yellow chariot. The chariot was success made visible. His decision to take the plunge and buy one (with all its attendant expenses of coachman, horses and stabling) was a counter-move provoked by the news that John Creed, his old rival for Sandwich's favour, had had the presumption to marry Lady Sandwich's niece.

[*On board ship on the way to Holland to bring back the King from exile.*] About 2 a-clock in the morning, letters came from London by our coxon; so they waked me, but I would not rise but bid him stay till morning, which he did; and then I rose and carried them in to my Lord, who read them a-bed. Among the rest, there was the writt and mandate for him to dispose to the Cinque Ports for choice of Parliament men. There was also one for me from Mr Blackburne, who with his own hand superscribes it to *S.P. Esqr.*, of which, God knows, I was not a little proud. (*25 March 1660*)

[*On board ship approaching Dover.*] I spoke with the Duke of York about business, who called me Pepys by name, and upon my desire did promise me his future favour. (*25 May 1660*)

[*In Dover harbour. The King and the Duke of York have gone to London leaving money to be distributed among the ship's company.*] Being with my Lord in the morning about business in his cabbin, I took occasion to give him thanks for his love to me in the share that he had given me of his Majestys money and the Dukes. He told me that he hoped to do me a more lasting kindness, if all things stand as they are now between him and the King – but says, "We must have a little patience and we will rise together. In the meantime I will do you all the good jobbs I can." Which was great content for me to hear from my Lord. (*2 June 1660*)

At noon [*with Navy Board colleagues*] by coach to the Tower, to Sir John Robinsons, to dinner. Where great good cheer. High company; among others, the Duchess of Albemerle, who is ever a plain, homely dowdy. I was much contented to ride in such state into the Towre and be received among such high company – while Mr Mount, my Lady Duchesses gentleman-usher, stood waiting at table, whom I ever thought a man so much above me in all respects. Also, to hear the discourse of so many high Cavaleers of things past – it was of great content and joy to me. (*8 March 1661*)

Talking long in bed with my wife about our frugall life for the time to come, proposing to her what I could and would do if I were worth 2000*l*; that is, be a Knight and keep my coach – which pleased her; and so I do hope we shall hereafter live to save something, for I am resolved to keep myself by rules from expences. (*Lord's Day, 2 March 1662*)

Up betimes and to my office; and at 9 a-clock (none of the rest going) I went alone to Deptford and there went on to pay Woolwich Yard; and so at noon dined well, being chief at the table, and do not see but everybody begins to give me as much respect and honour as any of the rest. After dinner to pay again and so till 9 at night – my great trouble being that I was forced to begin an ill practice of bringing down the wages of servants, for which people did curse me; which I do not love. At night, after I had eaten a cold pullet, I walked by brave mooneshine, with three or four armed [men] to guard me, to Redriffe – it being a joy to my heart to think of the condition that I am now in, that people should of themselfs provide this for me, unspoke to. (*19 September 1662*)

This night making an end wholly of Christmas, with a mind fully satisfyed with the great pleasures we have had by being abroad from home. And I do find my mind so apt to run to its old wont of pleasures, that it is high time to betake myself to my late vows [*against wine and plays*], which I will tomorrow, God willing, perfect and bind myself to, that so I may for a great while do my duty, as I have well begun, and encrease my good name and esteem in the world and get money, which sweetens all things and whereof I have much need. (*6 January 1663*)

To my great joy and with great thanks to Almighty God, I do find myself most clearly worth 1014*l* – the first time that ever I was worth 1000*l* before – which is the heighth of all that ever I have for a long time pretended to. So with praise to God for this state of fortune that I am brought to, I home to supper and to bed, desiring God to give me the Grace to make good use of what I have and continue my care and diligence to gain more. (*Lord's Day, 31 July 1664*)

So to my office a little; but being minded to make an end of my pleasure today, that I might fallow my business, I did take coach and to Jervas's again, thinking to avoir rencontré Jane; mais elle n'était pas dedans. So I back again to my office, where I did with great content faire a vow to mind my business and laisser aller les femmes for a month; and am with all my heart glad to find myself able to come to so good a resolution, that thereby I may fallow my business, which, and my honour thereby, lies a-bleeding. (*23 January 1665*)

Thence to Whitehall; where the King seeing me, did come to me, and calling me by name, did discourse with me about the ships in the river; and this is the first time that ever I knew the King did know me personally, so that hereafter I must not go thither but with expectation to be questioned, and to be ready to give good answers. (*17 April 1665*)

After dinner by coach to my Lord Chancellor's, and there a meeting – the Duke of York, the Duke of Albemarle, and several other Lords of the Commission of Tanger;

and there I did present a state of my accounts, and managed them well: and my Lord Chancellor did say, though he was in other things in an ill humour, that no man in England was of more method nor made himself better understood then myself. (*14 February 1667*)

At this time, my wife and I mighty busy laying out money in dressing up our best chamber and thinking of a coach and coachman and horses &c, and the more because of Creed's being now married to Mrs Pickering. (*20 October 1668*)

With Mr Povy spent all the afternoon going up and down among the coachmakers in Cow Lane, and did see several, and at last did pitch upon a little chariott, whose body was framed but not covered, at the widow's that made Mr Lowther's fine coach. And we are mightily pleased with it, it being light, and will be very gent and sober – to be covered with leather, but yet will hold four. (*5 November 1668*)

Up betimes, called up by my tailor, and there first put on a summer suit this year – but it was not my fine one of flowered tabby vest and coloured camelott tunic, because it was too fine with the gold lace at the hands, that I was afeared to be seen in it – but put on the stuff-suit I made the last year, which is now repaired; and so did go to the office in it and sat all the morning, the day looking as if it would be fowle. At noon home to dinner, and there find my wife extraordinary fine with her flowered tabby gown that she made two years ago, now laced exceeding pretty, and endeed was fine all over – and mighty earnest to go [*to the May Day parade in Hyde Park*], though the day was very lowering, and she would have me put on my fine suit, which I did; and so anon we went alone through the town with our new liverys of serge, and the horses' manes and tails tied with red ribbon and the standards thus gilt with varnish and all clean, and green raynes, that people did mightily look upon us; and the truth is, I did not see any coach more pretty, or more gay, then ours all the day. (*1 May 1669*)

The Theatre-goer

¶ THE THEATRES – closed since 1642 under the rule of the Puritans – were reopened after the King's return. By the end of 1660 there were two flourishing companies of actors in London licensed to perform in public, and (for the first time) to employ women in female parts (3 January 1661). They were the King's Company managed by Thomas Killigrew, and the Duke's Company managed by Sir William Davenant. The former, specialising in pre-1642 plays, performed in a theatre constructed from a tennis court in Vere St (usually referred to as 'the Theatre'), but moved in 1663 to a purpose-built theatre in Bridges St, off Drury Lane. The Duke's Company, specialising in new plays, settled in a theatre (again made from a tennis court) in Lincoln's Inn Fields equipped with elaborate scenery and stage machines, and known sometimes, from its 'works', as the 'Opera'. There were occasional productions by both companies in the evenings at Court, in the Great Hall of Whitehall Palace. In the theatres, plays were put on in the afternoons and ran for two or three days only.

Pepys had a passion for the theatre akin to his passion for music. He could rarely resist the temptation of a visit, and never tired of seeing the plays he liked. A little guilty at spending so much time in pleasure, and fearful of being criticised for neglecting his business, he attempted to bind himself against theatre-going by vows enforced by fines paid into his 'poor-box'. But to no great effect – he found ways of avoiding both the vows and the fines (see e.g. 8 May 1663). He rarely saw a play without passing judgement, and his comments are shrewd and comprehensive. He would criticise acting, production, plot and language.

Pepys came to know several actors and actresses, and was captivated in particular by the charm and vivacity of Nell Gwyn and Elizabeth Knepp.

To the Theatre, where was acted *Beggars Bush* [*by Fletcher and Massinger*], it being very well done; and here the first time that ever I saw women come upon the stage. (*3 January 1661*)

My wife and I to the Opera and there saw *Romeo and Julett*, the first time it was ever acted. But it is the play of itself the worst that ever I heard in my life, and the worst acted that ever I saw these people do; and I am resolved to go no more to see the first time of acting, for they were all of them out more or less. (*1 March 1662*)

To the King's Theatre, where we saw *Midsummers Nights Dreame*, which I have never seen before, nor shall ever again, for it is the most insipid ridiculous play that ever I saw in my life. I saw, I confess, some good dancing and some handsome women, which was all my pleasure. (*29 September 1662*)

To the Dukes House, where we saw [*Dryden's* The Slighted Mayde] well acted, though the play hath little good in it – being most pleased to see the little girl dance in boy's apparel, she having very fine legs; only, bends in the hams as I perceive all women do. (*23 February 1663*)

Thence to the new playhouse [*the Theatre Royal, Drury Lane*], the second day of its being opened. The play was *The Humorous Lieutenant* [*by Fletcher*] – a play that hath little good in it. In the dance, the tall Devil's actions was very pretty. And though my oath against going to plays doth not oblige me against this house, because it was not then in being, yet believing that at that time my meaning was against all public houses, I am resolved to deny myself the liberty of two plays at Court which are in arreare to me for the months of March and Aprill; which will more than countervail this excess. (*8 May 1663*)

Mr Creed dining with me, I got him to give my wife and me a play this afternoon, lending him money to do it – which is a fallacy that I have found now once to avoid my vowe with, but never to be more practised I swear. (*13 August 1664*)

After dinner we walked to the King's Playhouse, all in dirt, they being altering of the stage to make it wider – but God knows when they will begin to act again. But my business here was to see the inside of the stage and all the tiring roomes and machines; and endeed it was a sight worthy seeing. But to see their clothes and the various sorts, and what a mixture of things there was, here a wooden leg, there a ruff, here a hobby-horse, there a crowne, would make a man split himself to see with laughing – and perticularly Lacys wardrobe, and Shotrell's. But then again, to think how fine they show on the stage by candlelight, and how poor things they are to look now too nearhand, is not pleasant at all. The machines are fine, and the paintings very pretty. (*19 March 1666*)

[T. Killigrew] tells me how the audience at his house is not above half so much as it used to be before the late fire. That Knipp is like to make the best actor that ever came upon the stage, she understanding so well. That they are going to give her 30*l* a year more. That the stage is now by his pains a thousand times better and more glorious then ever heretofore. Now, wax-candles, and many of them; then [*i.e. under Charles I*], not above 3*lb* of tallow. Now, all things civil, no rudeness anywhere; then, as in a bear-garden. Then, two or three fiddlers; now, nine or ten of the best. Then, nothing but rushes upon the ground and everything else mean; and now, all otherwise. Then, the Queen seldom and the King never would come; now, not the King only for state, but all civil people do think they may come as well as any. (*12 February 1667*)

After dinner with my wife to the King's House, to see *The Mayden Queene*, a new play of Dryden's mightily commended for the regularity of it and the strain and wit; and the truth is, there is a comical part done by Nell, which is Florimell, that I never can hope ever to see the like done again by man or woman. The King and Duke of York was at the play; but so great performance of a comical part was never, I believe, in the world before as Nell doth this, both as a mad girle and then, most and best of all, when she comes in like a young gallant; and hath the motions and carriage of a spark the most that ever I saw any man have. It makes me, I confess, admire her. (*2 March 1667*)

At noon home to dinner; and presently my wife and I and Sir W. Penn to the King's playhouse, where the house extraordinary full; and there was the King and Duke of York to see the new play, *Queen Elizabeths Troubles, and The History of Eighty-Eight* [by Heywood]. I confess I have sucked in so much of the sad story of Queen Elizabeth from my cradle, that I was ready to weep for her sometimes. But the play is the most ridiculous that sure ever came upon stage, and endeed is merely a show; only, shows the true garbe of the Queens in those days, just as we see Queen Mary and Queen Elizabeth painted – but the play is merely a puppet-play acted by living puppets. Neither the design nor language better; and one stands by and tells us the meaning of things. Only, I was pleased to see Knipp dance among the milkmaids, and to hear her sing a song to Queen Elizabeth – and to see her come out in her nightgowne, with no locks on, but her bare face and hair only tied up in a knot behind; which is the comeliest dress that ever I saw her in to her advantage. (*17 August 1667*)

To the Duke of York's playhouse; but the House so full, it being a new play *The Coffee House* [*by St Cerfe*], that we could not get in, and so to the King's House; and there going in, met with Knipp and she took us up into the tireing-rooms and to the women's shift, where Nell was dressing herself and was all unready; and is very pretty, prettier than I thought; and so walked all up and down the House above, and then below into the Scene-room, and there sat down and she gave us fruit; and here I read the qu's to Knepp while she answered me, through all her part of *Flora's Figarys* [*by Rhodes*], which was acted today. But Lord, to see how they were both painted would make a man mad – and did make me loath them – and what base company of men comes among them, and how lewdly they talk – and how poor the men are in clothes, and yet what a show they make on the stage by candlelight, is very observable. But to see how Nell cursed for having so few people in the pit was pretty, the other House carrying away all the people at the new play, and is said nowadays to have generally most company, as being better players. By and by into the pit and there saw the play; which is pretty good, but my belly was full of what I had seen in the House. (*5 October 1667*)

Thence I after dinner to the Duke of York's playhouse, and there saw *Sir Martin Marrall* [*by Dryden*], which I have seen so often; and yet am mightily pleased with it and think it mighty witty, and the fullest of proper matter for mirth that ever was writ. And I do clearly see that they do improve in their acting of it. Here a mighty company of citizens, prentices and others; and it makes me observe that when I begin first to be able to bestow a play on myself, I do not remember that I saw so many by half of the ordinary prentices and mean people in the pit, at 2s.-6d. apiece, as now; I going for several years no higher then the 12d., and then the 18d. places, and though I strained hard to go in then when I did – so much the vanity and prodigality of the age is to be observed in this perticular. (*1 January 1668*)

I was prettily served this day at the playhouse door; where giving six shillings into the fellow's hand for us three, the fellow by legerdemain did convey one away, and with so much grace face me down that I did give him but five, that though I knew the contrary, yet I was overpowered by his so grave and serious demanding the other shilling that I could not deny him, but was forced by myself to give it him. (*24 February 1668*)

My wife and I by hackney to the King's playhouse and there, the pit being full, sat in a box above and saw *Catelin's Conspiracy* [*by Ben Jonson*] – yesterday being the first day – a play of much good sense and words to read, but that doth appear the worst upon the stage, I mean the least divertising, that ever I saw any, though most fine in clothes and a fine scene of the Senate and of a fight, that ever I saw in my life – but the play is only to be read. (*19 December 1668*)

The Virtuoso

¶ THE 'VIRTUOSO' in Pepys's day was a man of varied learning – not a polymath, and certainly not any sort of pedant, but a cultivated man with a variety of interests, in the manner of the 'universal man' of Renaissance times. Pepys was well qualified to be so described. In particular, he was excited by what we would call science, which was just becoming a part of general culture, though the word did not then exist in its modern meaning. The Royal Society of London ('Gresham College' from its place of meeting) was formally founded in 1660 and its meetings were attended not only by mathematicians and physicians, virtually the only members we would recognise as scientists, but also by amateur enthusiasts like Pepys. He became a Fellow in 1665 and served as President in 1684–6.

Sometimes Pepys's scientific curiosity is related to his personal or professional life (hence, for example, his interest in medicine and surgery, or in shipbuilding and navigation); but more often it arises from his love of knowledge in general, and especially of 'curious' knowledge. He held it to be one of the profoundest pleasures of London life to be able to observe the experiments conducted at meetings of the Royal Society and to share, if only as a listener, in the 'good discourse' of its Fellows. Among the virtuosi he came to know were some of the greatest figures of contemporary science and learning – Robert Boyle (of Boyle's Law), Robert Hooke, Secretary of the Society and the most gifted experimentalist of the age, Sir William Petty, political economist and ship designer, and John Wilkins, linguistic scholar and bishop. The subjects he found interesting ranged from the making of French bread to optics and from the propagation of frogs to the study of the stars.

With [Mr Shepley] and Mr Moore and John Bowles to the Renish winehouse, and there came Jonas Moore the mathematician to us. And there he did by discourse make us fully believe that England and France were once the same continent, by very good arguments. And spoke very many things, not so much to prove the Scripture false, as that the time therein is not well computed nor understood. From thence home by water and there shifted myself into my black silke sute (the first day I have put it on this year); and so to my Lord Mayors by coach, where a great deal of honourable company – and great entertainment. At table I had very good discourse with Mr Ashmole, wherein he did assure me that froggs and many other insects do often fall from the sky ready-formed. (*23 May 1661*)

About 11 a-clock Comissioner Pett and I walked to Chyrurgeons Hall (we being all invited thither and promised to dine there), where we were led into the Theatre; and by and by came the Reader, Dr Tearne, with the Maister and Company, in a very handsome manner; and all being settled, he begun his lecture, this being the second upon the kidnys, ureters, and yard, which was very fine; and his discourse being ended, we walked into the Hall; and there being great store of company we had a fine dinner and good learned company, many Doctors of Physique, and we used with extraordinary great respect. After dinner Dr Scarborough took some of his friends, and I went along with them, to see the body alone; which we did; he was a lusty fellow, a seaman that was hanged for a robbery. Thence we went into a private room, where I perceive they prepare the bodies, and there was the kidnys, ureters, yard, stones and semenary vessels upon which he read today. And Dr Scarborough, upon my desire and the company's, did show very clearly the manner of the disease of the stone and the cutting and all other questions that I could think of, and the manner of the seed, how it comes into the yard, and how the water into the bladder, through the three skinnes or coats, just as poor Dr Jolly had heretofore told me. Thence, with great satisfaccion to me, back to the Company, where I heard good discourse; and so to the afternoon lecture upon the heart and lungs, &c. And that being done, we broke up. (*27 February 1663*)

At noon to the coffee-house, where with Dr Allen some good discourse about physic and chymistry. And among other things, I telling him what Dribble the German Doctor do offer, of an instrument to sink ships, he tells me that which is more strange: that something made of gold, which they call in chymistry *Aurum Fulminans*; a grain, I think he said, of it put into a silver spoon and fired, will give a blow like a musquett and strike a hole through the spoon downward, without the least force upward. (*11 November 1663*)

Before I went to bed, I sat up till 2 a-clock in my chamber, reading of Mr Hookes Microscopical Observations, the most ingenious book that ever I read in my life. (*21 January 1665*)

At noon I to dinner at Trinity House – and thence to Gresham College where, first Mr Hooke read a second very curious lecture about the late comett, among other things, proving very probably that this is the very same comett that appeared before in the year 1618, and that in such a time probably it will appear again – which is a very new opinion – but all will be in print. Then to the meeting, where Sir G. Carterets two sons, his own and

Sir N. Slany, were admitted of the Society. And this day I did pay my admission money – 40s. – to the Society. Here was very fine discourses – and experiments; but I do lack philosophy enough to understand them, and so cannot remember them. Among others, a very perticular account of the making of the several sorts of bread in France, which is accounted the best place for bread in the world. (*1 March 1665*)

To Mr Hublands the merchant, where Sir W. Petty and abundance of most ingenious men, owners and freighters of the *Experiment* [*the double-bottomed ship designed by Petty*], now going with her two bodies to sea. Most excellent discourse. Among others, Sir Wm Petty did tell me that in good earnest, he hath in his will left such parts of his estate to him that could invent such and such things – as among others, that could discover truly the way of milk coming into the breasts of a woman – and he that could invent proper characters to express to another the mixture of relishes and tastes. And says that to him that invents gold, he gives nothing for the philosopher's stone; "for," says he, "they that find out that will be able to pay themselfs – but," says he, "by this means it is better then to give to a lecture. For here my executors, that must part with this, will be sure to be well convinced of the invention before they do part with their money." Then to Gresham College and there did see a kitlin killed almost quite (but that we could not quite kill her) with sucking away the ayre out of a receiver wherein she was put – and then the ayre being let in upon her, revives her immediately. Nay, and this ayre is to be made by putting together a liquor and some body that firments – the steam of that doth do the work. (*22 March 1665*)

At noon, going to the Change, met my Lord Brunkerd, Sir Robert Murry, Deane Wilkins, and Mr Hooke, going by coach to Coll. Blunt's to dinner. So they stopped and took me with them. Landed at the Tower Wharf and thence by water to Greenwich, and there coaches met us and to his house, a very stately seat for situation and brave plantations; and among others, a vineyard. No extraordinary dinner, nor any other entertainment good – but only, after dinner to the tryall of some experiments about making of coaches easy. And several we tried, but one did prove mighty easy (not here for me to describe, but the whole body of that coach lies upon one long spring) and we all, one after another, rid in it; and it is very fine and likely to take. These experiments were the intent of their coming, and pretty they are. (*1 May 1665*)

I to my Lord Brouncker and there spent the evening, by my desire, in seeing his Lordship open to pieces and make up again his wach, thereby being taught what I never knew before; and it is a thing very well worth my having seen, and am mightily pleased and satisfied with it. (*22 December 1665*)

At noon to dinner to the Popes Head, where my Lord Brouncker (and his mistress) dined, and Comissioner Pett, Dr Charleton, and myself entertained with a venison pasty by Sir W. Warren. Here, very pretty discourse of Dr Charleton concerning Nature's fashioning every creature's teeth according to the food she intends them. And that man's, it is plain, was not for flesh, but for fruit. And that he can at any time tell the food of a beast unknown, by the teeth. My Lord Brouncker made one or two objections to it; that creatures find their food proper for their teeth, rather then that the teeth was fitted for the food. But the Doctor, I think, did well observe that creatures do naturally, and from the first, before they have had experience to try, do love such a food rather then another. And that all children love fruit, and none brought to flesh but against their wills at first. Thence with my Lord to his coach-house, and there put in six horses into his coach and he and I alone to Highgate – all the way, going and coming, I learning of him the principles of optickes, and what it is that makes an object seem less or bigger. And how much distance doth lessen an object. And that it is not the eye at all, or any rule in optiques, that can tell distance; but it is only an act of reason, comparing of one mark with another. Which did both please and inform me mightily. (*28 July 1666*)

Discoursed with Mr Hooke a little, whom we met in the street, about the nature of sounds, and he did make me understand the nature of musicall sounds made by strings, mighty prettily; and told me that having come to a certain number of vibracions proper to make any tone, he is able to tell how many strokes a fly makes with her wings (those flies that hum in their flying) by the note that it answers to in musique during their flying. That, I suppose, is a little too much raffined; but his discourse in general of sound was mighty fine. (*8 August 1666*)

By and by comes by agreement Mr Reeves, and after him Mr Spong; and all day with them, both before and after dinner till 10 a-clock at night, upon opticke enquiries – he bringing me a frame with closes on, to see how the rays of light do cut one another, and in a dark room with smoake, which is very pretty. He did also bring a lantern, with pictures in glass to make strange things appear on a wall, very pretty. We did also at night see Jupiter and his girdle and satellites very fine with my 12-foot glass, but could not Saturne, he being very dark. Spong and I also had several fine discourses upon the globes this afternoon, perticularly why the fixed stars do not rise and set at the same hour all the year long, which he could not demonstrate, nor I neither, the reason of. So it being late, after supper they away home. But it vexed me to understand no more from Reeves and his glasses touching the nature and reason of the several refractions of the several figured glasses, he understanding the acting part but not one bit the theory, nor can make anybody understand it – which is a strange dullness methinks. (*19 August 1666*)

To the Popes Head, where all the Houblons were, and Dr Croone; and by and by to an exceeding pretty supper – excellent discourse of all sorts; and endeed, are a set of the finest gentlemen that ever I met withal in my life. Here Dr Croone told me that at the meeting at Gresham College tonight there was a pretty experiment, of the blood of one dogg let out (till he died) into the body of another on one side, while all his own run out on the other side. The first died upon the place, and the other very well, and likely to do well. This did give occasion to many pretty wishes, as of the blood of a Quaker to be let into an Archbishop, and such like. But, as Dr Croone says, [it] may if it takes be of mighty use to man's health, for the amending of bad blood by borrowing from a better body. (*14 November 1666*)

So to bed – mightily pleased with my reading Boyles Book of Colours today; only, troubled that some part of it, endeed the greatest part, I am not able to understand for want of study. (*28 April 1667*)

Dr Whistler told a pretty story related by Muffett, a good author, of Dr Cayus that built Key's College [*Caius College, Cambridge*]: that being very old and lived only at that time upon woman's milk, he, while he fed upon the milk of a angry fretful woman, was so himself; and then being advised to take of a good-natured patient woman, he did become so, beyond the common temper of his age. Thus much nutriment, they observed, might do. Their discourse was very fine; and if I should be put out of my office, I do take great content in the liberty I shall be at of frequenting these gentlemen's companies. (*21 November 1667*)

By coach to Arundell House to the elections of officers [*of the Royal Society*] for the next year; where I was near being chosen of the Council, but am glad I was not, for I could not have attended; though above all things, I could wish it, and do take it as a mighty respect to have been named there. The company great and elections long; and then to Cary House, a house of entertainment; and there, we after two hours' stay, sitting at the table with our napkins open, had our dinners brought; but badly done. But here was good company, I choosing to sit next Dr Wilkins, Sir George Ent, and others whom I value. And there talked of several things; among others, Dr Wilkins, talking of the universall speech, of which he hath a book coming out, did first inform me how man was certainly made for society, he being of all creatures the least armed for defence; and of all creatures in the world, the young ones are not able to do anything to help themselfs, nor can find the dug without being put to it, but would die if the mother did not help it. And he says were it not for speech, man would be a very mean creature. (*30 November 1667*)

To Eagle Court in the Strand and there met Mr Pierce the surgeon and Dr Clerke, Waldron, Turberville my physician for the eyes, and Lowre, to dissect several eyes of sheep and oxen, with great pleasure – and to my great information; but strange that this Turberville should be so great a man, and yet to this day had seen no eyes dissected, or but once, but desired this Dr Lowre to give him the opportunity to see him dissect some. (*3 July 1668*)

III

PEPYS'S WORLD

Ceremonies and Processions

¶ THE SERVICE AT CHARLES II'S CORONATION (23 April 1661) followed the traditional pattern which has remained materially unchanged since the Norman Conquest. The banquet which followed in Westminster Hall has not been held since the coronation of George IV.

The dispute about precedence between the representatives of the French and Spanish monarchs (30 September 1661) was of a type that occurred not infrequently until international agreement was reached at the Congress of Vienna in 1815. It was then decided that the order of precedence should be determined by the seniority by appointment of the local ambassadors, instead of by the supposed seniority by foundation of the monarchies themselves.

The new Queen, Catherine of Braganza, made her entry from Hampton Court into London by river (23 August 1662). She had landed at Portsmouth on 15 May. Whitehall 'Bridge' was a jetty.

The Russian embassy (27 November 1662) was a trade mission sent by the Tsar Alexis, father of Peter the Great.

Coronacion day. I lay with Mr Sheply, and about 4 in the morning I rose. And got to the Abby, where I fallowed Sir J. Denham the Surveyour with some company that he was leading in. And with much ado, by the favour of Mr Cooper his man, did get up into a great scaffold across the north end of the Abby – where with a great deal of patience I sat from past 4 till 11 before the King came in. And a pleasure it was to see the Abbey raised in the middle, all covered with red and a throne (that is a chaire) and footstoole on the top of it. And all the officers of all kinds, so much as the very fidlers, in red vests. At last comes in the Deane and Prebends of Westminster with the Bishops (many of them in cloth-of-gold copes); and after them the nobility all in their parliament robes,

[129]

which was a most magnificent sight. Then the Duke and the King with a Scepter (carried by my Lord of Sandwich) and Sword and Mond before him, and the Crowne too. The King in his robes, bare-headed, which was very fine. And after all had placed themselfs – there was a sermon and the service. And then in the quire at the high altar he passed all the ceremonies of the Coronacion – which, to my very great grief, I and most in the Abbey could not see. The Crowne being put upon his head, a great shout begun. And he came forth to the Throne and there passed more ceremonies: as, taking the oath and having things read to him by the Bishopp, and his lords (who put on their capps as soon as the King put on his Crowne) and Bishopps came and kneeled before him. And three times the King-at-Armes went to the three open places on the scaffold and proclaimed that if any one could show any reason why Ch. Steward should not be King of England, that now he should come and speak. And a generall pardon was also read by the Lord Chancellor; and meddalls flung up and down by my Lord Cornwallis – of silver; but I could not come by any. But so great a noise, that I could make but little of the musique; and endeed, it was lost to everybody. But I had so great a list to pisse, that I went out a little while before the King had done all his ceremonies and went round the Abby to Westminster Hall, all the way within rayles, and 10,000 people, with the ground coverd with blue cloth – and scaffolds all the way. Into the Hall I got – where it was very fine with hangings and scaffolds, one upon another, full of brave ladies. And my wife in one little one on the right hand.

Here I stayed walking up and down; and at last the King came in with his Crowne on and his Sceptre in his hand – under a canopy borne up by six silver staves, carried by Barons of the Cinqueports – and little bells at every end. And after a long time he got up to the farther end, and all set themselfs down at their several tables – and that was also a rare sight. And the King's first course carried up by the Knights of the Bath. And many fine ceremonies there was of the Heralds leading up people before him and bowing; and my Lord of Albimarles going to the kitchin and eat a bit of the first dish that was to go to the King's table. But above all was these three Lords, Northumberland and Suffolke and the Duke of Ormond, coming before the courses on horseback and staying so all dinner-time; and at last, to bring up (Dymock) the King's Champion, all in armor on horseback, with his speare and targett carried before him. And a herald proclaim that if any dare deny Ch. Steward to be lawful King of England, here was a Champion that would fight with him; and with those words the Champion flings down his gantlet; and all this he doth three times in his going up toward the King's table. At last, when he is come, the King drinkes to him and then sends him the cup, which is of gold; and he drinks it off and then rides back again with the cup in his hand. I went from table to table to see the Bishops and all others at their dinner, and was infinite pleased with it. And at the Lords' table I met with Wll Howe and he spoke to my Lord for me and he did give him four rabbits and a pullet; and so I got it, and Mr Creed and I got Mr Michell to give us some bread and so we at a stall eat it, as everybody else did what they could get. I took a great deal of pleasure to go up and down and look upon the ladies – and to hear the musique of all sorts; but above all, the 24 viollins. And strange it is, to think that these two days have held up fair till now that all is done and the King gone out of the Hall; and then it fell a-raining and thundering and lightening as I have not seen it do some years – which people did take great notice of God's blessing of the work of these two days – which is a foolery, to take too much notice of such things.

[To] Mr Bowyers, [where] a great deal of company; some I knew, others I did not. Here we stayed upon the leads and below till it was late, expecting to see the fireworkes; but they were not performed tonight. Only, the City had a light like a glory round about it, with bonefyres. To Axe Yard, in which, at the further end, there was three great bonefyres and a great many great gallants, men and women; and they laid hold of us and would have us drink the King's health upon our knee, kneeling upon a fagott; which we all did, they drinking to us one after another – which we thought a strange frolique. But these gallants continued thus a great while, and I wondered to see how the ladies did tiple. At last I sent my wife and her bedfellow to bed, and Mr Hunt and I went in with Mr Thornbury (who did give the company all their wines, he being yeoman of the wine-cellar to the King) to his house; and there we drank the King's health and nothing else, till one of the genlemen fell down stark drunk and there lay speweing. And I went to my Lord's pretty well. But no sooner a-bed with Mr Sheply but my head begun to turne and I to vomitt, and if ever I was foxed it was now – which I cannot say yet, because I fell asleep and sleep till morning – only, when I waked I found myself wet with my spewing. Thus did the day end, with joy everywhere.

Now after all this, I can say that besides the pleasure of

the sight of these glorious things, I may now shut my eyes against any other objects, or for the future trouble myself to see things of state and shewe, as being sure never to see the like again in this world. (*23 April 1661*)

I went into King Streete to the Red Lyon to drink my morning draught and there I heard of a fray between the two Embassadors of Spaine and France; and that this day being the day of the entrance of an Embassador from Sweden, they were entended to fight for the precedence [*in the procession*]. In Cheapeside hear that the Spaniard hath got the best of it and killed three of the French coach-horses and several men and is gone through the City next to our King's coach. At which it is strange to see how all the City did rejoice. And endeed, we do naturally all love the Spanish and hate the French. But I, as I am in all things curious, presently got to the waterside and there took oares to Westminster Palace, thinking to have seen them come in thither with all the coaches; but they being come and returned, I run after them with my boy after me, through all the dirt and the streets full of people; till at last at the Mewes I saw the Spanish coach go, with 50 drawne swords at least to guard it and our soldiers shouting for joy. And so I fallowed the coach, and then met it at Yorke House, where the Embassador lies; and there it went in with great state. So then I went to the French Ambassador's house, where I observe still that there is no men in the world of a more insolent spirit where they do well or before they begin a matter, and more abject if they do miscarry, then these people are. For they all look like dead men and not a word among them, but shake their heads. So having been very much dawbed with dirt, I got a coach and home – where I vexed my wife in telling of her this story and pleading for the Spaniard against the French. (*30 September 1661*)

Mr Creede by appointment being come, he and I went out together, and at an ordinary in Lumbard Streete dined together; and so walked down to the Styllyard and so all along Thames Streete, but could not get a boat: I offered 8*s*. for a boat to attend me this afternoon and they would not, it being the day of the Queenes coming to town from Hampton Court. So we fairly walked it to Whitehall; and through my Lord's lodgings we got into Whitehall garden, and so to the bowling-greene and up to the top of the new banqueting-house there over the Thames, which was a most pleasant place as any I could have got. And all the show consisted chiefly in the number of boats and barges – and two pageants, one of a King and another of a Queene, with her maydes of honour sitting at her feet very prettily. Anon came the King and Queene in a barge under a canopy, with 10,000 barges and boats I think, for we could see no water for them – nor discern the King nor Queen. And so they landed at Whitehall Bridge, and the great guns on the other side went off. (*23 August 1662*)

To the office – where we sat all the morning till noon; and then we all went to the next house upon Tower Hill to see the coming by of the Russia Embassador – for whose reception all the City trained bands do attend in the streets, and the King's Lifeguard, and most of the wealthy citizens in their black velvet coats and gold chains (which remain of their gallantry at the King's coming in); but they stayed so long that we went down again home to dinner. And after I had dined, I heard that they were coming, and so I walked to the conduict in the *Quarrefour* at the end of Gracious Street and Cornhill; and there (the spouts thereof running, very near me, upon all the people that were under it) I saw them pretty well go by. I could not see the Embassador in his coach – but his attendants in their habitts and fur caps very handsome comely men, and most of them with hawkes upon their fists to present to the King. But Lord, to see the absurd nature of Englishmen, that cannot forbear laughing and jeering at everything that looks strange. (*27 November 1662*)

Christmas

¶ IN THESE PASSAGES Pepys records Christmas dinners, with their familiar fare, and Christmas games. Twelfth Night marked the end of the season and was commonly the occasion for a party such as those described here. The guests chose slices from an elaborate Twelfth Night cake which contained tokens – one denoting the King who was to rule over the feast, another his Queen. Pepys's relatives the Strudwicks, who were professional bakers, made ideal hosts.

To my cousin Stradwick. Where, after a good supper, there being there my father, mother, brothers, and sister, my cousin Scot and his wife, Mr Drawwater and his wife and her brother, Mr Stradwick, we had a brave cake brought us, and in the choosing, Pall was Queen and Mr Stradwick was King. After that, my wife and I bid Adieu and came home, it being still a great frost. (*6 January 1660*)

This evening Mr Gauden [*the Navy Victualler*] sent me, against Christmas a great chine of beefe and three dozen of toungs. I did give 5s. to the man that brought it and half-crown to the porters. (*24 December 1662*)
Dined by my wife's bedside with great content, having a mess of brave plum-porridge, and a roasted pullett for dinner; and I sent for a mince-pie abroad, my wife not being well to make any herself yet. After dinner sat talking a good while with her, her [pain] being become less, and then to see Sir W. Penn a little; and so to my office, practising arithmetique alone with great content, till 11 at night; and so home to supper and to bed. (*Christmas Day, 1662*)

We had to dinner, my wife and I, a fine turkey and a mince-pie, and dined in state, poor wretch, she and I; and have thus kept our Christmas together, all alone almost — having not once been out. (*31 December 1663*)

To Sir W. Batten, where Mr Coventry and all our families here, women and all, and Sir R. Ford and his. And a great feast — and good discourse and merry. I here all the afternoon and evening till late. Then to my office to enter my day's work; and so home to bed, where my people and wife innocently at cards, very merry. And I to bed, leaving them to their sport and blindman's buff. (*26 December 1664*)

At night home, being Twelfenight, and there chose my piece of cake, but went up to my vial and then to bed, leaving my wife and people up at their sports, which they continue till morning, not coming to bed at all. (*6 January 1665*)

To church, where our parson Mills made a good sermon. Then home, and dined well on some good ribbs of beef roasted and mince pies; only my wife, brother, and Barker, and plenty of good wine of my own; and my heart full of true joy and thanks to God Almighty for the goodness of my condition at this day. (*Christmas Day, 1666*)

Church Uniformity Restored

¶ IN 1660, THE LEGAL FRAMEWORK of the Church was automatically restored with the return of monarchy. The Church was once more ruled by a supreme Governor and bishops. Since most of the pre-revolution bishops had died, a number of new ones were immediately appointed and consecrated (4 October 1660). More gradual was the return of the old Prayer Book services, with use of music and surplices – at first in the royal chapels, the cathedrals and college chapels, and later in the parish churches. Finally, in May 1662, an Act of Uniformity was passed requiring all the clergy without exception to use the Prayer Book, by now revised in Convocation. About 1000, mostly strict Presbyterians, refused and were expelled from their livings. (A farewell sermon by Dr William Bates is reported at 17 August 1662.) Bates and his like went out of the church to establish congregations of their own, forming thereby the basis of modern Nonconformity. A series of acts followed making non-Anglican worship illegal, to no avail. The King was averse to the policy (19 February 1663); so too was Pepys (7 August 1664).

The Solomon Eccles (of 29 July 1667) was the Quaker made famous by Defoe as Solomon Eagle in his *Journal of the Plague Year.*

To Whitehall to Chapel, where I got in with ease by going before the Lord Chancellor with Mr Kipps. Here I heard very good musique, the first time that I remember ever to have heard the organs and singing-men in surplices in my life. The Bishop of Chichester preached before the King and made a great flattering sermon, which I did not like that clergy should meddle with matters of state. (*Lord's Day, 8 July 1660*)

To Westminster Abbey, where we saw Dr Fruen translated to the Archbishopric of Yorke. Here I saw the Bishops of Winchester, Bangor, Rochester, Bath and

Wells, and Salisbury, all in their habitts, in King Henry the 7ths Chappell. But Lord, at their going out, how people did most of them look upon them as strange creatures, and few with any kind of love or respect. (*4 October 1660*)

In the morn to our own church, where Mr Mills did begin to nibble at the Common Prayer by saying "Glory be to the Father," &c after he had read the two psalms. But the people have beene so little used to it that they could not tell what to answer. (*Lord's Day, 4 November 1660*)

Coming home tonight, I met with Will Swan, who doth talk as high for the fanatiques as ever he did in his life; and doth pity my Lord Sandwich and me that we should be given up to the wickedness of the world, and that a fall is coming upon us all. For he finds that he and his company are the true spirit of the nation, and the greater part of the nation, too – who will have liberty of conscience in spite of this Act of Uniformity, or they will die; and if they may not preach abroad, they will preach in their own houses. He told me that certainly Sir H. Vane [*recently executed*] must be gone to Heaven, for he died as much a martyr and saint as ever any man died. And that the King hath lost more by that man's death then he will get again a good while. At all which, I know not what to think; but I confess I do think that the Bishops will never be able to carry it so high as they do. (*22 June 1662*)

I had a mind to hear Dr Bates's farewell sermon, and walked to St Dunstans, where, it being not 7 a-clock yet, the doors were not open; and so I went and walked an hour in the Temple garden. At 8 a-clock I went and crowded in at a back door among others, and the church being half-full almost before any doors were open publicly. And so got into the gallry besides the pulpit and heard very well. His text was, "Now the god of peace" – the last *Hebrews* and the 20 verse – he making a very good sermon and very little reflections in it to anything of the times. Besides the sermon, I was very well pleased with the sight of a fine lady that I have often seen walk in Grayes Inn Walks. After dinner to St Dunstan's again, and the church quite crouded before I came, which was just at one a-clock; but I got into the gallery again, but stood in a crowd and did exceedingly sweat all the while. He pursued his text again very well, and only at the conclusion told us after this manner – "I do believe that many of you do expect that I should say something to you in reference to the time, this being the last time that possibly I may appear here. You know it is not my manner to speak anything in the pulpit that is extraneous to my text and business. Yet this I shall say, that it is not my opinion, faction, or humour that keeps me from complying with what is required of us, but something which after much prayer, discourse and study yet remains unsatisfied and commands me herein. Wherefore, if it is my unhappinesse not to receive such an illuminacion as should direct me to do otherwise, I know no reason why men should not pardon me in this world, and am confident that God will pardon me for it in the next." And so he concluded. I hear most of the Presbyters took their leaves today. And the City is much dissatisfied with it. I pray God keep peace among us and make the Bishops careful of bringing in good men in their room, or else all will fly a-pieces; for bad ones will not down with the City. (*17 August 1662*)

Great talk among people how some of the fanatiques do say that the end of the world is at hand and that next Tuesday is to be the day – against which, whenever it shall be, good God fit us all. (*25 November 1662*)

This day I read the King's speech to the parliament yesterday; which is very short and not very obliging, but only telling them his desire to have a power of indulging tender consciences, not that he will yield to have any mixture in the uniformity of the Church discipline. And says the same for the Papist, but declares against their ever being admitted to have any offices or places of trust in the Kingdom – but God knows, too many have. (*19 February 1663*)

The Commons in parliament, I hear, are very high to stand to the Act of Uniformity, and will not indulge the Papists (which is endeavoured by the court party) nor the Presbyters. (*25 February 1663*)

While we were talking, came by several poor creatures, carried by by constables for being at a conventicle. They go like lambs, without any resistance. I would to God they would either conform, or be more wise and not be ketched. (*Lord's Day, 7 August 1664*)

To Westminster Hall, where the Hall full of people, the King being to come to speak to the House today. One thing extraordinary was this day, a man, a Quaker, came naked through the Hall, only very civilly tied about the privities to avoid scandal, and with a chafing-dish of fire and brimstone burning upon his head did pass through the Hall, crying, "Repent! Repent!" (*29 July 1667*)

The Court

¶ WHITEHALL PALACE was the main royal residence and the centre of government. It consisted of a series of buildings which, except for Inigo Jones's Banqueting House, no longer survive, having been destroyed by fire in 1698. St James's Palace, across the park, was the principal residence of the King's brother and heir-presumptive, James Duke of York, the Lord High Admiral. Pepys, as a government servant, was a frequent visitor to both. His own observations of court life were supplemented by information or gossip from well-placed friends such as James Pearse, a court surgeon, and Sarah, housekeeper of Sandwich's lodgings in Whitehall which happened to be next door to those of Lady Castlemaine, the beautiful and rapacious mistress of the King. Pepys's comments often reflect his disappointment at what he saw as the irresponsibility of the King and his entourage. At 27 August 1667, for instance, he reports the fall of the Lord Chancellor, Clarendon – a great man who had done more than anyone else to bring about a peaceful restoration of the King. He was now cast aside for younger and less able favourites.

The 'Portugall ladys' (25 May 1662) were the attendants of Catherine of Braganza whom the King had recently married.

'Tennis' (4 January 1664) was the indoor game of real (royal) tennis. The 'Tour' (19 March 1665) was the fashionable parade of coaches and riders round Hyde Park. The King's new fashion (15 October 1666) was a war measure designed in reaction to French fashions; Louis XIV's response was to put his valets into it, but it survived to become the ancestor of the modern male's jacket and waistcoat.

To Worcester House, where several Lords are met in council this afternoon. And while I am waiting there, in comes the King in a plain common riding-suit and velvet capp, in which he seemed a very ordinary man to one that had not known him. (*19 August 1661*)

My wife and I by water to Westminster; to my Lord's lodgeings, where she and I stayed, walking into White-hall garden; and in the Privy Garden saw the finest smocks and linen petticoats of my Lady Castlemaynes, laced with rich lace at the bottomes, that ever I saw; and did me good to look upon them. So to Wilkinsons, she and I and Sarah to dinner, where I had a good quarter of lamb and a salat. Here Sarah told me how the King dined at my lady Castlemayne, and supped, every day and night the last week. And that the night that the bonefires were made for joy of the Queenes arrivall, the King was there; but there was no fire at her door, though at all the rest of the doors almost in the street; which was much observed. And that the King and she did send for a pair of scales and weighed one another; and she, being with child, was said to be heavyest. (*21 May 1662*)

With Capt. Ferrers to Charing Cross; and there at the Triumph taverne he showed me some Portugall ladys which are come to towne before the Queene. They are not handsome, and their farthingales a strange dress. Many ladies and persons of quality come to see them. I find nothing in them that is pleasing. And I see they have learnt to kiss and look freely up and downe already, and I do believe will soon forget the recluse practice of their own country. They complain much for lack of good water to drink. (*Lord's Day, 25 May 1662*)

[*Pepys joins the crowds on the riverside at Whitehall to watch the arrival of the new Queen from Hampton Court.*] That which pleased me best was that my Lady Castlemayne stood over against us upon a piece of Whitehall, where I glutted myself with looking on her. But methought it was strange to see her Lord and her upon the same place, walking up and down without taking notice one of another; only, at first entry, he put off his hat and she made him a very civil salute – but afterwards took no notice one of another. But both of them now and then would take their child, which the nurse held in her armes, and dandle it. One thing more; there happend a scaffold below to fall, and we feared some hurt but there was none; but she, of all the great ladies only, run down among the common rabble to see what hurt was done, and did take care of a child that received some little hurt; which methought was so noble. Anon there came one there, booted and spurred, that she talked long with. And by and by, she being in her haire, she put on his hat, which was but an ordinary one, to keep the wind off. But methought it became her mightily, as everything else do. (*23 August 1662*)

Pierce the chyrurgeon tells me that my Lady Castlemayne is with child; but though it be the King's, yet her Lord being still in towne and sometime seeing of her, though never to eat or lie together, it will be laid to him. He tells me also how the Duke of York is smitten in love with my Lady Chesterfield (a virtuous lady, daughter of my Lord of Ormond); and so much, that the Duchesse of Yorke hath complained to the King and her father about it, and my Lady Chesterfield is gone into the country for it. At all which I am sorry; but it is the effect of idlenesse and having nothing else to imploy their great spirits upon. (*3 November 1662*)

To Whitehall Chappell, where Bishop Morly preached upon the Song of the Angels – "Glory to God on high –

on earth peace, and good will towards men." Methought
he made but a poor sermon, but long and reprehending
the mistaken jollity of the Court for the true joy that shall
and ought to be on these days. Perticularized concerning
their excess in playes and gameing, saying that he whose
office it is to keep the gamesters in order and within
bounds serves but for a second rather in a duell, meaning
the Groome Porter. Upon which, it was worth observing
how far they are come from taking the reprehensions of a
Bishop seriously, that they all laugh in the chapel when
he reflected on their ill actions and courses. The sermon
done, a good anthemne fallowed, with vialls; and then
the King came down to receive the Sacrament. (*Christmas
Day, 1662*)

Mr Povy and I to Whitehall, he carrying me thither on
purpose to carry me into the Ball this night before the
King. He brought me first to the Duke's chamber, where
I saw him and the Duchesse at supper, and thence into the
room where the Ball was to be, crammed with fine ladies,
the greatest of the Court. By and by comes the King and
Queen, the Duke and Duchesse, and all the great ones;
and after seating themselfs, the King takes out the
Duchess of Yorke, and the Duke the Duchesse of Buck-
ingham, the Duke of Monmouth my Lady Castlemayne,
and so other lords other ladies; and they danced the
bransle. After that, the King led a lady a single *coranto*; and
then the rest of the lords, one after another, other ladies.
Very noble it was, and great pleasure to see. Then to
country dances; the King leading the first which he called
for; which was – says he, *Cuckolds all a-row*, the old dance
of England. Of the ladies that danced, the Duke of
Monmouth's mistress and my Lady Castlemayne and a

daughter of Sir Harry De Vickes were the best. The manner was, when the King dances, all the ladies in the room, and the Queen herself, stands up; and endeed he dances rarely and much better then the Duke of Yorke. Having stayed here as long as I thought fit, to my infinite content, it being the greatest pleasure I could wish now to see at Court, I went out, leaving them dancing. (*31 December 1662*)

Capt. Ferrers [told] me, among other Court passages, how about a month ago, at a Ball at Court, a child was dropped by one of the ladies in dancing; but nobody knew who, it being taken up by somebody in their handkercher. The next morning all the Ladies of Honour appeared early at Court for their vindication, so that nobody could tell whose this mischance should be. But it seems Mrs Wells fell sick that afternoon and hath disappeared ever since, so that it is concluded it was her. Another story was how my Lady Castlemayne, a few days since, had Mrs Stuart to an entertainment, and at night begun a frolique that they two must be married; and married they were, with ring and all other ceremonies of church service, and ribbands and a sack-posset in bed and flinging the stocking. But in the close, it is said that my Lady Castlemayne, who was the bridegroom, rose, and the King came and took her place with pretty Mrs Stuart. This is said to be very true. (*8 February 1663*)

With Creede to the King's Head ordinary; but coming late, dined at the second table very well for 12*d.*; and a pretty gentleman in our company who confirms my Lady Castlemaynes being gone from Court, but knows not the reason. He told us of one wipe the Queene a little while ago did give her, when she came in and found the Queene under the dresser's hands and had been so long – "I wonder your Majesty," says she, "can have the patience to sit so long a-dressing." "Oh," says the Queene, "I have so much reason to use patience, that I can very well bear with it." (*4 July 1663*)

Hearing that the King and Queene are rode abroad with the Ladies of Honour to the parke, and seeing a great croude of gallants staying here to see their return, I also stayed, walking up and down. By and by, the King and Queene, who looked in this dress, a white laced waistcoat and a crimson short pettycoate and her hair dressed *a la negligence*, mighty pretty; and the King rode hand in hand with her. Here was also my Lady Castlemayne rode among the rest of the ladies, but the King took me-thought no notice of her; nor when they light did anybody press (as she seemed to expect, and stayed for it) to take her down, but was taken down by her own gentleman. She looked mighty out of humour, and had a yellow plume in her hat (which all took notice of) and yet is very handsome – but very melancholy; nor did anybody speak to her or she so much as smile or speak to anybody. I fallowed them up into Whitehall and into the Queenes presence, where all the ladies walked, talking and fidling with their hats and feathers, and changing and trying one another's, but on another's heads, and laughing. But it was the finest sight to me, considering their great beautys and dress, and ever I did see in all my life. But above all, Mrs Steward in this dresse, with her hat cocked and a red plume, with her sweet eye, little Roman nose, and excellent *taille*, is now the greatest beauty I ever saw I think in my life; and if ever woman can, doth exceed my Lady Castlemayne; at least, in this dresse. Nor do I wonder if the King changes, which I verily believe is the reason of his coldness to my Lady Castlemayne. (*13 July 1663*)

Thence to the Tennice Court and there saw the King play at tennis and others. But to see how the King's play was extolled without any cause at all, was a loathsome sight, though sometimes endeed he did play very well and deserved to be commended; but such open flattery is beastly. (*4 January 1664*)

Mr Povy and I in his coach to Hide Parke, being the first day of the Tour there – where many brave ladies. Among others, Castlemayne lay impudently upon her back in her coach, asleep with her mouth open. There was also my Lady Kerneeguy, once my Lady Anne Hambleton, that is said to have given the Duke [of York] a clap upon his first coming over. (*Lord's Day, 19 March 1665*)

The King did speak in contempt of the ceremoniousnesse of the King of Spain, that he doth nothing but under some ridiculous form or other; and will not piss but another must hold the chamber-pot. (*11 July 1666*)

This day the King begins to put on his vest, and I did see several persons of the House of Lords, and Commons too, great courtiers, who are in it – being a long cassocke close to the body, of black cloth and pinked with white silk under it, and a coat over it, and the legs ruffled with black riband like a pigeon's leg – and upon the whole, I wish the King may keep it, for it is a very fine and handsome garment. (*15 October 1666*)

Stayed till the Council was up, and attended the King and Duke of York round [St James's] Park. They stood a good while to see the ganders and geese tread one another in the water, the goose being all the while kept for a great while quite under water, which was new to me; but they did make mighty sport at it, saying (as the King did often), "Now you shall see a marriage between this and that" – which did not please me. (*17 February 1667*)

Sir H. Cholmly came to me this day, and tells me the Court is as mad as ever and that the night the Duch burned our ships, the King did sup with my Lady Castlemayne at the Duchess of Monmouth, and there were all mad in hunting of a poor moth. All the Court afeared of a Parliament; but he thinks nothing can save us but the King's giving up all to a Parliament. (*21 June 1667*)

[Mr Povey] tells me, speaking of the horrid effeminacy of the King, that the King hath taken ten times more care and pains making friends between my Lady Castlemayne and Mrs Steward when they have fallen out, then ever he did to save his kingdom. (*24 June 1667*)

This day Mr Pierce the surgeon was with me; and tells me how this business of my Lord Chancellors [*his dismissal*] was certainly designed in my Lady Castlemaine's chamber, and that when he went from the King on Monday morning, she was in bed (though about 12 a-clock) and ran out in her smock into her aviary looking into Whitehall garden, and thither her woman brought her her nightgown, and stood joying herself at the old man's going away. And several of the gallants of Whitehall (of which there was many staying to see the Chancellor return) did talk to her in her bird cage; among others, Blanckford, telling her she was the Bird of Paradise. (*27 August 1667*)

After dinner comes in Mr Townsend [*of the King's Wardrobe*]; and there I was witness of a horrid rateing, which Mr Ashburnham, as one of the Grooms of the King's Bedchamber, did give him for want of linen for the King's person; which he swore was not to be endured, and that the King would not endure it, and that the King his father would have hanged his wardrobe-man should he have been served so; the King having at this day no handkerchers and but three bands to his neck, he swore. Mr Townsend answered want of money and the owing of the linendraper 5000*l*; and that he hath of late got many rich things made, beds and sheets and saddles, and all without money, and he can go no further; but still this old man (endeed, like an old loving servant) did cry out for the King's person to be neglected. But when he was gone, Townsend told me that it is the grooms taking away the King's linen at the quarter's end, as their fees, which makes this great want. (*2 September 1667*)

By and by I met with Mr Brisban; and having it in my mind this Christmas to do (what I never can remember that I did) go to see the manner of the gaming at the Groome Porter's, he did lead me thither; where after staying an hour, they begin to play at about 8 at night – where to see how differently one man took his losing from another, one cursing and swearing, and another only muttering and grumbling to himself, a third without any appearing discontent at all – to see how the dice will run good luck in one hand for half an hour together – and another have no good luck at all. To see how easily here, where they play nothing but guinnys, 100*l* is won or lost. To see two or three gentlemen come in there drunk, and putting their stock of gold together – one 22 pieces, the second 4, and the third 5 pieces; and these to play one with another, and forget how much each of them brought, but he that brought the 22 think that he brought no more then the rest. To see the different humours of gamesters to change their luck when it is bad – how ceremonious they are as to call for new dice – to shift their places – to alter their manner of throwing; and that with great industry, as if there was anything in it. To see how some gamesters, that have no money now to spend as formerly, do come and sit and look on; as among others, Sir Lewes Dives, who was here and hath been a great gamester in his time. To hear their cursing and damning to no purpose; as one man, being to throw a seven if he could and failing to do it after a great many throws, cried he would be damned if ever he flung seven more while he lived, his despair of throwing it being so great, while others did it as their luck served, almost every throw. To see how persons of the best quality do here sit down and play with people of any, though meaner; and to see how people in ordinary clothes shall come hither and play away 100, or 2 or 300 guinnys, without any kind of difficulty. And lastly, to see the formality of the Groome Porter, who is their judge of all disputes in play and all quarrels that may arise therein; and how his under-officers are there to observe true play at each table and to give new dice, is a consideration I never could have thought had been in the world, had I not now seen it. And mighty glad I am that I did see it;

and it may be will find another evening, before Christmas be over, to see it again; when I may stay later, for their heat of play begins not till about 11 or 12 a-clock; which did give me another pretty observation, of a man that did win mighty fast when I was there: I think he won 100*l* at single pieces in a little time; while all the rest envied him his good fortune, he cursed it, saying, "A pox on it that it should come so early upon me! For this fortune two hours hence would be worth something to me; but then, God damn me, I shall have no such luck." This kind of profane, mad entertainment they give themselfs. And so I having enough for once, refusing to venture, though Brisband pressed me hard and tempted me with saying that no man was ever known to lose the first time, the Devil being too cunning to discourage a gamester; and he offered me also to lend me ten pieces to venture, but I did refuse and so went away. (*1 January 1668*)

The Fire

¶ THE GREAT FIRE OF 1666 was the most destructive catas-
trophe in the history of London before the Great Blitz of
1941. It occurred after a summer of drought and during a
spell of strong easterly winds. Four days and nights of
virtually uncontrolled conflagration laid waste the City,
destroying almost all its public buildings, including St Paul's
Cathedral and eighty-four parish churches, together with
countless homes. Mercifully, few lives were lost. Disasters
such as this were not unique in days when towns lacked
good water supplies and efficient fire-fighting apparatus.
Half of Northampton, for instance, was burnt down in
1675.

In the case of London the hope that a new and splendid
capital city, with wide boulevards, would arise from the
ashes, was not realised, and was not in fact practicable, short
of a radical rearrangement by statute of property rights. But
the City recovered quickly, though not before some trade
had moved to Westminster. Rebuilding was well under way
by 1670, and the beauty of the new Wren churches did
something to compensate for the loss of so much of an
earlier London.

Pepys's account of the Fire shows his powers of pictorial
description at their best. His house and office in Seething
Lane escaped unscathed, but his birthplace in Salisbury
Court off Fleet Street was destroyed.

Some of our maids sitting up late last night to get things
ready against our feast today, Jane called us up, about 3 in
the morning, to tell us of a great fire they saw in the City.
So I rose, and slipped on my nightgown and went to her
window, and thought it to be on the back side of Marke
Lane at the furthest; but being unused to such fires as
fallowed, I thought it far enough off, and so went to bed
again and to sleep. About 7 rose again to dress myself, and
there looked out at the window and saw the fire not so
much as it was, and further off. So to my closet to set

things to rights after yesterday's cleaning. By and by Jane comes and tells me that she hears that above 300 houses have been burned down tonight by the fire we saw, and that it was now burning down all Fish Street by London Bridge. So I made myself ready presently, and walked to the Tower and there got up upon one of the high places, Sir J. Robinsons little son going up with me; and there I did see the houses at that end of the bridge all on fire, and an infinite great fire on this and the other side the end of the bridge – which, among other people, did trouble me for poor little Michell and our Sarah on the Bridge. So down, with my heart full of trouble, to the Lieutenant of the Tower, who tells me that it begun this morning in the King's bakers house in Pudding Lane, and that it hath burned down St Magnes Church and most part of Fish Streete already. So I down to the waterside and there got a boat and through the bridge, and there saw a lamentable fire. Poor Michells house, as far as the Old Swan, already burned that way and the fire running further, that in a very little time it got as far as the Stillyard while I was there. Everybody endeavouring to remove their goods, and flinging into the river or bringing them into lighters that lay off. Poor people staying in their houses as long as till the very fire touched them, and then running into boats or clambering from one pair of stair by the waterside to another. And among other things, the poor pigeons I perceive were loath to leave their houses, but hovered about the windows and balconies till they were some of them burned, their wings, and fell down.

Having stayed, and in an hour's time seen the fire rage every way, and nobody to my sight endeavouring to quench it, but to remove their goods and leave all to the fire; and having seen it get as far as the Steeleyard, and the

wind mighty high and driving it into the City, and
everything, after so long a drougth, proving combustible, even the very stones of churches, and among other
things, the poor steeple by which pretty Mrs [Horsley]
lives, and whereof my old schoolfellow Elborough is
parson, taken fire in the very top and there burned till it
fall down – I to Whitehall with a gentleman with me
who desired to go off from the Tower to see the fire in
my boat – to Whitehall, and there up to the King's closet
in the chapel, where people came about me and I did give
them an account dismayed them all; and word was
carried in to the King, so I was called for and did tell the
King and Duke of York what I saw, and that unless his
Majesty did command houses to be pulled down, nothing
could stop the fire. They seemed much troubled, and the
King commanded me to go to my Lord Mayor from him
and command him to spare no houses but to pull down
before the fire every way. The Duke of York bid me tell
him that if he would have any more soldiers, he shall; and
so did my Lord Arlington afterward, as a great secret.
Here meeting with Capt. Cocke, I in his coach, which he
lent me, and Creed with me, to Pauls; and there walked
along Watling Street as well as I could, every creature
coming away loaden with goods to save – and here and
there sick people carried away in beds. Extraordinary
good goods carried in carts and on backs. At last met my
Lord Mayor in Canning Streete, like a man spent, with a
handkercher about his neck. To the King's message, he
cried like a fainting woman, "Lord, what can I do? I am
spent! People will not obey me. I have been pull[ing]
down houses. But the fire overtakes us faster then we can
do it." That he needed no more soldiers; and that for
himself, he must go and refresh himself, having been up

all night. So he left me, and I him, and walked home – seeing people all almost distracted and no manner of means used to quench the fire. The houses too, so very thick thereabouts, and full of matter for burning, as pitch and tar, in Thames Street – and warehouses of oyle and wines and brandy and other things. Here I saw Mr Isaccke Houblon, that handsome man – prettily dressed and dirty at his door at Dowgate, receiving some of his brothers things whose houses were on fire; and as he says, have been removed twice already, and he doubts (as it soon proved) that they must be in a little time removed from his house also – which was a sad consideration. And to see the churches all filling with goods, by people who themselfs should have been quietly there at this time. By this time it was about 12 a-clock, and so home and there find my guests, which was Mr Wood and his wife, Barbary Shelden, and also Mr Moone. While at dinner, Mrs Batelier came to enquire after Mr Woolfe and Stanes (who it seems are related to them), whose houses in Fish Street are all burned, and they in a sad condition. She would not stay in the fright.

As soon as dined, I and Moone away and walked through the City, the streets full of nothing but people and horses and carts loaden with goods, ready to run over one another, and removing goods from one burned house to another – they now removing out of Canning Street (which received goods in the morning) into Lumbard Streete and further; and among others, I now saw my little goldsmith Stokes receiving some friend's goods, whose house itself was burned the day after. We parted at Pauls, he home and I to Pauls Wharf, where I had appointed a boat to attend me; and took in Mr Carcasse and his brother, whom I met in the street, and carried them below and above bridge, to and again, to see the fire, which was now got further, both below and above, and no likelihood of stopping it. Met with the King and Duke of York in their barge, and with them to Queenhith and there called Sir Rd Browne to them. Their order was only to pull down houses apace, and so below bridge at the waterside; but little was or could be done, the fire coming upon them so fast. Good hopes there was of stopping it at the Three Cranes above, and at Buttolphs Wharf below bridge, if care be used; but the wind carries it into the City, so as we know not by the waterside what it doth there. River full of lighter[s] and boats taking in goods, and good goods swimming in the water; and only, I observed that hardly one lighter or boat in three that had goods of a house in, but there was a pair of virginalls in it. Having seen as much as I could now, I away to Whitehall by appointment, and there walked to St James's Park, and there met my wife and Creed and Wood and his wife and walked to my boat, and there upon the water again, and to the fire up and down, it still increasing and the wind great. So near the fire as we could for smoke; and all over the Thames, with one's face in the wind you were almost burned with a shower of firedrops – this is very true – so as houses were burned by these drops and flakes of fire, three or four, nay five or six houses, one from another. When we could endure no more upon the water, we to a little alehouse on the Bankside over against the Three Cranes, and there stayed till it was dark almost and saw the fire grow; and as it grow darker, appeared more and more, and in corners and upon steeples and between churches and houses, as far as we could see up the hill of the City, in a most horrid malicious bloody flame, not like the fine flame of an ordinary fire. We stayed till, it being darkish, we saw the fire as only one entire arch of fire from this to the other side of the bridge, and in a bow up the hill, for an arch of above a mile long. It made me weep to see it. The churches, houses, and all on fire and flaming at once, and a horrid noise the flames made, and the cracking of houses at their ruine.

So home with a sad heart, and there find everybody discoursing and lamenting the fire; and poor Tom Hater came with some few of his goods saved out of his house, which is burned upon Fish Street Hill. I invited him to lie at my house, and did receive his goods: but was deceived in his lying there, the noise coming every moment of the growth of the fire, so as we were forced to begin to pack up our own goods and prepare for their removal. And did by mooneshine (it being brave, dry, and moonshine and warm weather) carry much of my goods into the garden, and Mr Hater and I did remove my money and iron chests into my cellar – as thinking that the safest place. And got my bags of gold into my office ready to carry away, and my chief papers of accounts also there, and my tallies into a box by themselfs. So great was our fear, as Sir W. Batten had carts come out of the country to fetch away his goods this night. We did put Mr Hater, poor man, to bed a little; but he got but very little rest, so much noise being in my house, taking down of goods. (*Lord's Day, 2 September 1666*)

Sir W. Batten, not knowing how to remove his wind [*wine*], did dig a pit in the garden and laid it in there; and I took the opportunity of laying all the papers of my office that I could not otherwise dispose of. And in the evening Sir W. Penn and I did dig another and put our wine in it, and I my Parmazan cheese as well as my wine and some other things. The Duke of York was at the office this day at Sir W. Penn's, but I happened not to be within. This afternoon, sitting melancholy with Sir W. Penn in our garden and thinking of the certain burning of this office without extraordinary means, I did propose for the sending up of all our workmen from Woolwich and Deptford yards (none whereof yet appeared), and to write to Sir W. Coventry to have the Duke of York's permission to pull down houses rather then lose this office, which would much hinder the King's business. So Sir W. Penn he went down this night, in order to the sending them up tomorrow morning; and I wrote to Sir W. Coventry about the business, but received no answer. (*4 September 1666*)

Much terrified in the nights nowadays, with dreams of fire and falling down of houses. (*15 September 1666*)

Up betimes, and shaved myself after a week's growth; but Lord, how ugly I was yesterday and how fine today. (*17 September 1666*)

[Sir Tho. Crew] doth, from what he hath heard at the Committee for examining the burning of the City, conclude it as a thing certain, that it was done by plot – it being proved by many witnesses that endeavours were made in several places to encrease the fire, and that both in City and country it was bragged by several papists that upon such a day or in such a time we should find the hottest weather that ever was in England, and words of plainer sense. (*5 November 1666*)

It is observable that within these eight days I did see smoke remaining, coming out of some cellars, from the late great Fire, now above six months since. (*16 March 1667*)

[I] do observe the great streets in the City are marked out with piles drove into the ground; and if ever it be built in that form, with so fair streets, it will be a noble sight. (*29 March 1667*)

Houses and Gardens

¶ PEPYS REPORTS AN INTERESTING COMMENT by Hugh
May, the architect, on English gardens, at 22 July 1666, but
he was himself no gardener. Neither of his two gardens at
Seething Lane and Brampton receives more than a passing
mention in the diary. Buildings, however, he was interested
in, and he greatly preferred the new 'regular' style of
architecture to the Elizabethan or Gothic.

Audley End (8 October 1667) was the largest of the
houses mentioned here, and was reputedly the biggest
private residence in the country. It had been built by the 1st
Earl of Suffolk, Lord Treasurer in the reign of James I, who
is said to have remarked of it that only a Lord Treasurer –
certainly no King – could afford to live in it. Much of it was
pulled down in the eighteenth century, but it remains
imposing and palatial.

Hinchingbrooke, close by Huntingdon (13 October 1662;
20 September 1663) was originally a nunnery and had been
converted into a house in the late sixteenth and early
seventeenth centuries. The alterations carried out by Sandwich were designed by, or under the direction of, Sir John
Denham, architect and poet.

Clarendon House, in Piccadilly (14 February 1666) was
designed by Roger Pratt. After Clarendon's fall in 1667 it
was acquired by Albemarle's son, the 2nd Duke, who had it
pulled down in the 1680s to make room for several streets of
houses (among them Albemarle Street).

Pepys's house at Brampton, near Huntingdon (9 October
1667) was a small Tudor farmhouse (extended in the
eighteenth century and still surviving) which he inherited
from his uncle Robert Pepys, a bailiff employed by the
Mountagus, in 1661. In moments of depression he thought
of retiring there.

Thomas Povey's house (19 January, 4 September 1663)
was one of the smaller houses on the east side of Lincoln's
Inn Fields, a fashionable area, built in 1657. The 'perspective'
was an illusionist picture by Hoogstraten.

John Evelyn, Pepys's friend and fellow diarist, wrote
voluminously on gardens, arboriculture and similar subjects.
He created his own garden at Sayes Court, near Deptford.

The holly hedge mentioned at 5 October 1665 has its own place in history. It was the hedge through which Peter the Great of Russia, on his stay there, learning shipbuilding at Deptford, had himself pushed in a wheelbarrow.

To Audly End and did go all over the house and garden; and mighty merry we were. The house endeed doth appear very fine, but not so fine as it hath heretofore to me. Perticularly, the ceilings are not so good as I alway took them to be, being nothing so well wrought as my Lord Chancellors are; and though the figure of the house without be very extraordinary good, yet the stayre case is exceeding poor; and a great many pictures, and not one good one in the house but one of Harry the 8th done by Holben; and not one good suit of hangings in all the house, but all most ancient things, such as I would not give the hanging-up of in my house; and the other furniture, beds and other things, accordingly. Only, the gallery is good; and above all things, the cellars, where we went down and drunk of much good liquor, and endeed the cellars are fine; and here my wife and I did sing to my great content, and then to the garden and there eat many grapes, and took some with us; and so away thence, exceeding well satisfied, though not to that degree that by my old esteem of the house I ought and did expect to have done – the situation of it not pleasing me. (*8 October 1667*)

Up to Hinchingbrooke and there with Mr Sheply did look all over the house; and I do, I confess, like well of the alterations and do like the staircase; but there being nothing done to make the outside more regular and moderne, I am not satisfied with it, but do think it to be too much to be laid out upon it. (*13 October 1662*)

To Hinchingbrooke, and there my Lord took me with the rest of the company and singly demanded my opinion, in the walks in his garden, about the bringing of the crooked wall on the mount to a shape. (*Lord's Day, 20 September 1663*)

[Mr Evelyn] showed me his gardens, which are, for variety of evergreens and hedge of holly, the finest things I ever saw in my life. Thence in his coach to Greenwich, and there to my office, all the way having fine discourse of trees and the nature of vegetables. (*5 October 1665*)

I took Mr Hill to my Lord Chancellors new house that is building, and went with trouble up to the top of it and there is there the noblest prospect that ever I saw in my life, Greenwich being nothing to it. And in everything is a beautiful house – and most strongly built in every respect – and as if, as it hath, it had the Chancellor for its maister. (*14 February 1666*)

Walked up and down with Hugh May, who is a very ingenious man – among other things, discoursing of the present fashion of gardens, to make them plain – that we have the best walks of gravell in the world – France having none, nor Italy; and our green of our bowling-alleys is better then any they have. So our business here being ayre, this is the best way, only with a little mixture of statues or pots, which may be handsome, and so filled with another pot of such or such, a flower or greene, as the season of the year will bear. And then for flowers, they are best seen in a little plat by themselfs; besides, their borders spoil the walks of any other garden. And then for fruit, the best way is to have walls built circularly, one within another, to the south, on purpose for fruit, and leaving the walking-garden only for that use. (*Lord's Day, 22 July 1666*)

Came to Brampton at about noon, and up and down to see the garden with my father, and the house, and do altogether find it very pretty – especially the little parlour and the summer-houses in the garden. Only, the wall doth want greens upon it and the house is too low-roofed; but that is only because of my coming from a house with higher ceilings; but altogether is very pretty and I bless God that I am like to have such a pretty place to retire to. And I did walk with my father without doors and do find a very convenient way of laying out money there in building, which will make a very good seat; and the place deserves it, I think, very well. (*9 October 1667*)

By coach to Mr Povys. He seems to set off his rest in the neatness of his house; which he after dinner showed me from room to room, so beset with delicate pictures, and above all, a piece of per[s]pective in his closet in the low parler. His stable, where was some most delicate horses, and the very racks painted, and mangers, with a neat leaden painted cistern and the walls done with Dutch tiles like my chimnies. (*19 January 1663*)

About one o'clock went to Povys; and by and by in comes he, and so we sat down to dinner, and his lady whom I never saw before (a handsome old woman that brought him money, that makes him do as he does).

After dinner down to see his new cellars which he hath made so fine, with so noble an arch and such contrivances for his barrels and bottles, and in a room next to it such a grotto and fountayne, which in summer will be so pleasant as nothing in the world can be almost. But to see how he himself doth pride himself too much in it, and commend and expect to have all admired, though indeed everything doth highly deserve it, is a little troublesome. (*4 September 1663*)

Marvels and Mysteries

¶ CURIOUS ABOUT EVERYTHING, Pepys was always fasci-
nated by what was unusual or not easily to be explained. But
his wonder stopped well short of credulity.

To the Hill House at Chatham, where I never was before.
And I find a pretty pleasant house – and am pleased with
the armes that hang up there. Here we supped very
merry, and late to bed. Sir Wm [Batten] telling me that
old Edgeborow, his predecessor, did die and walk in my
chamber did make me somewhat afeared, but not so
much as for mirth sake I did seem. So to bed in the
Treasurer's chamber and lay and sleep well till 3 in the
morning, and then waking; and by the light of the moon
I saw my pillow (which overnight I flung from me) stand
upright, but not bethinking myself what it might be, I
was a little afeared. But sleep overcame all, and so lay till
high morning – at which time I had a caudle brought me
and a good fire made. (*8–9 April 1661*)

At the office in the morning and did business. By and by
we are called to Sir W. Battens to see the strange creature
that Capt. Holmes hath brought with him from Guiny; it
is a great baboone, but so much like a man in most things,
that (though they say there is a species of them) yet I
cannot believe but that it is a monster got of a man and
she-baboone. I do believe it already understands much
English; and I am of the mind it might be tought to speak
or make signs. (*24 August 1661*)

At noon to my Lord Crewes – where one Mr Templer
(an ingenious [man] and a person of honour he seems to
be) dined; and discoursing of the nature of serpents, he
told us of some that in the waste places of Lancashire do

grow to a great bigness, and that do feed upon larkes, which they take thus – they observe when the lark is soared to the highest, and do crawle till they come to be just underneath them; and there they place themselfs with their mouths uppermost, and there (as is conceived) they do eject poyson up to the bird; for the bird doth suddenly come down again in its course of a circle, and falls directly into the mouth of the serpent – which is very strange. (*4 February 1662*)

[Capt. Minnes] and the other Captains that were with us tell me that negros drownded look white and lose their blacknesse – which I never heard before. (*11 April 1662*)

Both at and after dinner we had great discourses of the nature and power of spirits and whether they can animate dead bodies; in all which, as of the general appearing of spirits, my Lord Sandwich is very scepticall. He says the greatest warrants that ever he had to believe any, is the present appearing of the Devil in Wiltshire, much of late talked of, who beats a drum up and down; there is books of it, and they say very true. But my Lord observes that though he doth answer to any tune that you will play to him upon another drum, yet one tune he tried to play and could not; which makes him suspect the whole, and I think it is a good argument. (*15 June 1663*)

After breakfast [*at Woolwich*], Mr Castle and I walked to Greenwich, and in our way met some gypsys who would needs tell me my fortune, and I suffered one of them – who told me many things common, as others do, but bid me beware of a John and a Thomas, for they did seek to do me hurt. And that somebody should be with me this day sennit to borrow money of me, but I should lend them none. She got ninepence of me; and so I left them. (*22 August 1663*)

Walked to Redriffe and so home. In my way, overtaking of a beggar or two on the way that looked like gypsys, it came into my head what the gypsys eight or nine days ago had foretold, that somebody that day sennit should be with me to borrow money, but I should lend none; and looking, when I came to my office, upon my Journall, that my brother John had brought me a letter that day from my brother Tom to borrow 20*l* more of me, which had vexed me so, that I had sent the letter to my father into the country, to acquaint him of it. (*3 September 1663*)

This evening with Mr Brisband speaking of inchantments and spells, I telling him some of my charmes, he told me this of his own knowledge at Bourdeaux in France. The words these –

> *Voicy un corps mort*
> *Royde comme un baston*
> *Froid comme marbre*
> *Leger comme un esprit,*
> *Levons te au nom de Jesus Christ.*

He saw four little girles, very young ones, all kneeling, each of them upon one knee; and one begin the first line, whispering in the eare of the next, and the second to the third, and the third to the fourth, and she to the first. Then the first begun the second line, and so round quite through. And putting each one finger only to a boy that lay flat upon his back on the ground, as if he was dead. At the end of the words, they did with their four fingers raise this boy as high as they could reach. And he being there and wondering at it (as also being afeared to see it – for they would have had him to have bore a part in saying the words in the room of one of the little girls, that was so young that they could hardly make her learn to repeat the words), did, for fear there might be some sleight used in it by the boy, or that the boy might be light, called the cook of the house, a very lusty fellow, as Sir G. Carteret's cooke, who is very big, and they did raise him just in the same manner. This is one of the strangest things I ever heard, but he tells it me of his own knowledge and I do heartily believe it to be true. I enquired of him whether they were Protestant or Catholique girls, and he told me they were Protestant – which made it the more strange to me. (*31 July 1665*)

By and by to dinner, where very good company. Among other discourse, we talked much of Nostradamus his prophecy of these times and the burning of the City of London, some of whose verses are put into Bookers Almanac this year. And Sir G. Carteret did tell a story, how at his death he did make the town swear that he should never be dug up, or his tomb opened, after he was buried; but they did after 60 years do it, and upon his breast they found a plate of brasse, saying what a wicked and unfaithful people the people of that place were, who after so many vows should disturb and open him such a day and year and hour – which if true, is very strange. (*3 February 1667*)

With Sir W. Penn by coach to Islington to the [King's Head], where his lady and Madam Lowder and her mother-in-law did meet us and two of Mr Lowther's brothers; and here dined upon nothing but pigeon pyes – which was such a thing for him to invite all that company to, that I was ashamed of it; but after dinner was all our sport, when there came in a jugler, who endeed did show us so good tricks as I have never seen in my life, I think, of legerdemaine, and such as my wife hath since seriously said that she would not believe but that he did them by the help of the Devil. (*24 May 1667*)

Griffin did tell me that it is observed, and is true, in the late Fire of London, that the fire burned just as many parish churches as there were hours from the beginning to the end of the fire; and next, that there were just as many churches left standing as there were taverns left standing in the rest of the City that was not burned; being, I think he told me, thirteen in all of each – which is pretty to observe. (*31 January 1668*)

All the morning at the office, and at noon my clerks dined with me; and there do hear from them how all the town is full of the talk of a meteor, or some fire that did on Saturday last to fly over the City at night; which doth put me in mind that being then walking in the dark an hour or more myself in the garden after I had done writing, I did see a light before me come from behind me, which made me turn back my head and I did see a sudden fire or light running in the sky, as it were toward Cheapside-ward, and vanished very quick; which did make me bethink myself what holiday it was; and took it for some rocket, though it was much brighter then any rocket, and so thought no more of it; but it seems Mr Hater and Gibson, going home that night, did meet with many clusters of people talking of it, and many people of the towns about the City did see it, and the world doth make much discourse of it – their apprehensions being mighty full of the rest of the City to be burned, and the papists to cut our throats – which God prevent. (*21 May 1668*)

Matters of State

¶ PEPYS WAS A KEEN OBSERVER of politics. His work brought him into close touch with the political world, and his sociable habits provided him with the means of acquiring a remarkable knowledge of public opinion.

The political story of 1660–9, as he tells it, is one of growing disillusion. The Restoration had been hailed with relief. The government treated the leading revolutionaries with unusual clemency. Except for the regicides (such as Harrison, the Fifth Monarchist: 13 October 1660), and the dangerous republican Vane (14 June 1662), there were no executions. But Cavaliers and Roundheads found difficulty in living and working together amicably. Much might have been done by a generous distribution of offices and pensions, but there was not enough of either to go round. In any case, many of the Royalists were unfit for office, having had no experience of government (24 June 1663). The King, for his part, though conciliatory, was lazy and irresponsible. Clarendon, Lord Chancellor and chief minister, was the wisest head among the politicians, but lacked the King's full confidence, and failed to build up a power base for himself in the Council and Parliament. Moreover, his position was gravely weakened soon after the Restoration by the marriage of his daughter Anne to the Duke of York, the heir presumptive to the throne, which led to the fear that he was becoming overpowerful (24 June 1667). In 1667, he fell an easy victim to the anger provoked by the Dutch invasion of the Medway (11 November 1667). By that time everything that Clarendon stood for was at risk. The Duke of York was suspected of favouring the creation of a militarised monarchy on the French model (12 July 1667), and there were many who began to look back on the 'late times' with admiration, even nostalgia, and to yearn for the return of the iron discipline of Cromwell and the Puritans.

To my Lord's in the morning, where I met with Capt. Cuttance. But my Lord not being up, I went out to Charing Cross to see Maj.-Gen. Harrison hanged, drawn, and quartered – which was done there – he looking as cheerfully as any man could do in that condition. He was presently cut down and his head and his heart shown to the people, at which there was great shouts of joy. It is said that he said that he was sure to come shortly at the right hand of Christ to judge them that now have judged him. And that his wife doth expect his coming again. Thus it was my chance to see the King beheaded at Whitehall and to see the first blood shed in revenge for the blood of the King at Charing Cross. (*13 October 1660*)

Up by 4 a-clock in the morning and upon business at my office. Then we sat down to business; and about 11 a-clock, having a room got ready for us, we all went out to the Tower Hill; and there, over against the scaffold made on purpose this day, saw Sir Henry Vane brought. A very great press of people. He made a long speech, many times interrupted by the Sheriffe and others there; and they would have taken his paper out of his hand, but he would not let it go. But they caused all the books of those that writ after him [*sc. wrote down his speech*] to be given the Sheriffe; and the trumpets were brought under the scaffold, that he might not be heard. Then he prayed, and so fitted himself and received the blow. But the scaffold was so crowded that we could not see it done. But Boreman, who had been upon the scaffold, came to us and told us that first he begun to speak of the irregular proceeding against him; that he was, against Magna Charta, denied to have his excepcions against the endictment allowed. And that there he was stopped by the Sheriffe. Then he drow out his paper of notes and begun to tell them; first, his life, that he was born a gentleman, that he was bred up and had the qualitys of a gentleman, and to make him in the opinion of the world more a gentleman, he had been, till he was seventeen year old, a goodfellow. But then it pleased God to lay a foundacion of Grace in his heart, by which he was persuaded against his worldly interest to leave all preferment and go abroad, where he might serve God with more freedom. Then he was called home and made a member of the Long Parliament; where he never did, to this day, anything against his conscience, but all for the glory of God. Here he would have given them an account of the proceedings of the Long Parliament, but they so often interrupted him, that at last he was forced to give over; and so fell into prayer for England in generall, then for the churches in England, and then for the City of London. And so fitted himself for the block and received the blow. He had a blister or issue upon his neck, which he desired them not to hurt. He changed not his colour or speech to the last, but died justifying himself and the cause he had stood for; and spoke very confidently of his being presently at the right hand of Christ. And in all things appeared the most resolved man that ever died in that manner, and showed more of heate than cowardize, but yet with all humility and gravity. One asked him why he did not pray for the King: he answered, "Nay," says he, "you shall see I can pray for the King; I pray, God bless him." (*14 June 1662*)

[Sir W. Coventry] discoursed of the condition of the King's party at present; who, as the Papists, though otherwise fine persons, yet being by law kept for these four score years out of imployment, they are now wholly uncapable of business; and so the Cavalers for 20 years – who, says he, for the most part have either given themselfs over to look after country and family business,

[175]

and those the best of them, and the rest to debauchery &c. (*24 June 1663*)

Thence with Creede to hire a coach to carry us to Hide Parke, today there being a general muster of the King's Guards, horse and foot, where a goodly sight to see so many fine horse and officers, and the King, Duke and others come by a-horseback. And after long being there, I light and walked to the place where the King, Duke, &c. did stand to see the horse and foot march by and discharge their guns, to show a French Marquesse (for whom this muster was caused) the goodness of our firemen; which endeed was very good, though not without a slip now and then (and one broadside close to our coach we had going out of the park, even to that neerenesse as to be ready to burn our hairs); yet me-thought all these gay men are not the soldiers that must do the King's business, it being such as these that lost the old King all he had and were beat by the most ordinary fellows that could be. (*4 July 1663*)

Mr Blackeburne [*a leading naval official under the Common-wealth*] and I fell to talk of many things; wherein I did speak so freely to him in many things agreeing with his sense, that he was very open to me in all things. First, in that of religion, he makes it great matter of prudence for the King and Council to suffer liberty of conscience. And imputes the loss of Hungary to the Turke from the Emperors denying them this liberty of their religion. He says that many pious Ministers of the word of God – some thousands of them, do now beg their bread. And told me how highly the present clergy carry themselfs everywhere, so as that they are hated and laughed at by everybody. He tells me that the King, by name, with all his dignities, is prayed for by them that they call fanatiques, as heartily and powerfully as in any of the other churches that are thought better. And that let the King think what he will, it is them that must help him in the day of warr – for, as they are the most, so generally they are the most substantiall sort of people, and the soberest. And did desire me to observe it to my Lord Sandwich, among other things, that of all the old army now, you cannot see a man begging about the street. But what? You shall have this captain turned a shoemaker; the lieutenant, a baker; this, a brewer; that, a haberdasher; this common soldier, a porter; and every man in his apron and frock, &c., as if they never had done anything else – whereas the [Cavaliers] go with their belts and swords, swearing and cursing and stealing – running into people's houses, by force oftentimes, to carry away something. And this is the difference between the temper of one and the other; and concludes (and I think with some reason) that the spirits of the old Parliament-soldier[s] are so quiet and contented with God's providences, that the King is safer from any evil meant him by them, a thousand times more then from his own discontented Cavalier[s]. (*9 November 1663*)

This morning Mr Burgby, one of the writing clerks belonging to the Council, was with me about business, a knowing man. He complains how most of the Lords of the Council do look after themselfs and their own ends and none the public, unless Sir Edw. Nicholas. Sir G. Carteret is diligent, but all for his own ends and profit. My Lord Privy Seale, a destroyer of everybody's business and doth no good at all to the public. The Archbishop of

[177]

Canterbury speaks very little nor doth much, being now come to the highest pitch that he can expect. Talks much of [the Chancellor's] neglecting the King and making the King to trot every day to him, when he is well enough to go to visit his cosen, Chief Justice Hide, but not to the Council or King. He commends my Lord of Ormond mightily in Ireland; but cries out cruelly of Sir G. Lane for his corruption and that he hath done my Lord great dishonour by selling of places here, which are now all taken away and the poor wretches ready to starve. That nobody almost understands or judges of business better then the King, if he would not be guilty of his father's fault, to be doubtful of himself and easily be removed from his own opinion. That my Lord Lauderdale is never from the King's eare nor counsel and that he is a most cunning fellow. Upon the whole, that he finds things go very bad everywhere; and even in the Council, nobody minds the public. (*2 March 1664*)

Good discourse among the old men [at the Trinity House]. Among other things, they observed that there are but two seamen in the Parliament house, *viz.*, Sir W. Batten and Sir W. Pen – and not above 20 or 30 merchants; which is a strange thing in an island, and no wonder that things of trade go no better nor are better understood. (*23 March 1664*)

Anon comes the King and passed the bill for repealing the Triennial Act, and another about writts of errour. I crowded in and heard the King's speech to them; but he speaks the worst that ever I heard man in my life – worse then if he read it all, and he had it in writing in his hand. (*5 April 1664*)

Among other things, Sir R. Ford did make me understand how the House of Commons is a beast not to be
understood – it being impossible to know beforehand the
success almost of any small plain thing – there being so
many to think and speak to any business, and they of so
uncertain minds and interests and passions. He did tell
me, and so did Sir W. Batten, how Sir Allen Brodericke
and Sir Allen Apsly did come drunk the other day into
the House, and did both speak for half an hour together,
and could not be either laughed or pulled or bid to sit
down and hold their peace – to the great contempt of the
King's servants and cause – which I am aggrieved at with
all my heart. (*19 December 1666*)

Public matters in a most sad condition. Seamen discouraged for want of pay, and are become not to be
governed. Nor, as matters are now, can any fleet go out
next year. Our enemies, French and Duch, great, and
grow more, by our poverty. The Parliament backward in
raising, because jealous of the spending, of the money.
The City less and less likely to be built again [*after the
Fire*], everybody settling elsewhere, and nobody encour-
aged to trade. A sad, vicious, negligent Court, and all
sober men there fearful of the ruin of the whole Kingdom
this next year – from which, good God deliver us. (*31
December 1666*)

Capt. Cocke tells me how the King was vexed the other
day for having no paper laid him at the Council table as
was usual; and that Sir Rd Browne did tell his Majesty he
would call the person whose work it was to provide it –
who being come, did tell His Majesty that he was but a
poor man, and was out 4 or 500*l* for it, which was as

[179]

much as he is worth; and that he cannot provide it any longer without money, having not received a penny since the King's coming in. So the King spoke to my Lord Chamberlaine; and many such mementos the King doth nowadays meet withal, enough to make an ingenuous [man] mad. (*22 April 1667*)

Mr Povy tells me that the Duke's family is in horrible disorder by being in debt, by spending above 60,000*l* per annum when he hath not 40,000*l*. That the Duchesse is not only the proudest woman in the world, but the most expenseful; and that the Duke of York's marriage with her hath undone the kingdom by making the Chancellor so great above reach, who otherwise would have been but an ordinary man, to have been dealt with by other people, and he would have been careful of managing things well, for fear of being called to account; whereas now, he is secure and hath let things run to wrack, as they now appear. (*24 June 1667*)

[*Sir H. Cholmley says that the King*] is now raising of a land army, which this Parliament and Kingdom will never bear. But the design is, and the Duke of York he says is hot for it, to have a land army, and so to make the government like that of France; but our princes have not brains, or at least care and forecast enough, to do that. It is strange how he and everybody doth nowadays reflect upon Oliver and commend him, so brave things he did and made all the neighbour princes fear him; while here a prince, come in with all the love and prayers and good liking of his people, and have given greater signs of loyallty and willingness to serve him with their estates then ever was done by any people, hath lost all so soon, that it is a miracle what way a man could devise to lose so much in so little time. (*12 July 1667*)

[Sir G. Carteret] doth say that the Court is in a way to ruin all for their pleasures; and says that he himself hath once taken the liberty to tell the King the necessity of having at least a show of religion in the government, and sobriety; and that it was that that did set up and keep up Oliver, though he was the greatest rogue in the world. And that it is so fixed in the nature of the common Englishman, that it will not out of him. He tells me that while all should be labouring to settle the Kingdom, they are at Court all in factions, some for and others against my Lord Chancellor, and another for and against another man; and the King adheres to no man, but this day delivers himself up to this and the next to that, to the ruin of himself and business. (*27 July 1667*)

G. Carteret and I toward the Temple in coach together, and there he did tell me how the King doth all he can in the world to overthrow my Lord Chancellor, and that notice is taken of every man about the King that is not seen to promote the ruine of the Chancellor. He tells me that as soon as Secretary Morrice brought the Great Seale from my Lord Chancellor, Babb May fell upon his knees and ketched the King about the legs and joyed him, and said that this was the first time that ever he could call him King of England, being freed this great man – which was a most ridiculous saying. (*11 November 1667*)

My wife having a mind to see the play, *Bartholomew Fayre* with puppets, which we did, and it is an excellent play; the more I see it, the more I love the wit of it – only, the business of abusing the Puritans begins to grow stale, and of no use, they being the people that at last will be found the wisest. (*4 September 1668*)

The Navy: Officers and Seamen

¶ IT WAS TAKEN FOR GRANTED in the seventeenth century that the officer class in the armed forces should be recruited from the upper ranks of society (4 June 1661). This principle worked better in the army than in the navy, where technical knowledge, for instance of navigation, was of major importance. Disaster might occur when it was lacking (4 April 1667). Opinion in the Admiralty was strongly in favour of appointing skilled seamen ('tarpaulins') to commissions. When Pepys rose to become Secretary to the Admiralty after 1673 he established a professional test by examination for appointment to a lieutenancy and a pay structure (including half-pay for periods when ships were laid up), which gave the sea officer continuous employment and a pension.

The passage about Penn (9 November 1663) is a piece of malicious libel. He owed his rise to his seamanship not to his puritanism, but Pepys could not forgive him his success and his influence with the Duke of York. Pepys is seen to better advantage in the passage concerning the poor seamen. They were paid by 'tickets' (12 March 1667) – always in arrear when their ship came into harbour and often cashed at a discount by ticket-mongers (such as innkeepers) who kept a proportion for themselves.

The 'press', which ended with the Napoleonic wars, was used for the recruitment of seamen and should have been applied only to fishermen, mariners and vagrants. Hence Pepys's distress (1 July 1666) at seeing 'housekeepers' and labourers taken on board by the recruiting officer and his men. The 'press-money' was the travelling allowance which by statute they were paid to enable them to be ready ('*prest*') at the rendezvous.

The purser (22 November 1665) was a warrant officer who received a low wage, varying with the rate of his ship, which was eked out by the wages of imaginary seamen and commissions on ships' supplies of food and clothing.

Fireships (13 June 1666) were small vessels crammed full of combustible material which were set on fire after being fastened alongside the enemy. It was a dangerous assignment for the fireship crew who had to escape by boat as best they could.

To my Lord Crew's to dinner with him. And had very good discourse about having of young noblemen and gentlemen to think of going to sea, as being as honourable service as the land war. (*4 June 1661*)

[Mr Blackborne and I] begun to talk of the Navy, and perticularly of Sir W. Pen – of whose rise [*during the Interregnum*] I had a mind to be informed. He told me he was alway a conceited man and one that would put the best side outward, but that it was his pretence of sanctity that brought him into play. Lawson and Portman and the Fifth Monarchy men, among whom he was a great brother, importuned that he might be general[-*at-sea*]; and it was pleasant to see how Blackburn himself did act it; how when the Comissioners of the Admiralty would enquire of the Captains and Admiralls of such and such men, how they would with a sithe and casting up the eye say, "Such a man fears the Lord" – or, "I hope such a man hath the Spirit of God," and such things as that. But he tells me that there was a cruel articling against Pen after one fight, for cowardice in putting himself within a coyle of cables, of which he had much ado to acquit himself. (*9 November 1663*)

Among other things, it pleased me to have it demonstrated that a purser without professed cheating is a professed loser, twice as much as he gets. (*22 November 1665*)

[184]

[The Duchess of Albemarle] cried mightily out against the having of gentlemen captains with feathers and ribbands, and wished the King would send her husband to sea with the old plain sea-captains that he served with formerly, that would make their ships swim with blood, though they could not make legs as captains nowadays can. (*10 January 1666*)

After dinner (being invited) to Sir Chr. Mings's funerall [*at Whitechapel*], and there heard the service and stayed till they buried him, and then out. And there met with Sir W. Coventry (who was there out of great generosity, and no person of quality there but he) and went with him into his coach; and being in it with him, there happened this extraordinary case – one of the most romantique that ever I heard of in my life, and could not have believed but that I did see it – which was this. About a dozen able, lusty, proper men came to the coach-side with tears in their eyes, and one of them, that spoke for the rest, begun and says to Sir W. Coventry – "We are here a dozen of us that have long known and loved and served our dead commander, Sir Chr. Mings, and have now done the last office of laying him in the ground. We would be glad we had any other to offer after him, and in revenge of him – all we have is our lives. If you will please to get his Royal Highness to give us a fireshipp among us all, here is a dozen of us, out of all which choose you one to be commander, and the rest of us, whoever he is, will serve him, and, if possible, do that that shall show our memory of our dead commander and our revenge." Sir W. Coventry was herewith much moved (as well as I, who could hardly abstain from weeping) and took their names; and so parted, telling me that he would move his

Royal Highness as in a thing very extraordinary, and so we parted. The truth is, Sir Chr. Mings was a very stout man, and a man of great parts and most excellent tongue among ordinary men; and as Sir W. Coventry says, could have been the most useful man in the world at such a pinch of time as this. He was come into great renowne here at home, and more abroad, in the West Indys. He had brought his family into a way of being great. But dying at this time, his memory and name (his father being always, and at this day, a shoomaker, and his mother a hoymans daughter, of which he was used frequently to boast) will be quite forgot in a few months, as if he had never been, nor any of his name be the better by it – he having not had time to coll[ect] any estate; but is dead poor rather then rich. (*13 June 1666*)

To the Tower several times about the business of the pressed men, and late at it, till 12 at night, shipping of them. But Lord, how some poor women did cry, and in my life I never did see such natural expression of passion as I did here – in some women's bewailing themselfs, and running to every parcel of men that were brought, one after another, to look for their husbands, and wept over every vessel that went off, thinking they might be there, and looking after the ship as far as ever they could by moonelight – that it grieved me to the heart to hear them. Besides, to see poor patient labouring men and house-keepers, leaving poor wifes and families, taken up on a sudden by strangers, was very hard; and that without press-money, but forced against all law to be gone. It is a great tyranny. (*1 July 1666*)

Up, and to the office, where busy all the morning sitting. At noon home to dinner, and then to the office, the yard being very full of women (I believe above 300) coming to get money for their husbands and friends that are prisoners in Holland; and they lay clamouring and swearing, and cursing us, that my wife and I were afeared to send a venison-pasty that we have for supper tonight to the cook's to be baked, for fear of their offering violence to it – but it went, and no hurt done. Then I took an opportunity, when they were all gone into the foreyard, and slipped into the office and there busy all the afternoon. But by and by the women got into the garden, and came all to my closet window and there tormented me; and I confess, their cries were so sad for money, and laying down the condition of their families and their husbands, and what they have done and suffered for the King, and how ill they are used by us, and how well the Duch are used here by the allowance of their masters, and what their husbands are offered to serve the Duch abroad, that I do most heartily pity them, and was ready to cry to hear them – but cannot help them; however, when the rest was gone, I did call one to me, that I heard complain only and pity her husband, and did give her some money; and she blessed me and went away. (*10 July 1666*)

[Sir W. Coventry] cries out upon the discipline of the fleet, which is lost. And that there is not, in any of the fourth-rates and under, scarce left one sea-comander, but all young gentlemen. (*Lord's Day, 16 December 1666*)

Upon Tower Hill saw about 3 or 400 seamen get together; and one, standing upon a pile of bricks, made his sign with his handkercher upon his stick, and called all the rest to him, and several shouts they gave. This made me afeared, so I got home as fast as I could – and hearing of no present hurt, did go to Sir Robt Viners about my plate again; and coming home, do hear of 1000 seamen said in the streets to be in armes. So in great fear home, expecting to find a tumult about our house, and was doubtful of my riches there – but I thank God, I found all well. But by and by Sir W. Batten and Sir R. Ford do tell me that the seamen have been at some prisons to release some seamen, and that the Duke of Albemarle is in armes, and all the Guards at the other end of the town; and the Duke of Albemarle is gone with some forces to Wapping to quell the seamen – which is a thing of infinite disgrace to us. (*19 December 1666*)

This day a poor seaman, almost starved for want of food, lay in our yard a-dying; I sent him half-a-crown – and we ordered his ticket to be paid. (*12 March 1667*)

Pretty, to hear how [the Duchess of Albemarle] talked against Capt. Du Tel, the Frenchman that the Prince and her husband put out last year; and how, says she, the Duke of York hath made for his good services his cupbearer; yet fired more shot into the Prince's ship, and others of the King's ships, then of the enemy. And the Duke of Albemarle did confirm it, and that somebody in the fight did cry out that a little Dutchman by his ship did plague him more then any other; upon which they were going to order him to be sunk, when they looked and found it was Du Tell, who, as the Duke of Albemarle says, had killed several men in several of our ships. He said, but for his interest which he knew he had at Court, he had hanged him at the yard's arm without staying for a court martiall. (*4 April 1667*)

[Sir W. Coventry, Penn and I] to talk of the loss of all affection and obedience now in the seamen, so that all power is lost. [Sir W. Coventry] told us that he doth concur in thinking that want of money doth do the most of it, but that that is not all; but the having of gentlemen captaines, who discourage all tarpaulins and have given out that they would in a little time bring it to that pass that a tarpaulin should not dare to aspire to more then to be a bosun or a gunner – that this makes the sea-captains to lose their own good affections to the service and to instil it into the seamen also, and that the seamen do see it themselfs and resent it. And tells us that it is notorious, even to his bearing of great ill will at Court, that he hath been the opposer of gentlemen-captains; and Sir W. Pen did put in and said that he was esteemed to have been the man that did instil it into Sir W. Coventry; which Sir W. Coventry did own also – and says that he hath alway told the gentlemen-captains his opinon of them; and that himself, who had now served to the business of the sea six or seven years, should know a little, and as much as them that had never almost been at sea; and that yet he found himself fitter to be a Bishop or Pope then to be a sea-commander, and so endeed he is. (*29 June 1667*)

Up, and by coach to Whitehall; and there attended the King and the Duke of York in the Duke of York's lodgings with the rest of the Officers [*of the Navy Board*] and many of the commanders of the fleet. Mr Wren whispered me in the eare, and said that the Duke of Albemarle did displace many commanders; among others, Captain Batts, who the Duke of York said was a very stout man, all the world knew; and that another was brought into his ship that had been turned off his place when he was a bosun not long before for being a drunkerd: this [Prince Rupert] took notice of, and would have been angry, I think, but they let their discourse fall; but the Duke of York was earnest in it and the Prince said to me, standing by me, "God damn me, if they will turn out every man that will be drunk, he must turn out all the commanders in the fleet. What is the matter if [he] be drunk, so when he comes to fight he doth his work? At least, let him be punished for his drunkenness, and not put out of his command presently," (*2 January 1668*)

The Navy at War

¶ THE ANGLO-DUTCH WAR OF 1665-7 was the second in a series of three naval wars in which the two nations fought for naval and commercial supremacy. The first (Oliver Cromwell's, 1652-4) was a clear British triumph; in the second, fortunes were more equal but the Dutch emerged victorious; the third (1672-4) was indecisive. All were costly in men, money and ships. One passage below (8 June 1665) describes the British victory of Lowestoft; another (4 June 1666) gives an account of the first two days of the Four Days Fight – the longest and most exciting battle of the whole series. What appeared at first to be an English victory turned out to be a defeat. Penn drew from this engagement the same lesson he had drawn in the Cromwellian war – that fleets had to fight in line if they were to maximise the effect of their broadsides (4 July 1666). This now became the classical doctrine of fighting at sea for a century and more.

The subject of the remaining extracts is the remarkable Dutch exploit in invading the Thames and Medway in June 1667, in which a force under De Ruyter broke the defensive chain that had been slung across the Medway, burnt some of our great ships and towed away the greatest of them all, the *Royal Charles*. To Pepys the disaster was due entirely to shortage of money. In the early months of 1667 the Cabinet had decided it was too expensive to maintain a battle fleet in being. There were to be only scattered squadrons. It was a decision that laid us open to invasion.

Great talk there is of a fear of a war with the Duch; and we have order to pitch upon 20 ships to be forthwith set out; but I hope it is but a scarecrow to the world, to let them see that we can be ready for them; though God knows, the King is not able to set out five ships at this present without great difficulty, we neither having money, credit, nor stores. (*28 June 1662*)

To the coffee-house with Capt. Cocke, who discoursed well of the good effects in some kind of a Duch war and conquest (which I did not consider before but the contrary); that is, that the trade of the world is too little for us two, therefore one must down. (*1 February 1664*)

After the Council rose, Sir G. Carteret, my Lord Brunkard, Sir Tho. Harvy, and myself down to my Lord Treasurer's chamber to him and the Chancellor and the Duke of Albemarle. And there I did give them a large account of the charge of the Navy, and want of money. But strange, to see how they held up their hands, crying, "What shall we do?" Says my Lord Treasurer, "Why, what means all this, Mr Pepys? This is true, you say, but what would you have me to do? I have given all I can for my life. Why will not people lend their money? Why will they not trust the King as well as Oliver? Why do our prizes come to nothing, that yielded so much heretofore?" And this was all we could get, and went away without other answer. Which is one of the saddest things, that at such a time as this, with the greatest action on foot that ever was in England, nothing should be minded, but let things go on of themselfs – do as well as they can. (*12 April 1665*)

Victory over the Dutch, 3 June 1665

This day they engaged – the Dutch neglecting greatly the opportunity of the wind they had of us – by which they lost the benefit of their fireships. The Earl of Falmouth, Muskery, and Mr Rd Boyle killed on board the Dukes ship, the *Royall Charles*, with one shot. Their blood and brains flying in the Duke's face – and the head of Mr Boyle striking down the Duke, as some say. Earle of Marlbrough, Portland, Rere-[A]dmirall Sansum (to

Prince Rupert) killed, and Captain Kirby and Ableson. Sir Jo. Lawson wounded on the knee – hath had some bones taken out, and is likely to be well again. Upon receiving the hurt, he sent to the Duke for another to command the *Royall Oake*. The Duke sent Jordan out of the *St George*, who did brave things in her. Captain Jer. Smith of the *Mary* was second to the Duke, and stepped between him and Captain Seaton of the *Urania* [*Oranje*] (76 guns and 400 men), who had sworn to board the Duke. Killed him, 200 men, and took the ship. Himself losing 99 men, and never an officer saved but himself and Lieutenant. His maister endeed is saved, with his leg cut off. Admirall Opdam blown up. Trump killed, and [*it is*] said, by Holmes. All the rest of their Admiralls, as they say, but Everson (whom they dare not trust for his affection to the Prince of Orange) are killed. We have taken and sunk, as is believed, about 24 of their best ships. Killed and taken near 8 or 10,000 men; and lost, we think, not above 700. A great victory, never known in the world. They are all fled; some 43 got into the Texell and others elsewhere, and we in pursuit of the rest.

Thence, with my heart full of joy, home, and to my office a little; then to my Lady Pen's, where they are all joyed and not a little puffed up at the good success of their father; and good service endeed is said to have been done by him. Had a great bonefire at the gate; and I with my Lady Pens people and others to Mrs Turner's great room, and then down into the street. I did give the boys 4*s* among them – and mighty merry; so home to bed – with my heart at great rest and quiet, saving that the consideration of the victory is too great for me presently to comprehend. (*8 June 1665*)

Sir Jo. Lawson, I hear, is worse then yesterday – the King
went to see him today, most kindly. It seems his wound is
not very bad, but he hath a fever, a thrush and a hickup
all three together; which are, it seems, very bad symp-
toms. [*He died on the 25th.*] (*17 June 1665*)

Up, and with Sir Jo. Minnes and Sir W. Pen to Whitehall
in the latter's coach – where when we came, we find the
Duke at St James's. So walking through the park, we saw
hundreds of people listening at the Gravell Pits, and to
and again in the park to hear the guns [*of the battle fleets at
sea*]. After wayting upon the Duke, Sir W. Penn and I
home – where no sooner come, but news is brought me
of a couple of men come to speak with me from the fleet.
So I down, and who should it be but Mr Daniel, all
muffled up, and his face as black as the chimney and
covered with dirt, pitch and tar, and powder, and
muffled with dirty clouts and his right eye stopped with
okum. He is come last night at 5 a-clock from the fleet,
with a comrade of his that hath endangered another eye.
They were set on shore at Harwich this morning at 2 a-
clock in a ketch, with about twenty more wounded men
from the *Royal Charles*. They being able to ride, took
post about 3 this morning and was here between 11 and
12. I went presently into the coach with them, and carried
them to Sumersett House Stairs and there took water (all
the world gazing upon us and concluding it to be news
from the fleet; and everybody's face appeared expecting
of news) to the Privy Stairs and left them at Mr
Coventry's lodging (he, though, not being there); and so
I into the park to the King, and told him [the Duke of
Albemarle] was well the last night at 5 o'clock, and
Prince [Rupert] come with his fleet and joyned with his

about 7. The King was mightily pleased with this news and so took me by the hand and talked a little of it – I giving him the best account I could; and then he bid me fetch the two seamen to him – he walking into the house. So I went and fetched the seamen into the Vane Room to him, and there he heard the whole account.

The Fight

How we found the Duch fleet at anchor on Friday, half-seas-over, between Dunkirke and Oastend, and made them let slip their anchors – they about 90, and we less then 60. We fought them and put them to the run, till they met with about 16 sail of fresh ships and so bore up again. The fight continued till night, and then again the next morning from 5 till 7 at night – and so too, yesterday morning they begun again, and continued till about 4 a-clock – they chasing us for the most part of Saturday and yesterday; we fleeing from them. The Duke himself, then those people, were put into the ketch, and by and by spied the Prince's fleet coming – upon which, De Ruyter called a little council (being in chase at this time of us); and thereupon their fleet divided into two squadrons, 40 in one and about 30 in the other (the fleet being at first about 90, but by one accident or other supposed to be lessened to about 70); the bigger to fallow the Duke, the less to meet the Prince. But the Prince came up with [Albemarle's] fleet, and the Dutch came together again and bore toward their own coast – and we with them. And now, what the consequence of this day will be, that we [hear] them fighting, we know not. The Duke was forced to come to anchor on Friday, having lost his sails and rigging. No perticular person spoken of to be hurt but Sir W. Clerke, who hath lost his leg, and bore it bravely. The Duke himself had a little hurt in his thigh, but signified little. The King did pull out of his pocket about twenty pieces in gold, and did give it Daniel for himself and his companion. And so parted, mightily pleased with the account he did give him of the fight and the success it ended with – of the Prince's coming – though it seems the Duke did give way again and again. The King did give order for care to be had of Mr Daniel and his companion; and so we parted. (*4 June 1666*)

[Sir W. Penn] says three things must [be] remedied, or else we shall be undone:

1. That we must fight in a line, whereas we fight promiscuously, to our utter and demonstrable ruine – the Duch fighting otherwise – and we, whenever we beat them.
2. We must not desert ships of our own in distress as we did, for that makes a captain desperate, and will fling away his ship when there is no hopes left him of succour.
3. That ships, when they are a little shattered, must not take the liberty to come in of themselfs; but refit themselfs the best they can, and stay out – many of our ships coming in with very small disablings.

He told me that our very commanders, nay, our very flag-officers, do stand in need of exercizing among themselfs and discoursing the business of commanding a fleet – he telling me that even one of our flagmen in the fleet did not know which tacke lost the wind or which kept it in the last engagement. He says it was pure dismaying and fear that made them all run upon the Galloper [Sand], not having their wits about them; and that it was a miracle they were not all lost. (*4 July 1666*)

Up, and with W. Penn to Whitehall by coach. Here the Duke of York did acquaint us (and the King did the like also, afterward coming in) with his resolution of altering the manner of the war this year; that is, that we shall keep what fleet we have abroad in several squadrons; so that now all is come out, but we are to keep it as close as we can, without hindering the work that is to be done in preparation to this. Great preparations there are to fortify Sheernesse and the yard at Portsmouth, and forces are drawing down to both those places, and elsewhere by the seaside; so that we have some fear of an invasion, and the Duke of York himself did declare his expectation of the enemy's blocking us up here in the River, and therefore directed that we should send away all the ships that we have [there]. (*6 March 1667*)

At the office all the morning, where Sir W. Penn came, being returned from Chatham from considering the means of fortifying the River Medway, by a chain at the stakes and ships laid there, with guns to keep the enemy from coming up to burn our ships – all our care now being [to] fortify ourselfs against their invading us. (*23 March 1667*)

[Sir W. Coventry's] clerk Powell doth tell me that ill news is come to Court of the Dutch breaking the chaine at Chatham, which struck me to the heart, and to Whitehall to hear the truth of it; and there, going up the park stairs, I did hear some lackeys speaking of sad news come to Court, saying that hardly anybody in the Court but doth look as if they cried; and [I] would not go into the house for fear of being seen, but slunk out and got into a coach. And so home, where all our hearts do now ake; for the news is true, that the Dutch have broke the chain and burned our ships, and perticularly the *Royall Charles*; other perticulars I know not, but most sad to be sure. (*12 June 1667*)

A man of Mr Gawden's came from Chatham last night and tells me that he himself (I think he said) did hear many Englishmen on board the Dutch ships, speaking to one another in English, and that they did cry and say, "We did heretofore fight for tickets; now we fight for dollers!" and did ask how such and such a one did, and would commend themself to them – which is a sad consideration. And several seamen came this morning to me to tell me that if I would get their tickets paid, they would go and do all they could against the Dutch; but otherwise they would not venture being killed and lose all they have already fought for – so that I was forced to try what I could do to get them paid. And endeed, the hearts as well as affections of the seamen are turned away; and in the open streets in Wapping, and up and down, the wifes have cried publicly, "This comes of your not paying our husbands; and now your work is undone, or done by hands that understand it not;" and Sir W. Batten told me that he was himself affronted with a woman in language of this kind himself on Tower Hill publicly yesterday; and we are fain to bear it – and to keep one at the office-door to let no idle people in, for fear of firing of the office and doing us mischief. The City is troubled at their [trainbands] being put upon duty: summoned one hour and discharged two hours after and then again summoned two hours after that, to their great charge as well as trouble; and Pelling the pothecary tells me the world says all over that less charge then what the kingdom is put to, of one kind or other, by this business, would have set out all our great ships. It is said they did in open streets yesterday, at Westminster, cry, "A Parliament! A Parliament!"; and do believe it will cost blood to answer for these miscarriages. We do not hear that the Duch are come to Gravesend, which is a wonder; but a wonderful thing it is that to this day we have not one word yet from Brouncker or P. Pett or J. Mennes of anything at Chatham; the people that come hither to hear how things go make me ashamed to be found unable to answer them, for I am left alone here at the office; and the truth is, I am glad my station is to be here – near my own home and out of danger, yet in a place of doing the King good service. (*14 June 1667*)

The Plague

¶ TOGETHER WITH THE BLACK DEATH OF 1348–9 the Plague
of 1665 is the best-known outbreak in British history of
bubonic plague (so-called from the bubos, or swellings, it
caused). It was also the last outbreak – for reasons which are
still a matter for debate. It made its first appearance in
Westminster in the early summer, then spread eastwards to
reach its peak in the hot weather that followed. In the winter
of 1665–6 it subsided but in 1666 it spread outside the capital
to parts of the South East. Its progress in London was
recorded (though inaccurately) in the weekly 'bills of
mortality' produced by the Parish Clerks' Company (29
June).

Those who could, fled the pestilence – the Court to
Oxford, the Navy Office to Greenwich, Pepys and his wife
to Woolwich (though Pepys regularly commuted back to
the city to his office there). Altogether a quarter of London's
population died.

There was no remedy (though tobacco was held to be a
useful prophylactic) and the victims mostly died after a few
days. The bacillus was spread by fleas carried by rats, but the
authorities, under the impression that it was spread by con-
tagion or infection, required all members of the victims,
households to be immured in their houses for forty days.

This day, much against my will, I did in Drury Lane see
two or three houses marked with a red cross upon the
doors, and "Lord have mercy upon us" writ there –
which was a sad sight to me, being the first of that kind
that to my remembrance I ever saw. It put me into an ill
conception of myself and my smell, so that I was forced
to buy some roll tobacco to smell to and chaw – which
took away the apprehension. (*7 June 1665*)

In the evening home to supper, and there to my great
trouble hear that the plague is come into the City (though
it hath these three or four weeks since its beginning been

wholly out of the City); but where should it begin but in my good friend and neighbour's, Dr Burnett in Fanchurch Street – which in both points troubles me mightily. (*10 June 1665*)

I out of doors a little to show forsooth my new suit, and back again; and in going, saw poor Dr Burnets door shut. But he hath, I hear, gained great goodwill among his neighbours; for he discovered it himself first, and caused himself to be shut up of his own accord – which was very handsome. (*Lord's Day, 11 June 1665*)

The town grows very sickly, and people to be afeared of it – there dying this last week of the plague 112, from 43 the week before – whereof, one in Fanchurch Street and one in Broad Street by the [*Navy*] Treasurer's office. (*15 June 1665*)

It stroke me very deep this afternoon, going with a hackny-coach from my Lord Treasurer's down Holborne – the coachman I found to drive easily and easily; at last stood still, and came down hardly able to stand; and told me that he was suddenly stroke very sick and almost blind, he could not see. So I light and went into another coach, with a sad heart for the poor man and trouble for myself, lest he should have been stroke with the plague – being at that end of the town that I took him up. But God have mercy upon us all. (*17 June 1665*)

Up, and by water to Whitehall, where the Court full of waggons and people ready to go out of town. The mortality bill is come to 267 – which is about 90 more

then the last [week]; and of these, but 4 in the City –
which is a great blessing to us. (*29 June 1665*)

Thus this month ends, with great sadness upon the public
through the greatness of the plague, everywhere through
the kingdom almost. Every day sadder and sadder news
of its encrease. In the City died this week 7496; and of
them 6102 of the plague. But it is feared that the true
number of the dead this week is near 10,000 – partly from
the poor that cannot be taken notice of through the
greatness of the number, and partly from the Quakers
and others that will not have any bell ring for them. (*31
August 1665*)

Up, and put on my colourd silk suit, very fine, and my
new periwigg, bought a good while since, but darst not
wear it because the plague was in Westminster when I
bought it. And it is a wonder what will be the fashion
after the plague is done as to periwigs, for nobody will
dare to buy any haire for fear of the infection – that it had
been cut off of the heads of people dead of the plague.
After dinner I by water to Greenwich, where much ado
to be suffered to come into the town because of the
sickness, for fear I should come from London – till I told
them who I was. So up to the church, where my Lord
Brouncker, Sir J. Mennes, and I up to the Vestry at the
desire of the Justices of the Peace, Sir Th. Bidolph and Sir
W. Boreman and Ald. Hooker – in order to the doing
something for the keeping of the plague from growing;
but Lord, to consider the madness of people of the town,
who will (because they are forbid) come in crowds along
with the dead corps to see them buried. But we agreed on
some orders for the prevention thereof. Among other

stories, one was very passionate methought – of a complaint brought against a man in the town for taking a child from London from an infected house. Ald. Hooker told us it was the child of a very able citizen in Gracious Street, a sadler, who had buried all the rest of his children of the plague; and himself and wife now being shut up, and in despair of escaping, did desire only to save the life of this little child; and so prevailed to have it received stark naked into the arms of a friend, who brought it (having put it into new fresh clothes) to Grenwich; where, upon hearing the story, we did agree it should be permitted to be received and kept in the town. (*Lord's Day, 3 September 1665*)

But Lord, how empty the streets are, and melancholy, so many poor sick people in the streets, full of sores, and so many sad stories overheard as I walk, everybody talking of this dead, and that man sick, and so many in this place, and so many in that. And they tell me that in Westminster there is never a physitian, and but one apothecary left, all being dead – but that there are great hopes of a great decrease this week: God send it. (*16 October 1665*)

I was set down at Woolwich town's-end and walked through the town in the dark, it being now night. But in the street did overtake and almost run upon two women, crying and carrying a man's coffin between them: I suppose the husband of one of them, which methinks is a sad thing. (*Lord's Day, 29 October 1665*)

I, with my Lord Brouncker and Mrs Williams, by coach with four horses to London, to my Lord's house in Covent Guarden. But Lord, what staring to see a nobleman's coach come to town – and porters everywhere bow to us, and such begging of beggars. And a delightful thing it is to see the town full of people again, as now it is, and shops begin to open, though in many places, seven or eight together, and more, all shut; but yet the town is full compared with what it used to be – I mean the City-end, for Covent Gu[a]rden and Westminster are yet very empty of people, no Court nor gentry being there. (*5 January 1666*)

Popular Entertainments

¶ PEPYS PREFERRED THE GENTEEL DELIGHTS of pleasure gardens like Vauxhall to the rough sports of the rabble such as cock-fighting and bull-baiting which, after being officially prohibited under the rule of the Puritans, returned at the Restoration.

Bartholomew Fair was held annually in Smithfield for a fortnight from 23 August. The Bear Garden on Bankside (the Surrey side of the river) was an amphitheatre used for bull- and bear-baiting, and for prize-fights, which in Pepys's day took the form of fights with weapons rather than boxing.

Made my wife get herself presently ready, and so carried her by coach to [Bartholomew] Fair and showed her the munkys dancing on the ropes; which was strange, but such dirty sport that I was not pleased with it. There was also a horse with hoofes like rams hornes, a goose with four feet, and a cock with three. Thence to another place and saw some German clockeworks, the Salutacion of the Virgin Mary and several Scripture stories; but above all, there was at last represented the sea, with Neptune, Venus, mermaids, and Cupid on a dolphin, the sea rolling. (*4 September 1663*)

Being directed by sight of bills upon the walls, did go to Shooe Lane to see a cocke-fighting at a new pit there – a sport I was never at in my life. But Lord, to see the strange variety of people, from Parliament-man (by name Wildes, that was Deputy-Governor of the Tower when Robinson was Lord Mayor) to the poorest prentices, bakers, brewers, butchers, draymen, and what not; and all these fellows one with another in swearing, cursing, and betting. I soon had enough of it; and yet I would not but have seen it once, it being strange to observe the nature of those poor creatures, how they will fight till they drop down dead upon the table and strike after they are ready to give up the ghost – not offering to run away when they are weary or wounded past doing further. Whereas, where a dunghill brood comes, he will, after a sharp stroke that pricks him, run off the stage, and then they wring off his neck without more ado. Whereas the other they preserve, though their eyes be both out, for breed only of a true cock of the game. One thing more it is strange to see, how people of this poor rank, that look as if they had not bread to put in their mouths, shall bet 3 or 4*l* at one bet and lose it, and yet bet as much the next battell, as they call every make [*match*] of two cocks – so that one of them will lose 10 or 20*l* at a meeting. (*21 December 1663*)

By coach home, calling by the way at Charing Cross and there saw the great Dutchman that is come over, under whose arm I went with my hat on and could not reach higher than his eyebrows with the tip of my fingers, reaching as high as I could. He is a comely and well-made man, and his wife a very little but pretty comely Dutch woman. It is true he wears pretty high-heeled shoes, but not very high, and doth generally wear a turbant, which makes him show yet taller then he really is, though he is very tall as I have said before. (*15 August 1664*)

After dinner with my wife and Mercer to the Beare Garden, where I have not been I think of many years, and saw some good sport of the bull's tossing of the dogs – one into the very boxes. But it is a very rude and nasty pleasure. We had a great many Hectors in the same box with us (and one, very fine, went into the pit and played his dog for a wager, which was a strange sport for a gentleman), where they drank wine, and drank Mercer's health first, which I pledged with my hat off. (*14 August 1666*)

Then abroad by [water] and stopped at the Bear Garden Stairs, there to see a prize fought; but the house so full, there was no getting in there; so forced to [go] through an alehouse into the pit where the bears are baited, and upon a stool did see them fight, which they did very furiously, a butcher and a waterman. The former had the better all along, till by and by the latter dropped his sword out of his hand, and the butcher, whether not seeing his sword dropped or I know not, but did give him a cut over the wrist, so as he was disabled to fight any longer. But Lord, to see how in a minute the whole stage was full of watermen to revenge the foul play, and the butchers to defend their fellow, though most blamed him; and there they all fell to it, to knocking down and cutting many of each side. It was pleasant to see, but that I stood in the pit and feared that in the tumult I might get some hurt. At last the rabble broke up, and so I away to Whitehall. (*27 May 1667*)

Presently comes Creed, and he and I by water to Foxhall and there walked in Spring Garden; a great deal of company, and the weather and garden pleasant; that it is very pleasant and cheap going thither, for a man may go to spend what he will, or nothing, all as one – but to hear the nightingale and other birds, and here fiddles and there a harp, and here a jews trump, and here laughing, and there fine people walking, is mighty divertising. Among others, there were two pretty women alone, that walked a great while; which [being] discovered by some idle gentlemen, they would needs take them up; but to see the poor ladies, how they were put to it to run from them, and they after them; and sometimes the ladies put themselfs along with other company, then the others drew back; at last, the ladies did get off out of the house and took boat and away. I was troubled to see them abused so; and could have found my heart, as little desire of fighting as I have, to have protected the ladies. (*28 May 1667*)

Went into Holborne and there saw the woman that is to be seen with a beard; she is a little plain woman, a Dane, her name, Ursula Dyan, about forty years old, her voice like a little girl's, with a beard as much as any man I ever saw, as black almost, and grizzly. They offered [to] show my wife further satisfaction if she desired it, refusing it to men that desired it there, but there is no doubt but by her voice she is a woman. It begun to grow at about seven years old – and was shaved not above seven months ago, and is now so big as any man almost that ever I saw, I say, bushy and thick. It was a strange sight to me, I confess, and what pleased me mightily. (*21 December 1668*)

St Valentine's Day

¶ A COMMON CONVENTION was that both men and women chose as their Valentine the first person they saw on St Valentine's Day. Hence Elizabeth's covering her eyes on that day in 1662 to avoid seeing the painters who were at work in her dining room. Another method was to draw lots (15 February 1669). Whatever the method of choice, the female Valentines claimed expensive presents.

Up earely and to Sir W. Battens. But would not go in till I had asked whether they that opened the doore was a man or a woman. And Mingo, who was there, answered "A woman;" which, with his tone, made me laugh. So up I went and took Mrs Martha for my Valentine (which I do only for complacency), and Sir W. Batten, he go[es] in the same manner to my wife. And so we were very merry. (*14 February 1661*)

In the afternoon my wife and I and Mrs Martha Batten, my Valentine, to the Exchange; and there, upon a payre of embroydered and six payre of plain white gloves, I laid out 40s. upon her. (*18 February 1661*)

I did this day purposely shun to be seen at Sir W. Battens – because I would not have his daughter to be my Valentine, as she was the last year, there being no great friendship between us now as formerly. This morning in comes W. Bowyer, who was my wife's Valentine, she having (at which I made good sport to myself) held her hands all the morning, that she might not see the paynters that were at work in gilding my chimny-piece and pictures in my dining-room. (*14 February 1662*)

This morning comes betimes Dicke Pen to be my wife's Valentine, and came to our bedside. By the same token, I had him brought to my side, thinking to have made him kiss me; but he perceived me, and would not. So went to his Valentine – a notable, stout, witty boy. I up, about business; and opening the doore, there was Bagwell's wife, and she had the confidence to say she came with a hope to be time enough to be my Valentine. (*14 February 1665*)

This morning came up to my wife's bedside, I being up dressing myself, little Will Mercer to be her Valentine; and brought her name writ upon blue paper in gold letters, done by himself, very pretty – and we were both well pleased with it. But I am also this year my wife's Valentine, and it will cost me 5*l* – but that I must have laid out if we had not been Valentines. (*14 February 1667*)

To my cousin Turner's; where, having the last night been told by her that she had drawn me for her Valentine, I did this day call at the New Exchange and bought her a pair of green silk stockings and garters and shoe-strings, and two pair of jessimy-gloves, all coming to about 28*s*. – and did give them her this noon. (*15 February 1669*)

Sports and Contests

¶ A WIDE RANGE OF SPORTS, old and new, princely and popular, are mentioned here. The most royal of all was stag-hunting – and the forests within easy reach of London (such as those of Windsor and Richmond) must be those referred to at 11 August 1661 and 22 June 1663. The King and the Duke – young men of 30 and 28 at the Restoration – also led the latest sporting fashion, yacht racing on the river (5 September 1662) which they had learned to enjoy while in exile. (The word 'yacht' was of Dutch origin.) The equivalent water sport for rowing men (including the professional watermen who plied for hire on the river) was the occasional boat race, rowed in galleys, the fastest of all river craft (18 May 1661). No doubt for Pepys himself the most interesting of aquatic events was the series of contests between the double-keeled vessel designed by Sir William Petty, which claimed (succesfully) to be faster than any single-keeled ship (31 July 1663).

Two of the other sports mentioned here have connections with the Court – pall-mall (4 January 1664; a form of croquet, played in St James's Park, where it gave its name to the road) and 'real' or 'royal' tennis (2 September 1667). Skating, another Dutch-inspired fashion, was also a common pastime in St James's Park, on the canal constructed in 1660–1 (1 December 1662).

The sports represented here which come nearest to being spectator sports in the modern sense are wrestling matches (28 June 1661) and foot-races (10 August 1660; 30 July 1663) in which footmen were often contestants. They were sometimes employed for their athleticism: 'running footmen' accompanied their masters' coaches to make a show in town and to help to protect them against spills in the country roads. Irishmen were reputedly fast runners.

Horse-racing was well established by this time, but was a country diversion, out of Pepys's range as an observer of town life.

With Mr Moore and Creed to Hide Parke by coach and saw a fine foot-race, three times round the park, between an Irishman and Crow that was once my Lord Clay-pooles footman. Crow beat the other above two miles. (*10 August 1660*)

Being through bridge, I find the Thames full of boats and gallys; and upon enquiry find that there was a wager to be run this morning. So spying of Payne in a galley, I went into him and there stayed, thinking to have gone to Chelsy with them; but upon the start, the wager-boats fell foul one of another, till at last one of them goes over, pretending foule play; and so the other rew away alone – and all our sport lost. (*18 May 1661*)

Sir W. Penn in his coach and I, we went to Moorefields and there walked; and stood and saw the wrestling, which I never saw so much of before – between the North and West countrymen. (*28 June 1661*)

To Grayes Inn Walks where I met with Ned Pickering, who told me what a great match of hunting of a stagg the King had yesterday; and how the King tired all their horses and came home with not above two or three able to keep pace with him. (*Lord's Day, 11 August 1661*)

Up by break-a-day at 5 a-clock, and down by water to Woolwich; in my way saw the yacht lately built by our virtuosoes, my Lord Brunkard and others, with the help of Comissioner Pett also, set out from Greenwich with the little Dutch *Bezan*, to try for mastery; and before they got to Woolwich, the Duch beat them half-a-mile (and I hear this afternoon that in coming home it got above three mile); which all our people are glad of. (*5 September 1662*)

I to my Lord Sandwiches, and then over the parke (where I first in my life, it being a great frost, did see people sliding with their sckeates, which is a very pretty art) to Mr Coventry's chamber to St James's, where we all met to a venison pasty; and were here very merry. (*1 December 1662*)

Thence to walk in the parke a good while – the Duke [of York] being gone a-hunting; and by and by came in and shifted himself, he having in his hunting, rather than go about, light and led his horse through a river up to his breast, and came so home. (*22 June 1663*)

The town talke this day is of nothing but the great foot race run this day on Bansted Downes, between Lee, the Duke of Richmonds footman, and a tyler, a famous runner. And Lee hath beat him – though the King and Duke of Yorke, and all men almost, did bet three or four to one upon the tyler's head. (*30 July 1663*)

Mr Grant showed me letters of Sir Wm Pettys, wherein he says that his vessel which he hath built upon two keeles (a modell whereof, built for the King, he showed me) hath this month won a wager of 50*l* in sailing between Dublin and Holyhead with the pacquett-boat, the best ship or vessel the King hath there; and he offers to lay with any vessel in the world. It is about 30 ton in burden and carries 30 men with good accomodacion (as much more as any ship of her burden) and so shall carry any vessel of this figure more men, with better accommodation by half, then any other ship. This carries also ten guns of about five tons weight. In their coming back from Holyhead, they started together; and this vessel

[213]

came to Dublin by 5 at night and the pacquet-boat not before 8 the next morning; and when they came they did believe that this vessel had been drownded or at least behind, not thinking she could have lived in that sea. (*31 July 1663*)

To St James's Park and there spent an hour or two, it being a pleasant day, seeing people play at Pell Mell – where it pleased me mightily to hear a gallant, lately come from France, swear at one of his companions for suffering his man (a spruce blade) to be so saucy as to strike a ball while his master was playing on the Mall. (*4 January 1664*)

I went to see a great match at tennis between Prince Rupert and one Capt. Cooke against Bab May and the elder Chichly, where the King was and Court, and it seems are the best players at tennis in the nation. But this puts me in mind of what I observed in the morning: that the King, playing at tennis, had a steeleyard carried to him, and I was told it was to weigh him after he had done playing; and at noon Mr Asnburnham told me that it is only the King's curiosity, which he usually hath, of weighing himself before and after his play, to see how much he loses in weight by playing; and this day he lost 4½lb. (*2 September 1667*)

Street Life

¶ THERE ARE SOME FEATURES of London street life missing from the diary. Pepys never expresses disgust, for instance, at the smells of the open sewers. Perhaps he was too well hardened to them. What is more mysterious is the virtual absence of the poor. Pepys never records being accosted by beggars, and we might reasonably have expected a man of such marked humanity to have shown distress at the sight of the ragged poor who undoubtedly existed, and of the squalid alleyways and rookeries in which they lived. But he never does so. Does he take them for granted like the smells? The rag-picker (25 March 1661) and the occasional robber and prostitute are the only characters to emerge into the diary from London's underworld.

Two features of street life are made clear by implication in these passages – the narrowness of the streets (27 November 1660) and the lack of an efficient police force (22 August 1668).

The beating of the parish bounds (23 May 1661) was a ceremony carried out annually on Ascension Day and was meant to keep the position of the boundary marks clear in the public mind.

Public executions (21 January 1664) were not abolished until 1868. In the case of felonies (as here) they were at this time held in a public place near to the scene of the crime or to the home of the criminal.

Thence home, where I found my wife and maid a-washing. I sat up till the bell-man came by with his bell, just under my window as I was writing of this very line, and cried, "Past one of the clock, and a cold, frosty, windy morning." I then went to bed and left my wife and the maid a-washing still. (*16 January 1660*)

In King Streete, there being a great stop of coaches, there was a falling-out between a drayman and my Lord Chesterfield's coachman, and one of his footmen killed. (*27 November 1660*)

So homewards and took up a boy that had a lanthorn, that was picking up of rags, and got him to light me home. And had great discourse with him how he could get sometimes three or four bushels of rags in a day, and gat 3*d.* a bushel for them. And many other discourses, what and how many ways there are for poor children to get their livings honestly. (*25 March 1661*)

This day was kept a Holyday through the towne. And it pleased me to see the little boys go up and down in procession with their broomestaffes in their hands, as I have myself long ago gone. (*Ascension Day, 23 May 1661*)

Driving through the backside of the Shambles in New-gate Market, my coach plucked down two pieces of beef into the dirt; upon which the butchers stopped the horses, and a great rout of people in the street − crying that he had done him 40*s.* and 5*l* worth of hurt; but going down, I saw that he had done little or none; and so I gave them a shilling for it and they were well contented, and so home. (*15 December 1662*)

So home, and there find my wife come home and seeming to cry; for bringing home in a coach her new ferradin waistcoat, in Cheapside a man asked her whether that was the way to the Tower, and while she was answering him, another on the other side snatched away her bundle out of her lap, and could not be recovered − but ran away with it − which vexes me cruelly, but it cannot be helped. (*28 January 1663*)

So home; and being called by a coachman who had a fare in him, he carried me beyond the Old Exchange and there set down his fare, who would not pay him what was his due because he carried a stranger with him; and so after wrangling, he was fain to be content with 6*d*.; and being vexed, the coachman would not carry me home a great while, but set me down here for the other 6*d*. But with fair words he was willing to it; and so I came home and to my office. (*6 February 1663*)

Up; and after sending my wife to my aunt Wight's to get a place to see Turner hanged, I to the office, where we sat all the morning. And at noon, going to the Change and seeing people flock in that, I enquired and found that Turner was not yet hanged; and so I went among them to Leadenhall Street at the end of Lyme Street, near where the robbery was done, and to St Mary Axe, where he lived; and there I got for a shilling to stand upon the wheel of a cart, in great pain, above an hour before the execution was done – he delaying the time by long discourses and prayers one after another, in hopes of a reprieve; but none came, and at last was flung off the lather in his cloak. A comely-looked man he was, and kept his countenance to the end – I was sorry to see him. It was believed there was at least 12 or 14,000 people in the street. So I home all in a sweat. (*21 January 1664*)

[Sir W. Batten] tells me also how, upon occasion of some prentices being put in the pillory today for beating of their master, or some suchlike thing, in Cheapeside – a company of prentices came and rescued them and pulled down the pillory; and they being set up again, did the like again. So that the Lord Mayor and Maj.-Gen. Browne was fain to come and stay there to keep the peace; and drums all up and down the City was beat to raise the trainbands for to quiet the town. (*26 March 1664*)

Great discourse of the fray yesterday [*St James's Day*] in Moorefields, how the butchers at first did beat the weavers (between whom there hath been ever an old competition for mastery), but at last the weavers rallied and beat them. At first the butchers knock down all the weavers that had green or blue aprons, till they were fain to pull them off and put them in their breeches. At last, the butchers were fain to pull off their sleeves, that they might not be known, and were soundly beaten out of the field, and some deeply wounded and bruised – till at last the weavers went out tryumphing, calling, "A hundred pound for a butcher!" (*26 July 1664*)

I carried [Mrs Pierce and Mrs Knipp] to Fish Street and there treated them with prawns and lobsters; and it beginning to grow dark, we away; but the jest is, our horses would not draw us up the hill, but we were fain to light and stay till the coachman had made them draw down to the bottom of the hill, thereby warming their legs; and then they came up cheerfully enough, and we got up and I carried them home. (*18 April 1666*)

In the evening, out with my wife and my aunt Wight to take the ayre, and happened to have a pleasant race between our hackny-coach and a gentleman's. (*14 May 1666*)

To Westminster, in the way meeting many milkmaids with their garlands upon their pails, dancing with a fiddler before them, and saw pretty Nelly [Gwyn] standing at her lodgings door in Drury Lane in her smock-sleeves and bodice, looking upon one – she seemed a mighty pretty creature. (*1 May 1667*)

Before we got to Islington, between that and Kingsland, there happened an odd adventure; one of our coach-horses fell sick of the staggers, so as he was ready to fall down. The coachman was fain to light and hold him up and cut his tongue to make him bleed, and his tail – the horse continued shakeing every part of him, as if he had been in an ague a good while, and his blood settled in his tongue, and the coachman thought and believed he would presently drop down dead. Then he blew some tobacco in his nose; upon which the horse sneezed, and by and by grows well and draws us the rest of the way as well as ever he did; which was one of the strangest things of a horse I ever observed – but he says it is usual. It is the staggers. (*Lord's Day, 18 August 1667*)

Going through Leadenhall, it being market-day, I did see a woman ketched that had stolen a shoulder of mutton off of a butcher's stall, and carrying it wrapped up in a cloth in a basket. The jade was surprized, and did not deny it; and the woman so silly that took it as to let her go, only taking the meat. (*22 August 1668*)

Travellers' Tales

¶ SEA-CAPTAINS AND MERCHANTS were the source of most
of these stories. The 'slaves' referred to at 8 February 1661
were the prisoners taken by the pirates who governed the
Berber (Barbary) kingdoms of North Africa. They were
released by ransoms raised by public subscription. The
Genoese galley which carried slaves (26 June 1663) had been
captured by the pirates. The myth that swallows hibernated
under water (11 December 1663) was still commonly
believed in the late eighteenth century. The 'East Country'
merchants (11 December 1663) traded with the Baltic;
'Quinsborough' was Königsberg in East Prussia. Henry
Sheeres (27 September 1667) was a member of Sandwich's
staff during his embassy to Spain.

At noon to the Exchange. Here I met with many sea-
commanders; and among others, Capt. Cuttle, and Curtis
and Mootham; and I went to the Fleece tavern to drink
and there we spent till 4 a-clock telling stories of Algier
and the manner of the life of slaves there; and truly, Capt.
Mootham and Mr Dawes (who have been both slaves
there) did make me full acquainted with their condition
there. As how they eat nothing but bread and water. At
their redempcion, they pay so much for the water that
they drink at the public fountaynes during their being
slaves. How they are beat upon the soles of the feet and
bellies at the liberty of their *padron*. How they are all at
night called into their master's bagnard, and there they
lie. How the poorest men do use their slaves best. How
some rogues do live well, if they do endent to bring their
masters in so much a week by their industry or theft; and
then they are put to no other work at all. And theft there
is counted no great crime at all. (*8 February 1661*)

Dined with Capt. Lambert and had much talk of Portugall from whence he is lately come, and he tells me that it is a very poor dirty place – I mean the City and Court of Lisbone. That the King is a very rude and simple fellow; and for reviling of somebody a little while ago and calling of him cuckold, was run into the cods with a sword, and had been killed had he not told them that he was their King. That there is there no glass windows, nor will have any. That the King hath his meat sent up by a dozen of lazy guards, and in pipkins sometimes, to his own table – and sometimes nothing but fruits, and now and then half a hen. And that now the Infanta is becoming our Queene, she is come to have a whole hen or goose to her table – which is not ordinary. (*17 October 1661*)

To Sir Wm Battens, where in discourse I heard the custome of the eleccion of the Dukes of Genoa, who for two years are every day attended in the greatest state and 4 or 500 men always waiting upon him as a King. And when the two years are out and another is chose, a messenger is sent to him, who stands at the bottom of the stairs, and he at the top, and says, *Vostra Illustrissima Serenidad sta finita et puede andar en casa* – "Your serenity is now ended; and now you may be going home;" and so claps on his hat and the old Duke (having by custome sent his goods home before) walks away, it may be but with one man at his heels, and the new one brought immediately in his room, in the greatest state in the world. Another account was told us, how in the Dukedome of Regusa in the Adriatique (a state that is little, but more ancient they say then Venice, and is called the mother of Venice and the Turkes lie round about it) – that they change all the officers of their guard, for fear of conspiracy, every 24 houres, so that nobody knows who shall be captain of the guard tonight; but two men come to a man, and lay hold of him as a prisoner and carry him to the place; and there he hath the keys of the garrison given him, and he presently issues his orders for that night's watch; and so always, from night to night. (*11 January 1662*)

Stokes told us that notwithstanding the country of Gambo [*The Gambia*] is so unhealthy, yet the people of that place live very long, so as the present King there is 150 years old, which they count by raynes because every year it rains continually four months together. He also told us that the kings there have above 100 wives apiece, and offered him the choice of any of his wifes to lie with, and so he did Capt. Holmes. (*16 January 1662*)

This day, among other stories, [Capt. Cocke] told me how despicable a thing it is to be a hangman in Poleland, although it be a place of credit. And that in his time there was some repairs to be made of the gallowes there, which was very fine of stone; but nobody could be got to mend it till the Burgo-Maister or Mayor of the towne, with all the companies of those trades which were necessary to be used about those repairs, did go in their habits, with flags, in solemn procession to the place, and there the Burgo-Maister did give the first blow with the hammer upon the wooden work, and the rest of the Maisters of the Companies upon the works belonging to their trades, that so, workmen might not be ashamed to be imployed upon doing of the gallows-works. (*3 August 1662*)

Calling in at Mr Rawlinsons, he stopped me to dine with him and two East India officers of ships and Howell our turner. With the officers I had good discourse, perticularly of the people at the Cape of Good Hope – of whom they of their own knowledge do tell me these one or two things, *viz.*, that when they come to age, the men do cut off one of the stones of each other, which they hold doth help them to get children the better and to grow fat. That they never sleep lying, but always sitting upon the ground. That their speech is not so articulate as ours, but yet understand one another well. That they paint themselfs all over with the grease the Duch sell them (who have a fort there) and sutt. (*30 December 1662*)

To the Trinity House and there dined – where, among other discourse worth hearing among the old seamen, they tell us that they have ketched often in Greenland in fishing whales, with the iron grapnells that had formerly been struck into their bodies covered over with fat – that they have had eleven hogsheadds of oyle out of the tongue of a whale. (*6 May 1663*)

Sir Wm Rider did tell a story of his own knowledge, that a Genoese gally in Legorne Roade was struck by thunder so as the mast was broke a-pieces and the shackle upon one of the slaves was melted clear off of his leg, without hurting his leg. Sir Wm went on board the vessel and would have contributed toward the release of the slave whom Heaven had thus set free, but he could not compass it and so he was brought to his fetters again. (*26 June 1663*)

Then I sat by Mr Harrington and some East Country merchants; and talking of the country about Quinsborough and thereabouts – he told us himself that for fish, none there, the poorest body, will buy a dead fish; but must be alive, unless it be in winter; and then they told us the manner of putting their nets into the water through holes made in the thicke ice; they will spread a net of half a mile long, and he hath known 130 and 170 barrells of fish taken at one draught. And then the people comes with sledges upon the ice, with snow at the bottome, and lay the fish in and cover them with snow, and so carry them to market. And he hath seen when the said fish have been frozen in the sled, so as that he hath taken a fish and broke a-pieces, so hard it hath been; and yet the same fishes, taken out of the snow and brought into a hot room, will be alive and leap up and down. Swallow often are brought up in their nets out of the mudd from under water, hanging together to some twigg or other, dead in ropes; and brought to the fire, will come to life. Fowl killed in December (Ald. Barker said) he did buy; and putting into the box under his sled, did forget to take them out to eate till Aprill next, and they then were found there and were, through the frost, as sweet and fresh and eat as well as at first killed. (*11 December 1663*)

To the coffee-house, where I heard Lieut.-Coll. Baron tell very good stories of his travels over the high hills in Asia above the cloudes. How clear the heaven is above them. How thick, like a mist, the way is through the cloud, that wets like a sponge one's clothes. The ground above the clouds all dry and parched, nothing in the world growing, it being only a dry earth. Yet not so hot above as below the clouds. The stars at night most delicate bright and a fine clear blue sky. But cannot see the earth at any time through the clouds, but the clouds look like a world below you. (*1 February 1664*)

In Moorefields met Mr Pargiter, and then walked into the fields as far almost as Sir G. Whitmores, all the way talking of Russia – which he says is a sad place; and though Mosco is a very great city, yet it is, from the distance between house and house, and few people compared with this – and poor sorry houses, the Emperor himself living in a wooden house – his exercise only flying a hawke at pigeons and carrying pigeons ten or twelve mile off and then laying wagers which pigeon shall come soonest home to her house. All the winter within doors, some few playing at chesse but most drinking their time away. Women live very slavishly there. And it seems, in the Emperor's Court no room hath above two or three windows, and those the greatest not a yard wide or high – for warmth in winter time. And that the general cure for all diseases there is their sweating-houses – or people that are poor, they get into their ovens, being heated, and there lie. Little learning among things of any sort – not a man that speaks Latin, unless the Secretary of State by chance. (*16 September 1664*)

With Capt. Erwin, discoursing about the East Indys, where he hath often been. And among other things, he tells me how the King of Syam seldom goes out without 30 or 40,000 people with him, and not a word spoke nor a hum or cough in the whole company to be heard. He tells me the punishment frequently there for malefactors is cutting off the crowne of their head, which they do very dexterously, leaving their brains bare, which kills them presently. He told me, what I remember he hath once done heretofore – that everybody is to lie flat down at the coming by of the King, and nobody to look upon him, upon pain of death. And that he and his fellows, being strangers, were invited to see the sport of taking of a wild eliphant. And they did only kneel and look toward the King. Their druggerman did desire them to fall down, for otherwise he should suffer for their contempt of the King. The sport being ended, a messenger comes from the King, which the druggerman thought had been to have taken away his life. But it was to enquire how the strangers liked the sport. The druggerman answered that they did cry it up to be the best that ever they saw, and that they never heard of any prince so great in everything as this King. The messenger being gone back, Erwin and his company asked their druggerman what he had said, which he told them. "But why," say they, "would you say that without our leave, it being not true?" "It is no matter for that," says he, "I must have said it, or have been hanged, for our King doth not live by meat nor drink, but by having great lyes told him." (*17 August 1666*)

It was pretty to hear [Mr Progers] tell me of his own accord, as a matter of no shame, that in Spain he had a pretty woman his mistress; whom, when money grew scarce with him, he was forced to leave, and afterward heard how she and her husband lived well, she being kept by an old fryer who used her as his whore. But this, says he, is better then as our ministers do, who have wives that lay up their estates and do no good nor relieve any poor;

no, not our greatest prelates – and I think he is in the right
for my part. (*17 February 1667*)

[Lord Arlington] talked much of the plain habit of the
Spaniards; how the King and lords themselfs wear but a
cloak of Colchester bayze, and the ladies mantles, in cold
weather, of white flannel. And that the endeavours
frequently of setting up the manufacture of making these
stuffs there have only been prevented by the Inquisition –
the English and Duchmen that have been sent for to work
being taken with a Psalm-book or Testament, and so
clapped up and the house pulled down by the Inquisitors,
and the greatest lord in Spain dare not say a word against
it – if the word "Inquisition" be but mentioned. (*Lord's
Day, 24 February 1667*)

Sheres dined with me; and we had a great deal of pretty
discourse of the ceremoniousness of the Spaniards –
whose ceremonies are so many and so known, that he
tells me, upon all occasions of joy or sorrow in a
grandee's family, my Lord Embassador is fain to send one
with an *en hora buena* (if it be upon a marriage or birth of
a child) or a *pesa me*, if it be upon the death of a child or
so. And these ceremonies are so set, and the words of the
compliment, that he hath been sent from my Lord when
he hath done no more then send in word to the grandee
that one was there from the Embassador; and he knowing
what was his errand, that hath been enough, and he hath
never spoken with him. Nay, several grandees, having
been to marry a daughter, have wrote letters to my Lord
to give him notice and out of the greatness of his wisdom
to desire his advice, though people he never saw; and then
my Lord, he answers by commending the greatness of his

[227]

discretion in making so good an alliance, and so ends. He says that it is so far from dishonour to a man to give private revenge for an affront, that the contrary is a disgrace; they holding that he that receives an affront is not fit to appear in the sight of the world till he hath revenged himself; and therefore, that a gentleman there that receives an affront oftentimes never appears again in the world till he hath by some private way or other revenged himself; and that on this account, several have fallowed their enemy privately to the Indys, thence to Italy, thence to France and back again, watching for an opportunity to be revenged. He says my Lord was fain to keep a letter from the Duke of York to the Queen of Spain a great while in his hands before he could think fit to deliver it, till he had learnt whether the Queen would receive it, it being directed to his "Cosen." He says that many ladies in Spain, after they are found to be with child, do never stir out of their beds or chambers till they are brought to bed – so ceremonious they are in that point also. He tells of their wooing by serenades at the window, and that their friends do alway make the match; but yet that they have opportunities to meet at masse at church, and there they make love. That the Court there hath no dancings, nor visits at night to see the King or Queene, but is always just like a cloyster, nobody stirring in it. (*27 September 1667*)

IV

PEPYS THE
STORY-TELLER

The Bashful Lovers

¶ IN THE SUMMER OF 1665 Pepys, as Sandwich's man of business, arranged the terms of a match between Lady Jemima Mountagu, Sandwich's eldest daughter, and Philip, eldest son of Sir George Carteret, Treasurer of the Navy. He was glad of the chance of improving his standing with both. His opposite number, who acted for Carteret, was Dr Timothy Clarke, physician to the Court and also to the Commission for Sick and Wounded Seamen. Carteret (because of the Plague) was living mainly at this time in the Navy Treasurer's official lodgings at Deptford. 'Dagenhams', near the modern Dagenham, was the country house of Lady Wright, sister of Lady Sandwich and daughter of Lord Crew. Both the young people, as it happened, suffered from forms of physical disablement – Philip from lameness and Lady Jemima from a malformation of the neck for which she had once worn a surgical collar. Hence perhaps the shyness which made them such tongue-tied lovers. After their marraige, they settled down to country life in Bedfordshire, Philip occupying himself with painting and mending watches. Viscount Carteret, who succeeded Walpole as George II's Prime Minister, was their grandson.

23 JUNE. My Lord did begin to tell me how much he was concerned to dispose of his children, and would have my advice and help; and propounded to match my Lady Jemimah to Sir G. Careterets eldest son – which I approved of, and did undertake the speaking with him about it as from myself; which my Lord liked. I did [agree] that I should first, by another hand, break my intentions to Sir G. Carteret. I pitched upon Dr Clerke, which my Lord liked – and so I endeavoured, but in vain, to find him out tonight.

24 JUNE. *Midsummer Day.* Up very betimes, by 6, and at Dr Clerkes at Westminster by 7 of the clock, having overnight by a note acquainted him with my intention of

coming. And there I, in the best manner I could, broke my errand about [the] match – which he (as I knew he would) took with great content; and we both agreed that my Lord and [Sir George], being both men relating to the sea under a kind aspect of His Majesty – already good friends, and both virtuous and good families, their allyance might be of good use to us. And he did undertake to find out Sir George this morning, and put the business in execution. Thence I to Sir G. Carteret at his chamber [*in Whitehall*], and in the best manner I could, and most obligingly, moved that business; he received it with great respect and content and thanks to me, and promised that he would do what he could possibly for his son, to render him fit for my Lord's daughter. And showed great kindness to me, and sense of my kindness to him herein.

25 JUNE. *Lord's Day*. Back through bridge to Whitehall – where after I had again visited Sir G. Carteret and received his (and now his Lady's) full content in my proposal, I went to my Lord Sandwich; and having told him how Sir G. Carteret received it, he did direct me to return to Sir G. Carteret and give him thanks for his kind reception of this offer, and that he would the next day be willing to enter discourse with him about that business. Which message I did presently do, and so left the business, with great joy to both sides. My Lord, I perceive, entends to give 5000*l* with her, and expects about 800*l* per annum joynture.

28 JUNE. This morning I met with Sir G. Carteret, who tells me how all things proceed between my Lord Sandwich and himself to full content, and both sides depend upon having the match finished presently. And

professed great kindness to me, and said that now we were something akinned. I am mightily, both with respect to myself and much more of my Lord's family, glad of this alliance.

9 JULY, *Lord's Day*. About 10 a-clock by water to Sir G. Carteret [*at Deptford*]. We are received with most extraordinary kindness by my Lady Carteret and her children, and dined most nobly. After dinner I took occasion to have much discourse with Mr Ph. Carteret, and find him a very modest man, and I think verily of mighty good nature – and pretty understanding. Down to my Lady Carteret, where mighty merry and great pleasantness between my Lady Sandwich and the young ladies and me; and all of us mighty merry, there never having been in the whole world, sure, a greater business of general content then this match proposed between Mr Carter[e]t and my Lady Jemimah. But withal, it is mighty pretty to think how my poor Lady Sandwich, between her and me, is doubtful whether her daughter will like of it or no, and how troubled she is for fear of it; which I do not fear at all and desire her not to do it. But her fear is the most discreet and pretty that ever I did see.

14 JULY. I by water to Sir G. Carteret, and there find my Lady Sandwich and her buying things for my Lady Jem's wedding. And my Lady Jem is beyond expectation come to Dagenhams, where Mr Carteret is to go to visit her tomorrow; and my proposal of waiting on him, he being to go alone to all persons strangers to him, was well accepted and so I go with him. But Lord, to see how kind my Lady Carteret is to her – sends her most rich jewells, and provides bedding and things of all sorts most richly for her – which makes my Lady and me out of our wits

almost, to see the kindness she treats us all with, as if they would buy the young lady.

15 JULY. Mr Carteret and I to the ferry-place at Greenwich and there stayed an hour, after crossing the water to and again to get our coach and horses over, and by and by set out and so toward Dagenham. But Lord, what silly discourse we had by the way as to matter of love-matters, he being the most awkerd man I ever I met withal in my life as to that business. Thither we came by time it begin to be dark, and were kindly received by my Lady Wright and my Lord Crew; and to discourse they went, my Lord discoursing with him, asking of him questions of travell, which he answered well enough in a few words. But nothing to the lady from him at all. To supper, and after supper to talk again, he yet taking no notice of the lady. My Lord would have had me have consented to leaving the young people together tonight to begin their amours, his staying being but to be little. But I advised against it, lest the lady might be too much surprized. So they led him up to his chamber, where I stayed a little to know how he liked the lady; which he told me he did mightily, but Lord, in the dullest insipid manner that ever lover did. So I bid him good-night, and down to prayers with my Lord Crew's family. And after prayers, my Lord and Lady Wright and I to consult what to do; and it was agreed at last to have them go to church together as the family used to do, though his lameness was a great objection against it; but at last my Lady Jem sent me word by my Lady Wright that it would be better to do just as they used to do before his coming, and therefore she desired to go to church – which was yielded then to.

16 JULY. *Lord's Day.* I up, having lain with Mr Moore in the chaplins chamber. And having trimmed myself, down to Mr Carteret; and he being ready, we down and walked in the gallery an hour or two, it being a most noble and pretty house that ever for the bigness I saw. Here I taught him what to do; to take the lady alway by the hand to lead her; and telling him that I would find opportunity to leave them two together, he should make these and these compliments, and also take a time to do the like to my Lord Crew and Lady Wright. After I had instructed him, which he thanked me for, owning that he needed my teaching him, my Lord Crew came down and family, the young lady among the rest; and so by coaches to church, four mile off where a pretty good sermon – and a declaration of penitence of a man that had undergone the Church censure for his wicked life. Thence back again by coach – Mr Carteret having not had the confidence to take his lady once by the hand, coming or going; which I told him of when we came home, and he will hereafter do it. So to dinner. My Lord excellent discourse. Then to walk in the gallery and to sit down. By and by my Lady Wright and I go out (and then my Lord Crew, he not by design); and lastly my Lady Crew came out and left the young people together. And a little pretty daughter of my Lady Wright's most innocently came out afterward, and shut the door to, as if she had done it, poor child, by inspiration – which made us without have good sport to laugh at. They together an hour; and by and by church time, whither he led her into the coach and into the church; and so at church all the afternoon. Several handsome ladies at church – but it was most extraordinary hot that ever I knew it. So home again and to walk in the gardens, where we left the

young couple a second time; and my Lady Wright and I to walk together, who to my trouble tells me that my Lady Jem must have something done to her body by Scott before she can be married, and therefore care must be had to send him – also, that some more new clothes must of necessity be made her, which, and other things, I took care of. After Mr Carteret carried to his chamber, we to prayers again and then to bed.

17 JULY. Up, all of us, and to billiards – my Lady Wright, Mr Carter[e]t, myself and everybody. By and by the young couple left together. Anon to dinner, and after dinner Mr Carteret took my advice about giving to the servants, and I led him to give 10*l* among them, which he did by leaving it to the chief manservant, Mr Medows, to do for him. Before we went, I took my Lady Jem apart and would know how she liked this gentleman and whether she was under any difficulty concerning him. She blushed and hid her face awhile, but at last I forced her to tell me; she answered that she could readily obey what her father and mother had done – which was all she could say or I expect. In our way Mr Carteret did give me mighty thanks for my care and pains for him, and is mightily pleased – though the truth is, my Lady Jem hath carried herself with mighty discretion and gravity, not being forward at all in any degree but mighty serious in her answers to him, as by what he says and I observed, I collect. To London to my office and there took letters from the office, where all well; and so to the Bridge, and there he and I took boat and to Deptford, where mighty welcome, and brought the good news of all being pleased to them. Mighty mirth at my giving them an account of all; but the young man could not be got to say one word

before me or my Lady Sandwich of his adventures; but by what he afterward related to his father and mother and sisters, he gives an account that pleases them mightily. Here Sir G. Carteret would have me lie all night, which I did most nobly, better then ever I did in my life – Sir G. Carteret being mighty kind to me, leading me to my chamber; and all their care now is to have the business ended; and they have reason, because the sickness puts all out of order and they cannot safely stay where they are.

24 JULY. By appointment to Deptford to Sir G. Carteret between 6 and 7 a-clock, where I found him and my Lady almost ready; and by and by went over to the Ferry and took coach and six horses nobly for Dagenhams, himself and Lady and their little daughter Louisonne and myself in the coach – where when we came, we were bravely entertained and spent the day most pleasantly with the young ladies, and I so merry as never more. Here with great content all the day, as I think I ever passed a day in my life, because of the contentfulness of our errand – and the nobleness of the company and our manner of going. But I find Mr Carteret yet as backward almost in his caresses as he was the first day. At night, about 7 a-clock, took coach again; but Lord, to see in what a pleasant humour Sir G. Carteret hath been, both coming and going; so light, so fond, so merry, so boyish (so much content he takes in this business), it is one of the greatest wonders I ever saw in my mind. But once, in serious discourse, he did say that if he knew his son to be a debauch, as many and most are nowadays about the Court, he would tell it, and my Lady Jem should not have him.

3 1 JULY. Up, and very betimes, by 6 a-clock, at Deptford; and there find Sir G. Carteret and my Lady ready to
go – I being in my new coloured-silk suit and coat,
trimmed with gold buttons and gold broad lace round
my hands, very rich and fine. By water to the Ferry,
where, when we came, no coach there – and tide of ebb
so far spent as the horse-boat could not get off on the
other side the river to bring away the coach. So we were
fain to stay there in the unlucky Isle of Doggs – in a chill
place, the morning cool and wind fresh, above two if not
three hours, to our great discontent. Yet being upon a
pleasant errand, and seeing that could not be helped, we
did bear it very patiently; and it was worth my observing, I thought as ever anything, to see how upon these
two scores, Sir G. Carteret, the most passionate man in
the world and that was in greatest haste to be gone, did
bear with it, and very pleasant all the while, at least not
troubled much so as to fret and storm at it. We fearing
the canonicall hour would be past before we got thither,
did with a great deal of unwillingness send away the
licence and wedding-ring. So that when we came,
though we drove hard with six horses, yet we found
them gone from home; and going toward the church,
met them coming from church – which troubled us. But
however, that trouble was soon over – hearing it was well
done. The young lady mighty sad, which troubled me;
but yet I think it was only her gravity, in a little greater
degree then usual. All saluted her, but I did not till my
Lady Sandwich did ask me whether I had not saluted her
or no. So to dinner, and very merry we were; but yet in
such a sober way as never almost any wedding was in so
great families – but it was much better. After dinner,
company divided, some to cards – others to talk. At night

to supper, and so to talk and, which methought was the most extraordinary thing, all of us to prayers as usual, and the young bride and bridegroom too. And so after prayers, soberly to bed; only, I got into the bridegroom's chamber while he undressed himself, and there was very merry – till he was called to the bride's chamber and into bed they went. I kissed the bride in bed, and so the curtaines drawne with the greatest gravity that could be, and so good-night.

Buried Gold

¶ IN JUNE 1667 LONDON WAS SHOCKED by the news of the Dutch raid on the Medway. Pepys feared that an angry mob would attack the Navy Office. In his alarm he sent £2,400 of his life savings in gold pieces to be buried in the garden of his house at Brampton. Two attempts have been made in modern times to recover the twenty or thirty pieces which he says he never found. The second attempt was made with the help of a metal detector. Both failed.

13 JUNE. No sooner up but hear the sad news confirmed, of the *Royall Charles* being taken by [the Dutch] and that another fleet is come up into the Hope; which put me into such fear that I presently resolved of my father's and wife's going into the country; and at two hours' warning they did go by the coach this day – with about 1300*l* in gold in their night-bag. Pray God give them good passage and good care to hide it when they come home, but my heart is full of fear. They gone, I continued in frights and fear what to do with the rest. W. Hewer hath been at the banquiers and hath got 500*l* out of Backe-well's hands of his own money; but they are so called upon that they will be all broke, hundreds coming to them for money – and their answer is, "It is payable at twenty days; when the days are out, we will pay you;" and those that are not so, they make tell over their money, and make their bags false on purpose to give cause to retell it and so spend time. I cannot have my 200 pieces of gold again for silver, all being bought up last night that were to be had – and sold for 24 and 25*s*. a-piece. So I must keep the silver by me, which sometimes I think to fling into the house of office – and then again, know not how I shall come by it if we be made to leave the office. I did about noon resolve to send Mr Gibson

[240]

away after my wife with another 1000 pieces. I also sent (my mind being in pain) Saunders after my wife and father, to overtake them at their night's lodging to see how matters go with them. I have also made a girdle, by which with some trouble I do carry about me 300*l* in gold about my body, that I may not be without something in case I should be surprized; for I think, in any nation but ours, people that appear (for we are not endeed so) so faulty as we would have their throats cut.

[*In the following October he sets off to recover his gold.*]

7 OCTOBER. Up betimes, and did do several things towards the settling all matters, both of house and office, in order for my journey this day; and did leave my chief care, and the key of my closet, with Mr Hater, with direction what papers to secure in case of fire or other accident; and so about 9 a-clock, I and my wife and Willett set out in a coach I have hired, with four horses, and W. Hewer and Murford rode by us on horseback; and so, my wife and she in their morning gowns, very handsome and pretty and to my great liking, we set out; and so out at Allgate and so to the Green Man and so on to Enfield and before night did come to Bishop Stafford, where to the Raynedeere, where Mrs Aynsworth (who lived heretofore at Cambrige and whom I knew better then they think for, doth live – it was the woman that, among other things, was great with my Cosen Barmston of Cottenham, and did use to sing to him and did teach me *Full forty times over*, a very lewd song) – a woman they are very well acquainted with, and is here what she was at Cambrige, and all the goodfellows of the country come hither. To supper and so to bed, my wife and I in one bed and the girl in another in the same room. And lay very

well, but there was so much tearing company in the house, that we could not see my landlady, so I had no opportunity of renewing my old acquaintance with her. But here we slept very well.

8 OCTOBER. Up pretty betimes, and broke our fast, and then took coach and away to Cambrige, it being foul, rainy weather; and there did take up at the Rose. Here we had a good chamber and bespoke a good supper; and then I took my wife and W. Hewer and Willett (it holding up a little) and showed them Trinity College and St Johns Library, and went to King's College Chapel to see the outside of it only, and so to our inne; and with much pleasure did this, they walking in their pretty morning gowns, very handsome, and I proud to find myself in condition to do this; and so home to our lodging, and there by and by to supper with much good sport, talking with the drawers concerning matters of the town and persons whom I remember; and so after supper to cards and then to bed, lying, I in one bed and my wife and girl in another in the same room; and very merry talking together and mightily pleased both of us with the girl.

9 OCTOBER. Up, and got ready and eat our breakfast and then took coach; and the poor, as they did yesterday, did stand at the coach to have something given them, as they do to all great persons, and I did give them something; and the town musique did also come and play; but Lord, what sad music they made — however, I was pleased with them, being all of us in very good humour; and so set forth and through the town, and observed at our college of Magdalen the posts new-painted, and understand that the Vice-Chancellor is there this year. And so away for Huntington, mightily pleased all along the road to

remember old stories; and came to Brampton at about noon and there find my father and sister and brother all well.

10 OCTOBER. My father and I with a dark lantern, it being now night, into the guarden with my wife and there went about our great work to dig up my gold. But Lord, what a tosse I was for some time in, that they could not justly tell where it was, that I begun heartily to sweat and be angry that they should not agree better upon the place, and at last to fear that it was gone; but by and by, poking with a spit, we found it, and then begun with a spudd to lift up the ground; but good God, to see how sillily they did it, not half a foot under ground and in the sight of the world from a hundred places if anybody by accident were near-hand, and within sight of a neighbour's window and their hearing also, being close by; only, my father says that he saw them all gone to church before he begun the work when he laid the money, but that doth not excuse it to me; but I was out of my wits almost, and the more from that upon my lifting up the earth with the spud, I did discern that I scattered the pieces of gold round about the ground among the grass and loose earth; and taking up the iron head-pieces wherein they were put, I perceive the earth was got among the gold and wet, so that the bags were all rotten, all the notes, that I could not tell what in the world to say to it, not knowing how to judge what was wanting or what had been lost by Gibson in his coming down; which, all put together, did make me mad; and at last was forced to take up the head-pieces, dirt and all, and as many of the scattered pieces as I could with the dirt discern by the candlelight, and carry them up into my

[243]

brother's chamber and there lock them up till I had eat a little supper. And then all people going to bed, W. Hewer and I did all alone, with several pales of water and basins, at last wash the dirt off of the pieces and parted the pieces and the dirt, and then begun to tell; and by a note which I had of the value of the whole (in my pocket) do find that there was short above 100 pieces, which did make me mad; and considering that the neighbour's house was so near, that we could not suppose we could speak one to another in the garden at the place where the gold lay (especially by my father being deaf) but they must know what we had been doing on, I feared that they might in the night come and gather some pieces and prevent us the next morning; so W. Hewer and I out again about midnight (for it was now grown so late) and there by candlelight did make shift to gather 45 pieces more – and so in and to cleanse them, and by this time it was past 2 in the morning; and so to bed, with my mind pretty quiet to think that I have recovered so many. I lay in the trundle-bed, the girl being gone to bed to my wife, in some disquiet all night, telling of the clock till it was daylight.

11 OCTOBER. And then rose and called W. Hewer, and he and I, with pails and a sive, did lock ourselfs into the garden and there gather all the earth about the place into pails, and then sive those pails in one of the summer-houses (just as they do for dyamonds in other parts of the world); and there to our great content did with much trouble by 9 a-clock, and by that time we emptied several pails and could not find one, we did make the last night's 45 up [to] 79; so that we are come to about 20 or 30 of what I think the true number should be, and perhaps

within less; and of them I may reasonably think that Mr Gibson might lose some, so that I am pretty well satisfied that my loss is not great and do bless God that it is so well; and do leave my father to make a second examination of the dirt – which he promises he will do; and poor man, is mightily troubled for this accident. But I declared myself very well satisfied, and so endeed I am and my mind at rest in it, it being but an accident which is unusual; and so gives me some kind of content to remember how painful it is sometimes to keep money, as well as to get it, and how doubtful I was how to keep it all night and how to secure it to London. And so got all my gold put up in bags; and so having the last night wrote to my Lady Sandwich to lend me John Bowles to go along with me my journy, not telling her the reason, but it was only to secure my gold, we to breakfast; and then about 10 a-clock took coach, my wife and I, and Willett and W. Hewer, and Murford and Bowles, and my brother John on horseback; and with these four I thought myself pretty safe. But before we went out, the Huntington music came to me and played, and it was better then that of Cambridge. Here I took leave of my father, and did give my sister 20s. She cried at my going; but whether it was at her unwillingness for my going or any unkindness of my wife's or no, I know not; but God forgive me, I take her to be so cunning and ill-natured that I have no great love for her; but only, is my sister and must be provided for. My gold, I put into a basket and set under one of the seats; and so my work every quarter of an hour was to look to see whether all was well, and did ride in great fear all the day; but it was a pleasant day and good company, and I mightily contented. Mr Sheply saw me beyond St Neotts and there parted, and we straight to Stevenage, through Baldock lanes, which are already very bad. And at Stevenage we came well before night, and all safe; and there with great care I got the gold up to the chamber, my wife carrying one bag and the girl another and W. Hewer the rest in the basket, and set it all under a bed in our chamber; and then sat down to talk and were very pleasant, satisfying myself, among [other] things from Jo. Bowles, in some terms of hunting and about deere, bucks, and does; and so anon to supper and very merry we were and a good supper; and after supper to bed. Brecocke alive still, and the best Host I know almost.

12 OCTOBER. Up, and eat our breakfast and set out about 9 a-clock; and so to Barnett, where we stayed and baited (the weather very good all day and yesterday) and by 5 a-clock got home, where I find all well; and did bring my gold, to my heart's content, very safe home.

The Dancing Master

¶ IN THE SPRING OF 1663 Pepys paid for two courses of
dancing lessons for Elizabeth, her teacher being Mr Pembleton, a dancing master who lived close by in St Olave's
parish. Rather unwillingly Pepys agreed to the further
expense of taking lessons himself. (It was two years since he
had danced for the first time.) He soon regretted his
liberality. He was racked by jealousy, and the fact that he
was himself frequently unfaithful only made him the more
fearful of being cuckolded in his turn.

Mary Ashwell, who took part in the dancing, was
Elizabeth's companion.

25 APRIL. After supper merrily practising to dance,
which my wife hath begun to learn this day of Mr
Pembleton; but I fear will hardly do any great good at it,
because she is conceited that she doth well already,
though I think no such thing.

28 APRIL. Stepped up to see my wife and her dancing-
maister and I think after all she will do pretty well at it.

4 MAY. The dancing maister came; whom standing by
seeing him instructing my wife, when he had done with
her he would needs have me try the steps of a *coranto*; and
what with his desire and my wife's importunity, I did
begin, and then was obliged to give him entry-money,
10s – and am become his scholler. The truth is, I think it is
a thing very useful for any gentleman and sometimes I
may have occasion of using it; and though it cost me,
which I am heartily sorry it should, besides that I must by
my oath give half as much more to the poor, yet I am
resolved to get it up some other way; and then it will not
be above a month or two in a year. So though it be
against my stomach, yet I will try it a little while; if I see it
comes to any great inconvenience or charge, I will fling it

off. After I had begun with the steps of half a *coranto*, which I think I shall learn well enough, he went away and we to dinner.

6 MAY. While at supper comes Mr Pembleton; and after supper, we up to our dancing room and there danced three or four country dances, and after that, a practice of my *coranto* I begun with him the other day; and I begin to think that I shall be able to do something at it in time. Late and merry at it; and so, weary to bed.

15 MAY. Home – where I find it almost night and my wife and the dancing maister alone above, not dancing but walking. Now, so deadly full of jealousy I am, that my heart and head did so cast about and fret, that I could not do any business possibly, but went out to my office; and anon late home again, and ready to chide at everything; and then suddenly to bed and could hardly sleep, yet durst not say anything; but was forced to say that I had bad news from the Duke concerning Tom Hater, as an excuse to my wife – who by my folly hath too much opportunity given her with that man; who is a pretty neat black man, but married. But it is a deadly folly and plague that I bring upon myself to be so jealous; and by giving myself such an occasion, more then my wife desired, of giving her another month's dancing – which however shall be ended as soon as I can possibly. But I am ashamed to think what a course I did take by lying to see whether my wife did wear drawers today as she used to do, and other things to raise my suspicion of her; but I found no true cause of doing it.

16 MAY. Up, with my mind disturbed and with my last night's doubts upon me. For which I deserve to be

beaten, if not really served as I am fearful of being; especially since, God knows, that I do not find honesty enough in my own mind but that upon a small temptation I could be false to her, and therefore ought not to expect more justice from her – but God pardon both my sin and my folly herein. After dinner comes Pembleton again; and I being out of humour, would not see him, pretending business; but Lord, with what jealousy did I walk up and down my chamber, listening to hear whether they danced or no or what they did; notwithstanding I afterwards knew, and did then believe that Ashwell was with them. So to my office awhile; and my jealousy still reigning, I went in and, not out of any pleasure but from that only reason, did go up to them to practise; and did make an end of *La Duchesse*, which I think [I] should with a little pains do very well. So broke up and saw him gone.

19 MAY. By water (taking Pembleton with us) over the water to the Halfway House, where we played at ninepins; and there my damned jealousy took fire, he and my wife being of a side and I seeing of him taking her by the hand in play; though I now believe he did only in passing and sport.

21 MAY. I home and danced with Pembleton and then the barber trimmed me; and so to dinner – my wife and I having high words about her dancing, to that degree that I did retire and make a vowe to myself, not to oppose her or say anything to dispraise or correct her therein as long as her month lasts, in pain of 2s-6d for every time; which if God please, I will observe, for this roguish business hath brought us more disquiet then anything hath happened a great while. After dinner to my office, where late, and

then home; and Pembleton being there again, we fell to dance a country dance or two, and so to supper and bed. But being at supper, my wife did say something that caused me to oppose her in; she used the word "Devil," which vexed me; and among other things, I said I would not have her to use that word, upon which she took me up most scornefully; which before Ashwell and the rest of the world, I know not nowadays how to check as I would heretofore, for less then that would have made me strike her. So that I fear, without great discretion, I shall go near to lose too my command over her; and nothing doth it more then giving her this occasion of dancing and other pleasure, whereby her mind is taken up from her business and finds other sweets besides pleasing of me. But if this month of her dancing were but out, I shall hope with a little pains to bring her to her old wont.

24 MAY, *Lord's Day*. To church. Over against our gallery I espied Pembleton and saw him leer upon my wife all the sermon, I taking no notice of him, and my wife upon him; and I observed she made a curtsey to him at coming out, without taking notice to me at all of it; which, with the consideration of her being desirous these two last Lord's Days to go to church both forenoon and afternoon, doth really make me suspect something more than ordinary, though I am loath to think the worst; but yet it put and doth still keep me at a great loss in my mind, and makes me curse the time that I consented to her dancing, and more, my continuing it a second month, which was more then she desired, even after I had seen too much of her carriage with him. But I must have patience and get her into the country, or at least to make an end of her learning to dance as soon as I can.

26 MAY. Up and to my office a while and then home,
where I find Pembleton; and by many circumstances I am
led to conclude that there is something more then
ordinary between my wife and him; which doth so
trouble me that I know not, at this very minute that I
now write this almost, what either I write or am doing
nor how to carry myself to my wife in it, being unwilling
to speak of it to her for making of any breach and other
inconveniences, nor let it pass for fear of her continuing
to offend me and the matter grow worse thereby. So that
I am grieved at the very heart, but I am very unwise in
being so. Nothing could get the business out of my head,
I fearing that this afternoon, by my wife's sending
every[one] abroad and knowing that I must be at the
office, she hath appointed him to come. This is my
devilish jealousy; which I pray God may be false, but it
makes a very hell in my mind; which the God of heaven
remove, or I shall be very unhappy. [*After dinner*] to the
office, where we sat a while. By and by, my mind being
in great trouble, I went home to see how things were; and
there I find as I doubted, Mr Pembleton with my wife
and nobody else in the house, which made me almost
mad. So in great trouble and doubt to the office; and Mr
Coventry nor Sir G. Carteret being there, I made a quick
end of our business and desired leave to be gone, pretending to go to the Temple, but it was home; and so up to
my chamber and, as I think, if they had any intentions of
hurt, I did prevent doing anything at that time; but I
continued in my chamber vexed and angry till he went
away, pretending aloud, that I might hear, that he could
not stay, and Mrs Ashwell not being within they would
not dance. And Lord, to see how my jealousy wrought so
far, that I went saftly up to see whether any of the beds

were out of order or no, which I found not; but that did
not content me, but I stayed all the evening walking, and
though anon my wife came up to me and would have
spoke of business to me, yet I construed it to be but
impudence; and though my heart was full, yet I did say
nothing, being in a great doubt what to do. So at night
suffered them to go all to bed, and late put myself to bed
in great discontent, and so to sleep.

27 MAY. So I waked by 3 a-clock, my mind being
troubled; and so took occasion by making water to wake
my wife, and after having lain till past 4 a-clock, seemed
going to rise, though I did it only to see what she would
do; and so going out of the bed, she took hold of me and
would know what ayled me; and after many kind and
some cross words, I begun to tax her discretion in
yesterday's business, but she quickly told me my owne,
knowing well enough that it was my old disease of
jealousy; which I disowned, but to no purpose. After an
hour's discourse, sometimes high and sometimes kind, I
find very good reason to think that her freedom with him
was very great and more then was convenient, but with
no evil intent. And so after a while I caressed her and
parted seeming friends, but she crying and in a great
discontent. So I up and by water to the Temple, and
thence with Comissioner Pett to St James's, where an
hour with Mr Coventree, and so home – where I find my
wife in a musty humour, and tells me before Ashwell that
Pembleton had been there and she would not have him
come in unless I was there, which I was ashamed of; but
however, I had rather it should be so then the other way.
So to my office to put things in order there. And by and
by comes Pembleton and word is brought me from my

wife thereof, that I might come home; so I sent word that I would have her go dance, and I would come presently. So being at a great loss whether I should appear to Pembleton or no, and which would most proclaim my jealousy to him, I at last resolved to go home; and took Tom Hater with me and stayed a good while in my chamber. After much discourse I sent him away and then went up; and there we danced country dances and single, my wife and I, and my wife paid him off for this month also, and so he is cleared.

3 JUNE. In the evening to the office and did some business. Then home and, God forgive me, did from my wife's unwillingness to tell me whither she had sent the boy, presently suspect that he was gone to Pembleton's, and from that occasion grew so discontented that I could hardly speak or sleep all night.

4 JUNE. Up betimes, and I did so watch to see my wife put on drawers, which poor soul she did, and yet I could not get off my suspicion, she having a mind to go into Fanchurch Street before she went out for good and all with me; which I must needs construe to be to meet Pembleton, when she afterward told me it was to buy a fan that she had not a mind that I should know of, and I believe it is so. Especially, I did by a wile get out of my boy that he did not yesterday go to Pembleton's or thereabouts, but only was sent at that time for some starch; and I did see him bring home some – and yet all this cannot make my mind quiet.

18 OCTOBER. *Lord's Day.* My wife, in her best gowne and new poynt, to church with me. I was troubled to see Pembleton there, but I thought it prudence to take notice

myself first of it and show my wife him; and so by little and little considering that it mattered not much his being there, I grew less concerned; and so mattered it not much, and the less when anon my wife showed me his wife, a pretty little woman and well-dressed, with a good jewell at her breast.

Deb Willet

¶ PEPYS'S LOVE AFFAIR with Deb Willet, Elizabeth's young companion, is the only serious one recorded in the diary, and the only one which he failed to conceal from his wife. Elizabeth, on making the discovery, was deeply wounded. She vented her fury on her husband in a succession of jealous scenes. Her threat to become a Roman Catholic (25 October 1668) was made plausible by the fact that when she was a girl, before Pepys had known her, she had spent some time in a Paris convent school. But the threat was never carried out – she died an Anglican just a year after these events, in November 1669.

Will Hewer, who acts as go-between in the quarrel, was Pepys's confidential clerk, and became his lifelong friend. Deb's later history is unknown.

1667

27 SEPTEMBER. While I was busy at the office, my wife sends for me to come home, and what was it but to see the pretty girl which she is taking to wait upon her; and though she seems not altogether so great a beauty as she had before told me, yet endeed she is mighty pretty; and so pretty, that I find I shall be too much pleased with it, and therefore could be contented as to my judgment, though not to my passion, that she might not come, lest I may be found too much minding her, to the discontent of my wife. She is to come next week. She seems by her discourse to be grave beyond her bigness and age, and exceeding well-bred as to her deportment, having been a scholar in a school at Bow these seven or eight year. To the office again, my [mind] running on this pretty girl.

1 OCTOBER. Home by coach; and there to sing and sup with my wife and look upon our pretty girl, and so to bed.

22 DECEMBER. *Lord's Day*. Up, and then to dress myself and down to my chamber to settle some papers; and thither came to me Willet with an errand from her mistress, and this time I first did give her a little kiss, she being a very pretty-humoured girl, and so one that I do love mightily.

1668

25 OCTOBER. *Lord's Day*. At night W. Batelier comes and sups with us; and after supper, to have my head combed by Deb, which occasioned the greatest sorrow to me that ever I knew in this world; for my wife, coming up suddenly, did find me imbracing the girl con my hand sub su coats. I was at a wonderful loss upon it, and the girl also; and I endeavoured to put it off, but my wife was struck mute and grew angry, and as her voice came to her, grew quite out of order; and I do say little, but to bed; and my wife said little also, but could not sleep all night; but about 2 in the morning waked me and cried, and fell to tell me as a great secret that she was a Roman Catholique and had received the Holy Sacrament; which troubled me but I took no notice of it, but she went on from one thing to another, till at last it appeared plainly her trouble was at what she saw; but yet I did not know how much she saw and therefore said nothing to her. But after her much crying and reproaching me with inconstancy and preferring a sorry girl before her, I did give her no provocations but did promise all fair usage to her, and love, and foreswore any hurt that I did with her – till at last she seemed to be at ease again; and so toward morning, a little sleep; and so I, with some little repose and rest, rose, and up and by water to Whitehall, but with my mind mightily troubled for the poor girl, whom

I fear I have undone by this, my [wife] telling me that she would turn her out of door.

9 NOVEMBER. Up, and I did, by a little note which I flung to Deb, advise her that I did continue to deny that ever I kissed her, and so she might govern herself. The truth [is], that I did adventure upon God's pardoning me this lie, knowing how heavy a thing it would be for me to be the ruin of the poor girl; and next, knowing that if my wife should know all, it were impossible ever for her to be at peace with me again – and so our whole lives would be uncomfortable. The girl read, and as I bid her, returned me the note, flinging it to me in passing by.

10 NOVEMBER. Up, and my wife still every day as ill as she is all night; will rise to see me out doors, telling me plainly that she dares not let me see the girl; and so I out to the office, where all the morning; and so home to dinner, where I find my wife mightily troubled again, more then ever, and she tells me that it is from her examining the girl and getting a confession now from her of all – which doth mightily trouble me, as not being able to foresee the consequences of it as to our future peace together. So my wife would not go down to dinner, but I would dine in her chamber with her; and there, after mollifying her as much as I could, we were pretty quiet and eat; and by and by comes Mr Hollier, and dines there by himself after we had dined. And he being gone, we to talk again, and she to be troubled, reproaching me with my unkindness and perjury, I having denied my ever kissing her – as also with all her old kindnesses to me, and my ill-using of her from the beginning, and the many temptations she hath refused out of faithfulness to me; whereof several she was perticular in, and especially from

my Lord Sandwich by the sollicitation of Captain Ferrer; and then afterward, the courtship of my Lord Hinchingbrooke, even to the trouble of his Lady. All which I did acknowledge and was troubled for, and wept; and at last pretty good friends again, and so I to my office and there late, and so home to supper with her; and so to bed, where after half-an-hour's slumber, she wakes me and cries out that she should never sleep more, and so kept raving till past midnight, that made me cry and weep heartily all the while for her, and troubled for what she reproached me with as before; and at last, with new vows, and perticularly that I would myself bid the girl be gone and show my dislike to her – which I shall endeavour to perform, but with much trouble. And so, this appeasing her, we to sleep as well as we could till morning.

13 NOVEMBER. My wife tells me that Deb hath been abroad today, and is come home and says she hath got a place to go to, so as she will be gone tomorrow morning. This troubled me; and the truth is, I have a great mind for to have the maidenhead of this girl, which I should not doubt to have if yo could get time para be con her – but she will be gone and I know not whither. Before we went to bed, my wife told me she would not have me to see her or give her her wages; and so I did give my wife 10l for her year and half-a-quarter's wages, which she went into her chamber and paid her; and so to bed, and there, blessed be God, we did sleep well and with peace, which I had not done in now almost twenty nights together.

14 NOVEMBER. Up, and had a mighty mind to have seen or given a note to Deb or to have given her a little money; to which purpose I wrapped up 40s in a paper,

thinking to give her; but my wife rose presently, and would not let me be out of her sight; and went down before me into the kitchen, and came up and told me that she was in the kitchen, and therefore would have me go round the other way; which she repeating, and I vexed at it, answered her a little angrily; upon which she instantly flew out into a rage, calling me dog and rogue, and that I had a rotten heart; all which, knowing that I deserved it, I bore with; and word being brought presently up that she was gone away by coach with her things, my wife was friends; and so all quiet, and I to the office with my heart sad, and find that I cannot forget the girl, and vexed I know not where to look for her – and more troubled to see how my wife is by this means likely for ever to have her hand over me, that I shall for ever be a slave to her; that is to say, only in matters of pleasure, but in other things she will make her business, I know, to please me and to keep me right to her – which I will labour to be endeed, for she deserves it of me, though it will be I fear a little time before I shall be able to wear Deb out of my mind. After dinner to the office, where all the afternoon and doing much business late; my mind being free of all troubles, I thank God, but only for my thoughts of this girl, which hang after her. And so at night home to supper, and there did sleep with great content with my wife. I must here remember that I have lain with my moher as a husband more times since this falling-out then in I believe twelve months before – and with more pleasure to her then I think in all the time of our marriage before.

15 NOVEMBER. I in the evening to my office again to make an end of my journall, and so home to supper and

to bed, with my mind pretty quiet; and less troubled about Deb then I was, though yet I am troubled I must confess, and would be glad to find her out – though I fear it would be my ruin. This evening there came to sit with us Mr Pelling, who wondered to see my wife and I so dumpish; but yet it went off only as my wife's not being well; and poor wretch, she hath no cause to be well, God knows.

16 NOVEMBER. I away to Holborne about Whetstones Park, where I never was in my life before, where I understand by my wife's discourse that Deb is gone; which doth trouble me mightily, that the poor girl should be in a desperate condition forced to go thereabouts; and there, not hearing of any such man as Allbon, with whom my wife said she now was, I to the Strand and there, by sending of Drumbleby's boy, my flagelette-maker, to Eagle Court, where my wife also by discourse lately let fall that he did lately live, I found that this Dr Allbon is a kind of a poor broken fellow that dare not show his head nor be known where he is gone.

18 NOVEMBER. Lay long in bed, talking with my wife, she being unwilling to have me go abroad, being and declaring herself jealous of my going out, for fear of my going to Deb; which I do deny – for which God forgive me, for I was no sooner out about noon but I did go by coach directly to Somerset House and there enquired among the porters there for Dr Allbun; and the first I spoke with told me he knew him, and that he was newly gone into Lincoln's Inn Fields, but whither he could not tell me, but that one of his fellows, not then in the way, did carry a chest of drawers thither with him, and that

when he comes he would ask him. This put me in some hopes; and therefore I away and walked up and down the Strand between the two turnstiles, hoping to see her out of a window; and then imployed a porter, one Osbeston, to find out this Doctors lodgings thereabouts; who by appointment comes to me to Hercules Pillars, where I dined alone, but tells me that he cannot find out any such but will enquire further. Thence back to Whitehall to the Treasury a while, and thence to the Strand; and towards night did meet with the porter that carried the chest of drawers with this Doctor, but he would not tell me where he lived, being his good maister he told me; but if I would have a message to him, he would deliver it. At last, I told him my business was not with him, but a little gent[le]woman, one Mrs Willet, that is with him; and sent him to see how she did, from her friend in London, and no other token. He goes while I walk in Somerset House – walk there in the Court; at last he comes back and tells me she is well, and that I may see her if I will – but no more. So I could not be commanded by my reason, but I must go this very night; and so by coach, it being now dark, I to her, close by my tailor's; and there she came into the coach to me, and yo did besar her [and] give her the best counsel I could, to have a care of her honour and to fear God and suffer no man para haver to do con her – as yo have done – which she promised. Yo did give her 20s and directions para laisser sealed in paper at any time the name of the place of her being, at Herringman's my bookseller in the Change – by which I might go para her. And so bid her good-night, with much content to my mind and resolution to look after her no more till I heard from her. And so home, and there told my wife a fair tale, God knows, how I spent the whole day; with which the poor wretch was satisfied, or at least seemed so.

19 NOVEMBER. Up, and at the office all the morning, with my heart full of joy to think in what a safe condition all my matters now stand between my wife and Deb and me; and at noon, running upstairs to see the upholsters, who are at work upon hanging my best room and setting up my new bed, I find my wife sitting sad in the dining-room; which inquiring into the reason of, she begun to call me all the false, rotten-hearted rogues in the world, letting me understand that I was with Deb yesterday; which, thinking impossible for her ever to understand, I did a while deny; but at last did, for the ease of my mind and hers, and for ever to discharge my heart of this wicked business, I did confess all; and above-stairs in our bed-chamber there, I did endure the sorrow of her threats and vows and curses all the afternoon. And which was worst, she swore by all that was good that she would slit the nose of this girl, and be gone herself this very night from me; and did there demand 3 or 400*l* of me to buy my peace, that she might be gone without making any noise, or else protested that she would make all the world know of it. So, with most perfect confusion of face and heart, and sorrow and shame, in the greatest agony in the world, I did pass this afternoon, fearing that it will never have an end; but at last I did call for W. Hewers, who I was forced to make privy now to all; and the poor fellow did cry like a child [and] obtained what I could not, that she would be pacified, upon condition that I would give it under my hand never to see or speak with Deb while I live, as I did before of Pierce and Knepp; and which I did also, God knows, promise for Deb too, but I have the

confidence to deny it, to the perjuring of myself. So before it was late, there was, beyond my hopes as well as desert, a tolerable peace; and so to supper, and pretty kind words, and to bed, and there yo did hazer con ella to her content; and so with some rest spent the night in bed, being most absolutely resolved, if ever I can maister this bout, never to give her occasion while I live of more trouble of this or any other kind, there being no curse in the world so great as this of the difference between myself and her; and therefore I do by the Grace of God promise never to offend her more, and did this night begin to pray to God upon my knees alone in my chamber; which God knows I cannot yet do heartily, but I hope God will give me the Grace more and more every day to fear Him, and to be true to my poor wife. This night the upholsters did finish the hanging of my best chamber, but my sorrow and trouble is so great about this business, that put me out of all joy in looking upon it or minding how it was.

20 NOVEMBER. This morning up, with mighty kind words between my poor wife and I; and so to Whitehall by water, W. Hewer with me, who is to go with me everywhere until my wife be in condition to go out along with me herself; for she doth plainly declare that she dares not trust me out alone, and therefore made it a piece of our league that I should alway take somebody with me, or her herself; which I am mighty willing to, being, by the grace of God resolved never to do her wrong more.

We landed at the Temple, and there I did bid him call at my Cosen Roger Pepys's lodgings, and I stayed in the street for him; and so took water again at the Strand Stairs and so to Whitehall, in my way I telling him plainly and truly my resolutions, if I can get over this evil,

never to give new occasion for it. He is, I think, so honest
and true a servant to us both, and one that loves us, that I
was not much troubled at his being privy to all this, but
rejoiced in my heart that I had him to assist in the making
us friends; which he did do truly and heartily, and with
good success – for I did get him to go to Deb to tell her
that I had told my wife all of my being with her the other
night, that so, if my wife should send, she might not
make the business worse by denying it. While I was at
Whitehall with the Duke of York doing our ordinary
business with him, W. Hewer did go to her and come
back again; and so I took him into St James's Park, and
there he did tell me he had been with her and found what
I said about my manner of being with her true, and had
given her advice as I desired. I did there enter into more
talk about my wife and myself, and he did give me great
assurance of several perticular cases to which my wife had
from time to time made him privy of her loyalty and
truth to me after many and great temptations, and I
believe them truly. I did also discourse the unfitness of
my leaving of my imployment now in many respects, to
go into the country as my wife desires – but that I would
labour to fit myself for it; which he thoroughly understands, and doth agree with me in it; and so, hoping to get
over this trouble, we about our business to Westminster
Hall.

But when I came home, hoping for a further degree of
peace and quiet, I find my wife upon her bed in a horrible
rage afresh, calling me all the bitter names; and rising, did
fall to revile me in the bitterest manner in the world, and
could not refrain to strike me and pull my hair; which I
resolved to bear with, and had good reason to bear it. So I
by silence and weeping did prevail with her a little to be

quiet, and she would not eat her dinner without me; but yet by and by into a raging fit she fell again worse then before, that she would slit the girl's nose; and at last W. Hewer came in and came up, who did allay her fury, I flinging myself in a sad desperate condition upon the bed in the blue room, and there lay while they spoke together; and at last it came to this, that if I would call Deb "whore" under my hand, and write to her that I hated her and would never see her more, she would believe me and trust in me – which I did agree to; only, as to the name of "whore" I would have excused, and therefore wrote to her sparing that word; which my wife thereupon tore it, and would not be satisfied till, W. Hewer winking upon me, I did write so, with the name of a whore, as that I did fear she might too probably have been prevailed upon to have been a whore by her carriage to me, and therefore, as such, I did resolve never to see her more. This pleased my wife, and she gives it W. Hewer to carry to her, with a sharp message from her. So from that minute my wife begun to be kind to me, and we to kiss and be friends, and so continued all the evening and fell to talk of other matters with great comfort, and after supper to bed, with good sleep and rest, my wife only troubled in her rest, but less then usual – for which the God of Heaven be praised. I did this night promise to my wife never to go to bed without calling upon God upon my knees by prayer; and I begun this night, and hope I shall never forget to do the like all my life – for I do find that it is much the best for my soul and body to live pleasing to God and my poor wife – and will ease me of much care, as well as much expense.

21 NOVEMBER. Up, with great joy to my wife and me, and to the office, where W. Hewer did most honestly bring me back that part of my letter under my hand to Deb wherein I called her "whore", assuring me that he did not show it her – and that he did only give her to understand that wherein I did declare my desire never to see her, and did give her the best Christian counsel he could; which was mighty well done of him. But by the grace of God, though I love the poor girl and wish her well, as having gone too far toward the undoing her, yet I will never enquire after or think of her more – my peace being certainly to do right to my wife.

1669

12 JANUARY. This evening I observed my wife mighty dull; and I myself was not mighty fond, because of some hard words she did give me at noon, out of a jealousy at my being abroad this morning; when, God knows, it was upon the business of the office unexpectedly; but I to bed, not thinking but she would come after me; but waking by and by out of a slumber, which I usually fall into presently after my coming into the bed, I found she did not prepare to come to bed, but got fresh candles and more wood for her fire, it being mighty cold too. At this being troubled, I after a while prayed her to come to bed, all my people being gone to bed; so after an hour or two, she silent, and I now and then praying her to come to bed, she fell out into a fury, that I was a rogue and false to her; but yet I could perceive that she was to seek what to say; only, she invented, I believe, a business that I was seen in a hackney-coach with the glasses up with Deb, but could not tell the time, nor was sure I was he. I did, as I

might truly, deny it, and was mightily troubled; but all would not serve. At last, about one a-clock, she came to my side of the bed and drow my curtaine open, and with the tongs, red hot at the ends, made as if she did design to pinch me with them; at which in dismay I rose up, and with a few words she laid them down and did by little and little, very sillily, let all the discourse fall; and about 2, but with much seeming difficulty, came to bed and there lay well all night, and long in bed talking together with much pleasure; it being, I know, nothing but her doubt of my going out yesterday without telling her of my going which did vex her, poor wretch, last night: and I cannot blame her jealousy, though it doth vex me to the heart.

13 APRIL. W. Hewer and I by water to Whitehall. But here, being with him in the courtyard, as God would have it I spied Deb, which made my heart and head to work; and I presently could not refrain, but sent W. Hewer away to look for Mr Wren (W. Hewer, I perceive, did see her, but whether he did see me see her I know not, or suspect my sending him away I know not) but my heart could not hinder me. And I run after her and two women and a man, more ordinary people, and she in her old clothes; and after hunting a little, find them in the lobby of the Chapel below-stairs; and there I observed she endeavoured to avoid me, but I did speak to her and she to me, and did get her para docere me ou she demeures now. And did charge her para say nothing of me that I had vu elle — which she did promise; and so, with my heart full of surprize, and disorder, I away, and so home to my wife. But, God forgive me, I hardly know how to put on confidence enough to speak as innocent,

having had this passage today with Deb, though only, God knows, by accident. But my great pain is lest God Almighty shall suffer me to find out this girl, whom endeed I love, and with a bad amour; but I will pray to God to give me grace to forbear it. So home to supper, where very sparing in my discourse, not giving occasion of any enquiry where I have been today, or what I have done; and so, without any trouble tonight more then my fear, we to bed.

15 APRIL. Up and to the office; and thence, before the office sat, to the Excise Office with W. Hewer, but found some occasion to go another way to the Temple upon business; and I, by Deb's direction, did know whither in Jewen Street to direct my hackney coachman, while I stayed in the coach in Aldersgate Street, to go thither first to enquire whether Mrs Hunt her aunt was in town, who brought me word she was not; I thought this was as much as I could do at once, and therefore went away, but going down Holburn Hill by the Conduit, I did see Deb on foot going up the hill; I saw her, and she me, but she made no stop, but seemed unwilling to speak to me; so I away on, but then stopped and light and after her, and overtook her at the end of Hosier Lane in Smithfield; and without standing in the street, desired her to fallow me, and I led her into a little blind alehouse within the walls; and there she and I alone fell to talk and besar la. I did give her in a paper 20s, and we did agree para meet again in the Hall at Westminster on Monday next; and so, giving me great hopes by her carriage that she continues modest and honest, we did there part.

19 APRIL. I to Westminster Hall and there walked from 10 a-clock to past 12, expecting to have met Deb; but

whether she had been there before, and missing me went away, or is prevented in coming and hath no mind to come to me (the last whereof, as being most pleasing, as showing most modesty, I should be most glad of) I know not; but she not then appearing, I being tired with walking went home.

V

ANECDOTES,
OBSERVATIONS AND
REFLECTIONS

Anecdotes

[Luellin] told me how the pretty woman that I always loved at the beginning of Cheapeside that sells children's coates was served by the Lady Bennett (a famous strumpet), who by counterfeiting to fall into a swoune upon the sight of her in her shop, became acquainted with her and at last got her ends of her to lie with a gallant that had hired her to procure this poor soul for him. (*22 September 1660*)

Mr Christmas my old schoolfellow did remember that I was a great Roundhead when I was a boy, and I was much afeared that he would have remembered the words that I said the day that the King was beheaded (that were I to preach upon him, my text should be: "The memory of the wicked shall rot"); but I found afterward that he did go away from schoole before that time. (*1 November 1660*)

By coach to Whitehall, and I met with Dr Tho. Fuller and took him to the Dogg, where he tells me to what perfection he hath now brought the art of memory; that he did lately to four eminently great schollars dictate together in Latin upon different subjects of their proposing, faster then they were able to write, till they were tired. And by the way, in discourse tells me that the best way of beginning a sentence, if a man should be out and forget his last sentence (which he never was), that then his last refuge is to begin with an *Utcunque*. (*22 January 1661*)

After dinner to the Theatre, where I saw again *The Lost Lady*, which doth now please me better then before. And here, I sitting behind in a dark place, a lady spat backward upon me by a mistake, not seeing me. But after seeing her to be a very pretty lady, I was not troubled at it at all. (*28 January 1661*)

Then to Whitehall; and among other things, met with Mr Townsend, who told of his mistake the other day to put both his legs through one of his knees of his breeches and went so all day. (*6 April 1661*)

To Dr Williams, who did carry me into his garden, where he hath abundance of grapes. And did show me how a dog that he hath doth kill all the cattes that come thither to kill his pigeons, and doth afterwards bury them. And doth it with so much care that they shall be quite covered, that if but the tip of the tail hangs out, he will take up the cat again and dig the hole deeper – which is very strange. And he tells me he doth believe that he hath killed above 100 cats. (*11 September 1661*)

[Mr Coventry] told me the passage of a Frenchman through London Bridge; where when he saw the great fall, he begun to cross himself and say his prayers in the greatest fear in the world; and as soon as he was over, he swore "*Morbleu c'est le plus grand plaisir du mond*" – being the most like a French humour in the world. (*8 August 1662*)

Among other pretty discourse, some was of Sir Jerom Bowes, Embassador from Queene Elizabeth to the Emperor of Russia – who, because some of the noblemen there would go up the stairs to the Emperor before him, he would not go up till the Emperor had ordered those two men to be dragged downstair, with their heads knocking upon every stair till they were killed. And when he was come up, they demanded his sword of him before he entered the room; he told them, if they would have his sword, they should have his boots too; and so caused his boots to be pulled off and his night-gown and night-cap and slippers to be sent for, and made the Emperor stay till he could go in his night-dress, since he might not go as a soldier. And lastly, when the Emperor in contempt, to show his command over his subjects, did command one to leap from the window down and broke his neck in the sight of our Embassador, he replied that his mistress did set more by and did make better use of the necks of her subjects; but said that to show what her subjects would do for her, he would, and did, fling down his gantlett before the Emperor and challenged all the nobility there to take it up in defence of the Emperor against his Queene. For which, at this very day, the name of Sir Jer. Bowes is famous and honoured there. (*5 September 1662*)

At noon to the Exchange and so home to dinner, where I find my wife hath been with Ashwell at La Roches to have her tooth drawn, which it seems akes much. But my wife could not get her to be contented to have it drawn after the first twich, but would let it alone; and so they came home with it undone, which made my wife and me good sport. (*7 April 1663*)

To Whitehall, and there did hear Betty Michell was at this end of the town; and so did stay to endeavour to meet with her and carry her home; but she did not come, so I lost my whole afternoon. But pretty, how I took another pretty woman for her, taking her a clap on the breech, thinking verily it had been her. (*1 October 1666*)

[275]

[Mr Hunt] dined with us, and told me some ridiculous pieces of thrift of Sir G. Downing's, who is their countryman – in inviting some poor people at Christmas last, to charm the country people's mouths; but did give them nothing but beef-porridge, pudding, and pork, and nothing said all dinner, but only his mother would say, "It's good broth, son." He would answer, "Yes, it is good broth." Then his lady confirm all and say, "Yes, very good broth." By and by he would begin and say, "Good pork;" "Yes," says the mother, "good pork." Then he cries, "Yes, very good pork." And so they said of all things; to which nobody made any answer, they going there not out of love or esteem of them, but to eat his victuals, knowing him to be a niggardly fellow – and with this he is jeered now all over the country. (*27 February 1667*)

I to Creeds chamber and thence out to Whitehall with him, in our way meeting with Mr Cooling, my Lord Chamberlaines secretary, on horseback, who stopped to speak to us; and he proved very drunk and did talk and would have talked all night with us, I not being able to break loose from him, he holding me so by the hand. [He] told us his horse was a bribe, and his boots a bribe; and told us he was made up of bribes, as a Oxford scholar is set out with other men's goods when he goes out of town, and that he makes every sort of tradesmen to bribe him; and invited me home to his house to taste of his bribe-wine. I never heard so much vanity from a man in my life. (*30 July 1667*)

After dinner, my wife and Willett and I to the King's House and there saw *Henry the Fourth*. The house full of

Parliament-men, it being holiday with them. And it was observable how a gentleman of good habitt, sitting just before us eating of some fruit, in the midst of the play did drop down as dead, being choked; but with much ado, Orange Mall did thrust her finger down his throat and brought him to life again. (*2 November 1667*)

To the King's House. Many fine faces here today. It pleased us mightily to see the natural affection of a poor woman, the mother of one of the children brought on the stage – the child crying, she by force got upon the stage, and took up her child and carried it away off of the stage from Hart. (*28 December 1667*)

Observations and Reflections

To tower Wharfe and there took boat; and we all walked to Halfeway House and there eat and drunk, and were pleasant; and so finally home again in the evening, and so good-night – this being a very pleasant life that we now lead, and have long done; the Lord be blessed and make us thankful. But though I am much against too much spending, yet I do think it best to enjoy some degree of pleasure, now that we have health, money and opportunities, rather than to leave pleasures to old age or poverty, when we cannot have them so properly. (*20 May 1662*)

To the Trinity House to dinner, where great variety of talk. Mr Prin, among many, had a pretty tale of one that brought in a bill in Parliament for the impowering him to dispose his land to such children as he should have that should bear the name of his wife – it was in Queen Elizabeth's time. One replied that there are many species of creatures where the male gives the denominacion to both sexes, as men and woodcockes, but not above one where the female doth, and that is a goose. (*15 June 1663*)

[Sir William Compton, Master of the Ordnance] died yesterday – at which I was most exceedingly surprized; he being, and so all the world saying that he was, one of the worthyest men and best officers of state now in England; and so in my conscience he was – of the best temper, valour, abilities of mind, integrity, birth, fine person, and diligence of any one man he hath left behind him in the three kingdoms; and yet not forty year old, or if so, that is all. I find the sober men of the Court troubled for him; and yet not so as to hinder or lessen their mirth, talking, laughing, and eating, drinking and doing everything else, just as if there was no such thing – which is as good an instance for me hereafter to judge of death, both as to the unavoydablenesse, suddenness, and little effect of it upon the spirits of others, let a man be never so high or rich or good; but that all die alike, no more matter being made of the death of one then another. (*19 October 1663*)

This noon Mr Coventry discoursed largely and bravely to me concerning the different sort of valours, the active and passive valour. For the latter, he brought as an instance General Blacke [*Blake*], who in the defending of Taunton and Lime for the Parliament did through his stubborn sort of valour defend it the most *opiniastrement* that ever any man did anything – and yet never was the man that ever made any attaque by land or sea, but rather avoyded it on all, even fair occasions. On the other side, Prince Rupert the boldest attaquer in the world for personal courage; and yet in the defending of Bristoll, no man did ever anything worse, he wanting the patience and seasoned head to consult and advise for defence and to bear with the evils of a siege. (*4 June 1664*)

Up by 4 a-clock and walked to Greenwich, where called at Capt. Cockes and to his chamber, he being in bed – where something put my last night's dream into my head, which I think is the best that ever was dreamed – which was, that I had my Lady Castlemayne in my armes and was admitted to use all the dalliance I desired with her, and then dreamed that this could not be awake but that it was only a dream. But that since it was a dream and that I took so much real pleasure in it, what a happy thing it would be, if when we are in our graves (as Shakespeere resembles it), we could dream, and dream but such dreams as this – that then we should not need to be so fearful of death as we are this plague-time. (*15 August 1665*)

Lay very long in bed, discoursing with Mr Hill of most things of a man's life, and how little merit doth prevail in the world, but only favour – and that for myself, chance without merit brought me in, and that diligence only keeps me so, and will, living as I do among so many lazy people, that the diligent man becomes necessary, that they cannot do anything without him. (*1 November 1665*)

Up; and being sent for by my Lady Batten, I to her and there she found fault with my not seeing her since her being a widow; which I excused as well as I could, though it is a fault, but it is my nature not to be forward in visits. But here she told me her condition (which is good enough, being sole executrix, to the disappointment of all her husband's children). And here do see what creatures widows are in weeping for their husbands, and then presently leaving off; but I cannot wonder at it, the cares of the world taking place of all other passions. (*17 October 1667*)

VI

THE DIARY ENDS

The Diary Ends

¶ PEPYS ENDED HIS DIARY in May 1669 convinced that the effort of writing its small shorthand characters was sending him blind. There are indications of his suffering from eye-strain as early as 1662, and by 1668 his complaints of pain and of watering in the eyes become frequent, and from about the same time his handwriting in the diary becomes larger and more widely spaced. He tried remedy after remedy, from green spectacles to paper tubes fitted with lenses, but to no avail. The defect from which his eyes suffered, acccording to modern opinion, was a combination of long-sightedness with astigmatism, and for that there was no known remedy until 1825 when it was discovered that it could be corrected by the use of cylindrical lenses. So Pepys's diary, begun in thankfulness for his release from pain from the stone ('Blessed be God', its first words run, 'at the end of the last year I was in very good health, without any sense of my old pain') now ends with a prayer for patience in the face of an approaching calamity worse than pain. His intention to continue the diary by means of dictation was never realised, and he never submitted himself to the routine of diary keeping again, except for a few months in 1683 when he wrote a shorthand diary of a journey to Tangier.

Although he did not know it, what was facing him in May 1669 was not years of blindness but over thirty years of active life, during which his eyes only occasionally troubled him and forced him to use the services of an assistant to read for him or to write at his dictation. In the summer and autumn of 1669 he took a holiday in the Low Countries and France, and by January of the next year – and possibly earlier – he was using shorthand again in his office work. Those marvellous eyes, which observed so much, were unextinguished. But his journal had come to a full stop and lay dormant on a library shelf.

And thus ends all that I doubt I shall ever be able to do with my own eyes in the keeping of my journall, I being not able to do it any longer, having done now so long as

[283]

to undo my eyes almost every time that I take a pen in my hand; and therefore, whatever comes of it, I must forbear; and therefore resolve from this time forward to have it kept by my people in longhand, and must therefore be contented to set down no more then is fit for them and all the world to know; or if there be anything (which cannot be much, now my amours to Deb are past, and my eyes hindering me in almost all other pleasures), I must endeavour to keep a margin in my book open, to add here and there a note in shorthand with my own hand. And so I betake myself to that course which [is] almost as much as to see myself go into my grave – for which, and all the discomforts that will accompany my being blind, the good God prepare me.

May. 31. 1669.   S.P.

Select Glossary

This list covers words which may give difficulty to the reader, especially in those cases where their meaning has changed since Pepys's time. It also includes a few names of persons and places.

ABLE: wealthy
ACCOUNTANT: official account-
    able to Exchequer
ADMIRE: wonder
AGUE: fever
ALPHABET: index
ANTIQUE: fantastic
ARCHED VIALL: viol played from
    keyboard
ARTICLING: indictment
ASHWELL: Elizabeth Pepys's
    companion
BAGNARD: prison
BAND: neckband
BARBER'S MUSIQUE: discordant m.
BATTEN, Sir William: Surveyor
    of the Navy
BLACK: dark-haired
BLIND: obscure
BOTARGO: dried fish-roe
BRANSLE: ceremonious round
    dance
BRIDGE: London Bridge
BRILL, the: Brielle, Holland
BROUNCKER, Viscount: Navy
    Commissioner
BY-DISCOURSE: incidental treatise
CALL: call for
CARTERET, Sir George: Treasurer
    of the Navy
CAUDLE: gruel
CHANCELLOR, the (Lord): the
    Earl of Clarendon

CHANGE: the Royal Exchange in
    the City or the New
    Exchange in Westminster
CHARACTERS: written symbols
CLAP: gonorrhoea
CLOSE: shutter
CLUB: subscription dinner; share
    of expenses
COACH: stateroom in ship
COG: wheedle
COLLECT: recollect
COMPLACENCY: civility
CONCEITED, to be: to have a
    conceit (idea, notion) that
CORANTO: dance involving
    running or gliding step
COUNTRY: county; parliamentary
    constituency
COUNTRYMAN: county neighbour
COVENTRY, Mr/Sir William:
    Secretary to the Duke of
    York, Lord High Admiral
CREW, Lord: Lady Sandwich's
    father
CUNNING: knowledgeable;
    knowing
CURIOUS: careful; skilful
DEAD COLOURING: preparatory
    layer of colour in painting
DRAUGHT: drawing
DRESS: cook
DRUGGERMAN: dragoman
DUKE, the: usually Duke of York

[285]

EASILY: slowly
EFFEMINACY: love of womanising
FAMILY: household
FECKAM: Fécamp
FERRANDIN: cloth of silk mixed with wool
FLAGG-MEN: flag officers
FOXED: drunk
FOXHALL: Vauxhall
FRIEND: member of family
GENIUS: inborn character
GENT: elegant
GIBB-CAT: tomcat
GLASS: telescope; window
GLISTER: clyster, enema
GOODFELLOW: good-timer
GOSSIP: godparent
HAND: cuff
HARPSICHON: harpsichord
HEADPIECE: helmet
HECTOR: bully, swashbuckler
HEWER, Will: Pepys's clerk
HOLLAND: variety of linen
HONEST: virtuous
HOPE, the: reach of Thames below Tilbury
HOUSE OF OFFICE: latrine
IMPERTINENTLY: irrelevantly
INSIPID: dull, stupid
JACKE: spit
JESIMY: jasmine
KITLIN: kitten
LACE: lace collar or scarf trimmed with gold or silver thread
LINK: torch
MAD: fantastic, extravagant
MAKE LEGS: bow and scrape
MEAT: food
MENNES, Sir John: Comptroller of the Navy

MERCHANT STRANGERS: foreign merchants
MEWES, the: royal stables, Charing Cross
MINGO: Sir W. Batten's black servant
MOHER (Span. *mujer*): wife
MOND: orb
MORECLACKE: Mortlake
MRS: mistress (prefix; used also of single women)
MY LORD/MY LADY: usually Lord/Lady Sandwich
NAVY: Navy Office
NEAT HOUSES: cottages and houses of entertainment near Chelsea
NEAT'S TONGUE: ox tongue
NELLY: Nell Gwyn, actress
NOISE OF MUSIC: band of performers
OF COURSE: as usual
OPERA: spectacular entertainment with scenery
ORDINARY: fixed price restaurant
PADRON: slave master
PAGEANT: decorated float
PALL: Paulina, Pepys's sister
PASSION: feeling
PASSIONATE: giving rise to compassion
PHILOSOPHY: science
PIECE: gold coin worth *c.* 20s.
PIPKIN: small earthenware pot
PLAT: position; plate (engraving); garden plot
POOR WRETCH: poor dear
POSSET: hot drink
POVEY, Thomas: government official

[286]

POYNT. thread lace made with needle
PRESENTLY: immediately
PRICK: write out music
PRINCE, the: Prince Rupert, Charles II's cousin
QU: cue (theatrical)
QUARREFOUR: crossroads
QUINSBOROUGH: Königsberg, East Prussia
REDRIFFE: Rotherhithe
RESEMBLE: represent
SACK: white wine
SANDWICH, Earl of: Pepys's patron
SCHOOL: scold
SEEM: pretend
SENNIT: week (seven-night)
SERPENT: firework
SERVANT: suitor
SET OFF ONE'S REST: make one's whole aim to be
SHAGG: cloth with velvet nap
SHIFT: change clothes
SHUT: shutter
SIR WMS BOTH: Sir William Batten and Sir William Penn

SITHE: sigh
SPUDD: spade
STAIRS: usually riverside jetty
STOUT: brave
STUFF SUIT: cloth suit
TABBY: variety of silk
TANSY: egg pudding
TARGETT: shield
TELL: count
TENT (Span. *tinto*): red wine
TONGUE: reputation
TOPS: turn-overs of stockings
TOYLE: snare
TRAINBANDS: militia
TRAPAN: trap, trick
TRIM: shave
TRYANGLE: triangular virginals
TURNER: woodworker
UNDERTAKER: contractor
UTCUNQUE: however
VEST: equivalent of modern waistcoat
WAISTCOAT: undergarment
WAYTES: town musicians
WIND-MUSIQUE: woodwind
WIPE: sarcastic remark
YARD: penis